CONVERSATIONS ON COUNSELLING

CONVERSATIONS ON COUNSELLING

between

A DOCTOR AND A PRIEST

by

MARCUS LEFÉBURE O.P.

HANS SCHAUDER

Third Edition

T&T CLARK
EDINBURGH

First Edition © Marcus Lefébure O.P., 1982
Second Edition © Marcus Lefébure O.P., 1985
Third Edition © Marcus Lefébure and Hans Schauder, 1990

All rights reserved. No part of this publication may be reproduced, stored in a retrieval system, or transmitted, in any form or by any means, electronic, mechanical, photocopying, recording or otherwise, without the prior permission of T&T Clark.

Third Edition First Published 1990

British Library Cataloguing in Publicaion Data
Conversations on counselling between a doctor and a priest.
—3rd. ed.
1. Medicine. Psychotherapy. Counselling Spiritual aspects
I. Lefébure, Marcus *1933*— II. Schauder, Hans
291.1'75

ISBN 0 567 29164 2 PB

Typesetting by Swanston Graphics Ltd, Derby
Printed and bound in Great Britain by Billing & Sons Ltd, Worcester

TO
OUR FRIENDS

(What is more glorious than gold? asked the king. –
The splendour of light, answered the serpent. –
What is more delectable than light? asked the former. –
The communion of dialogue, answered the latter. –)
Goethe *Das Märchen*

'We may say ... that the Self exists only in dynamic relation with the Other ...
The original pattern of personal behaviour is not merely a starting-point. It is not left behind as the child grows up. It remains the ground pattern of all personal motivation at every stage of development. If the *terminus a quo* of the personal life is a helpless total dependence on the Other, the *terminus as quem* is no independence, but a mutual interdependence of equals.'
John Macmurray *Persons in Relation*

'A man truly alive is the glory of God.'
St Irenaeus of Lyons

contents

	Page
Acknowledgements	viii
Publishers' Note	xii
Introduction	viii
Dialogue 1 : The Stages of Counselling	1
Dialogue 2 : Counselling and the Archetype of Human Dialogue	24
Dialogue 3 : Relationship and Solitude	41
Dialogue 4 : The Stages of the Spiritual Path	51
Dialogue 5 : Stages of Counselling in Relation to Stages of the Spiritual Path	68
Dialogue 6 : Counselling and Creativity	92
Dialogue 7 : Backwards and Forwards	111
Dialogue 8 : Personality and Power	141
Dialogue 9 : Growth and Morality	159
Dialogue 10 : Sex and Contemplation	181
11 : The Open End	205
Concluding Personal Postscript on Counselling and Friendship	214
Index of Works Cited	222

Acknowledgements

I should like to express my grateful acknowledgement to the following for the use of material quoted in this book: George Allen & Unwin and Harper & Row for quotations from *The Art of Loving* by Erich Fromm (New York, 1956, pp.103-104) and *Outlines of Indian Philosophy* by M. Hiriyanna (London, 1932, pp.18, 20-21, 24); David Bolt Associates Ltd for a quotation from *New Pathways in Psychology: Maslow and the Post-Freudians* by Colin Wilson (London, 1973, pp.22-23); Collins Publishers for a quotation from *Silent Music* by W. Johnston (London, 1974, p.120); Constable Publishers for quotations from *On Becoming a Person* by C. Rogers (London, 1967, pp.17 & 23-24) and *The True Wilderness* by H. Williams (London, 1965, p.12); the executors and the estate of W. Somerset Maugham, William Heinemann Ltd and Doubleday & Co. Inc. for an excerpt from *The Razor's Edge* by W. Somerset Maugham (copyright 1943, 1944 by McCall Corporation, copyright 1944 by W. Somerset Maugham, reprinted by permission of Doubleday & Company Inc., New York, 1944, p.186); Faber & Faber, Publishers for quotations from *The Art of Prayer* by Igumen Chariton of Valamo (London, 1966, p.140) and from *Persons in Relation* by J. Macmurray (London, 1961, pp.17, 61 & 66); Granada Publishing Limited for a quotation from *The Silva Method of Mind Control* by J. Silva and P. Miele (St Albans, Herts, 1980, p.172); William Heinemann Ltd for quotations from *Twentieth Century Mystics and Sages* by A. Bancroft (London, 1976, pp.76 & 157); Verlag Herder GmbH & Co., KG for a passage (in my own translation) from *Wissende, Verschwiegene, Ein-geweihte* by H.-J. Baden (Freiburg, 1981, pp.100-101);

Hutchinson Publishing Group Ltd for a quotation from *The Way of All Women* by E. Harding (London, 1971, pp.275-276); Insel Verlag for a passage (in my own translation) from *Briefe an einen jungen Dichter* by R. M. Rilke (Leipzig, No. 406, n.d. p.19); Mosaik Verlag for two passages (in my own translation) from *Meditation – Wege zum Selbst* by U. Reiter (Munich, 1976, p.45); Oxford University Press for quotations from *Arthur Schnitzler* by M. Swailes (Oxford, 1971, pp.125-126), *Hinduism* by R. C. Zaehner (Oxford, 1980, pp.125-126, 170-171, 180) and *Natural Law and Natural Rights* by J. Finnis (Oxford, 1980, p.143); Penguin Books for quotations from *Confessions* by St Augustine (Harmondsworth, Middlesex, 1968, pp.211-212) and *Hinduism* by K. M. Sen (Harmondsworth, Middlesex, 1981, pp.13 & 22-23); Prestel Verlag for a passage (in my own translation) from *Die Zauberflöte* by A. Rosenberg (Munich, 1972, p.8); Ernst Reinhardt GmbH & Co Verlag for a passage (in our own translation) from *Der Organismus der Seele* by C. G. Heyer (Munich, 1951, pp.11ff.); Rowohlt Taschenbuch Verlag for a passage (in my own translation) from *Max Reinhardt* by Leonhard M. Fiedler (published in the series 'rowohlts monographien', copyright © 1975 by Rowohlt Taschenbuch Verlag GmbH, Reinbeck bei Hamburg p.38); Search Press for a quotation from *The Dark Night of the Soul* by St John of the Cross (London, 1953, pp.82 & 318); Sheed & Ward for a quotation from *Interior Castle* by Saint Theresa of Avila (London, 1974, p.143); Anthony Sheill Associates Ltd for a quotation from *Travelling In* by Monica Furlong (London, 1971, p.32); Sheldon Press for a quotation from *Conjectures of a Guilty Bystander* by T. Merton (London, 1968, p.158); Rudolf Steiner Press for a quotation from *Knowledge of the Higher Worlds* by R. Steiner (London, 1969, pp.137-138); Rudolf Steiner Nachlassverwaltung for passages (in my own translation) from *Die Welt der Sinne und die Welt des Geistes* by R. Steiner and *Zu Rudolf Steiner's Lebensgang*, Bildband I (Dornoch bei Basel, Switzerland, 1959, pp.32 & 34 and 1971, p.136 respectively); Tavistock Publications for a quotation from *The Divided Self* by R. D. Laing (Pelican Books, Harmondsworth, Middlesex, 1965, p.173); Vendanta Press for quotations from *How to Know God* by Prabhavananada & C. Isherwood (Hollywood, 1966, pp.78-79, 198 & 204). Anthroposophic Press Inc., for a quotation from Rudolf Steiner: *Knowledge of the Higher Worlds* (pp.32-33, New York, 1947) and *Practical Training in Thought* (p.13, New York, 1948); J.M. Dent & Sons Limited for a quotation from R.C. Zaehner: *Hindu Scriptures* (pp.67-68, Everyman Library, London, 1966); Eyre & Spottiswode for a passage from St. Thomas Aquinas: *Summa Theologica Volume 7* (p.95, Andover, 1976); Rupert Hart-Davis for a quotation from Laurence Whistler: *The Initials in the Heart* (p.234, London, 1966); Mosaik Verlag for a quotation from Udo Reiter: *Meditation – Wege zum Selbst* (p.47, Munich, 1976); Princeton University Press for a quotation from Jolande Jacobi and R.F.C. Hull (Eds.): *C.G. Jung: Psychological Reflections: An Anthology* (p.71, Princeton, 1953); Routledge & Kegan Paul for quotations from the English Edition of Jolande Jacobi and R.F.C. Hull (Eds.): *C.G. Jung: Psychological Reflections: An Anthology* and also Hermann J. Weigand (Translator and Editor): *Goethe: Wisdom and Experience, Selections by Ludwig Curtius* (p.164, London 1949); Verlag Urachhaus for a section from Hermann Beckh: *Der Hingang des Vollendeten* (p.44, Stuttgart, 1960). I am also grateful to Mr J. M. Cohen for permission to publish an extract from his translation of *The Life of Saint Teresa* (at p. 210) and to Professor Gerard Rochford for permission to cite a phrase from his inaugural lecture.

I should like to add an expression of special thanks to Frau Susanne Kerkovius for her sensitive rendering of our two volumes into German.

Marcus Lefébure,
Summer 1989.

7 Life Processes.
Breathing   ♄ Saturn
Warming   ♃ Jupiter
Nourishing (Digesting) ♂
Circulating ☉ Ego - turning point   Secreting Essential / non-essential
Maintaining ☿ movement, healing
Growing   Maturation ♀ new impulse - Individualizing
                              harmony.
Reproducing ☾ Creating something new. Rebirth.

Publishers' Note

The present revised and enlarged edition originally appeared as two separate volumes: *Conversations on Counselling* in 1982, and in a second edition in 1985; and *Human Experience and the Art of Counselling* in 1985. Both volumes were subsequently translated successfully into German and Dutch. Now these two volumes, appropriately edited and revised, have been brought together for the first time in one edition. At the time these conversations take place, Fr Marcus Lefébure is Catholic Chaplain in the University of Edinburgh; Dr Hans Schauder is an independent counsellor associated with the Rudolf Steiner movement and various social work agencies.

Introduction

Our initial meeting was as seemingly random as most meetings. And the evident contrasts between us made it seem more fragile than most. Yet from the very first we felt drawn on by something else behind these superficial differences. The first meeting seemed to require a sequel, this sequel another, and so on, until a friendship ripened, and out of the friendship a series of at first episodic, then gradually more systematic conversations grew, and with it the confidence to record them on tape. The contrasts remained, but they came to be suffused by ever greater mutual sympathy.

Perhaps I can ask the reader to picture this at first unlikely encounter – between, on the one hand, a short, stocky, largely bald man with bright, penetrating, animated eyes, an experienced paediatrician and counsellor in his late sixties, and therefore now in semi-retirement, speaking with a broken, mid-European accent, somebody at once sharp and wise, and in this way alone revealing his Jewish background, and, on the other, a slim, bearded, alternately still and vivacious man some twenty years his junior, a Catholic priest speaking standard BBC English except for his crumpled 'R'. This last was the give-away: the defective 'R' betrayed at once his Austrian parentage and thereby also one important factor in the deep sympathy that was to develop over the years between the two men. For Dr Schauder had been born and brought up and done his medical studies in the same Vienna where my parents had been born and brought up, albeit on different sides of that Jewish world which had also nourished the young Freud.

We had discovered this link soon after we had been introduced to each other by one of my confrères at the Catholic university chaplaincy where I had been working since 1970 (and was destined to go on working for fifteen years in all). In this way a contact that had begun by being a professional courtesy soon became a deep personal friendship expressed in a series of fairly regular meetings over *Kaffee mit Schlag*, the Viennese coffee with cream, provided by Dr Schauder's wife, Lisl. Thus the only adequate term for these meetings as they developed was Dr Schauder's: each meeting was a *Gespräch*, a profound and mutually enriching *dialogue* of feelings, thought and talk.

It was during these soon fairly regular meetings, in Dr Schauder's simply furnished but book-lined study overlooking the hills, that the idea was first conceived and then gradually realised of devoting at least some conversations to topics of common concern and of recording them, at least for ourselves. Could we not explore together some of the deeper issues underlying the practice of counselling such as emerged from our different but possibly complementary vantage points as counsellor and priest, respectively? It was in this way that we devoted a number of, usually, Saturday mornings to such topics. We did not plan the whole series from the start but allowed the topics as it were to grow out of each other.

Not that these conversations flowed smoothly one from and into another, as the unbroken sequence of chapter headings in the Table of Contents might suggest. There are in fact two distinct, albeit intimately inter-related sequences of conversations, which originally appeared as two separate publications.

In the case of the first series of dialogues, I have already suggested that what began by chance soon began to take on an impetus of its own, and, moreover, an impetus that, at least in retrospect, seemed to be organic, almost inevitable. And, being organic, the series also developed a pattern of its own. The two pillars of the book, as Dr Schauder soon saw

INTRODUCTION

and so called them, are formed by the first and the fourth chapters on 'The Stages of Conselling' and 'The Stages of the Spiritual Path', which then developed into two corresponding sequels. These were then connected by two further chapters on relationship and solitude and the supreme relationship of woman and man. This is where we left the first series, and also the conversations, at least until the inward dynamic from within us and the success of the publication of the first volume of conversations drew us on to recommence.

In the second series of dialogues, here again there was the same combination of unforced dynamic, organic growth and retrospectively appearing pattern. This time, however, the pattern came about differently. Our immediate starting-point was the need we had begun to feel by then to explore further what animated but was not exhausted by even so suggestive a scheme as Dr Schauder's seven stages, namely, the *creativity* that underlay it all. So, in a sense, we went backwards in order to launch forwards. And this proved to be the pattern of the following dialogues: they were a series of cases of *reculer pour mieux sauter*. More specifically, we discussed further the implications of a forward and backward dimension to the creative process, the pervasive but for this very reason unexamined notion of the critical importance of the personality, the very bearing and being of the counsellor, and the consequent potentiality for abuse of that power, the frequent conflict between the inner need for personal growth and the external demands of a social code, and, finally, the tangle, or conflict, of sex and contemplation.

This second series I sought to round off, this time on my own, with a reflection on how, through this developing sequence, I had come to glimpse a series of relationships as it were in enfilade: from life to counselling, from counselling to friendship, and then, even beyond this, from friendship to something more yet. And so I came to conclude on that note which had already sounded early in the first series, only then to die away before returning again with amplified resonance, the note of trinity – meant in upper as well as lower case.

So there is a hidden caesura in the present volume between the fifth and the sixth dialogue, at once pause, break and connection.

All these chapters (except the last two) thus correspond to actual tape-recorded conversations and are broadly based on them. Further, they all represent conversations between Dr Schauder and myself, except the opening one, which was with another of Dr Schauder's friends, a social worker who appears here as Bridget.

Such was the provenance of our dialogues. They are about encounter. They are also the fruit of encounter. On re-reading them now, at an interval of some five years, what strikes me – and with some surprise – is how much I can still stand by their substance. A great deal of water has flowed under the bridge for us both – in fact at times it seemed more exact to talk of the bridge itself collapsing into the flood – and yet, apart from a shift of emphasis here and a clarification there, I would say much the same today, with one exception. The first volume, as I have already indicated, contained a chapter on 'Woman and Man'. Our own later hesitations about it were reinforced by comments from outside. So in the end we decided to omit it altogether from this edition.

Another change for this edition was to abandon the exclusive use of 'he' to denote gender. Instead we have adopted the convention of distributing the gender references equally by referring to the counsellor as 'he' and to the counselled as 'she'. A new objection may now arise – that by giving the supposedly inferior role to the female we are perpetuating the gender imbalance in a more sophisticated way. But this is clearly not our intention, since one of the main tenets of these conversations is that counselling is based on a profound equality and could even be said to be an initiation into equality. To avoid any possibility of misunderstanding, we could perhaps have reversed the gender usages. But since my friend Dr Schauder and I happen to be men, such a solution would have been rather forced and slightly absurd.

One last remark. In this new edition we have taken out most of the German quotations and expressions, retained previously to suggest something of the local colour of the original conversations, so as to make the book that little bit more accessible. At the same time, I must warn the reader that there remain passages where he or she might have to work hard. I should like to think that this is at least in part because the questions we have tried to open up are too new, the quest for a mutual integration of psychotherapy and spirituality too rudimentary, to allow easy formulation. In any case, our hope is that, by our exploration, we are being in our turn what the many witnesses we have cited have been for us: companions on a way that must go through dark as well as delightful places.

Perhaps this wrestling with difficulties underlines one of the book's essential points: that by the very struggle to wrest a comprehensive and coherent truth from initially dark and fractured glimpses we can put our readers in touch with the truth that both envelops and is beyond us all. As beings in faltering pursuit of the truth of dialogue, we show ourselves to be what we freely acknowledge we are, earthen vessels indeed – but vessels that carry a shining gift.

Marcus Lefébure
Autumn, 1989.

Dialogue 1: The Stages of Counselling

> ... the real matter, the regeneration of an atrophied personal centre, will not be achieved. This can only be done by one who grasps the buried latent unity of the suffering soul with the great glance of the doctor: and this can only be attained in the person-to-person attitude of the partner, not by the consideration and examination of an object.
>
> Martin Buber *I and Thou*

'I'm really interested to know how you prepare for your counselling sessions, Hans', Bridget began. 'Working in the Social Work Department as I do, I get the impression that people don't take time to prepare themselves for these sessions and that they don't realise how important it is. I wonder how you feel about this?'

'Well', replied Hans, 'I feel it is extremely important to *prepare*, and to prepare in a number of ways. First of all, I think it is very important to be aware of the fact that your general way of life is fundamental to successful counselling. And by "general way of life" I mean two distinct, though related, things. On the one hand, I think it is very important that the counsellor should have an all-round experience of life and human beings. In this connection I often think of a statement by Jung. It is to be found in an anthology of his writings selected by one of his disciples, Jolande Jacobi, and it goes as follows:

> The man who would learn the human mind will gain almost nothing from experimental psychology. Far better

for him to put away his academic gown, to say good-bye to the study, and to wander with human heart through the world. There, in the horrors of the prison, the asylum and the hospital, in the drinking-shops, brothels, and gambling hells, in the salons of the elegant, in the exchanges, socialist meetings, churches, religious revivals, and sectarian ecstasies, through love and hate, through the experience of passions in every form in his own body, he would reap richer stores of knowledge than text-books a foot thick could give him. Then would he know how to doctor the sick with real knowledge of the human soul.[1]

I should myself like to add here that some basic experience of the arts and of the great spiritual traditions of mankind will be essential as well. Great art and religion embody transforming and transcendental experiences. The counsellor must to some extent be familiar with them, as in the later stages of working with a client, it will be his task to help her to build a secure inner life. — On the other hand, having lived in youth and early middle age, through experiences of this kind, he who aims at becoming a counsellor must gradually acquire a balanced, disciplined, rather serene way of life. For example, I think it would be very disturbing if I allowed myself to indulge in a great deal of social gossip and uncontrolled talk or watch a television programme which lasts too long and so on. I could give you many more examples which show that the way of life is most important. This is the first thing which seems to me to be fundamental. In the more immediate sense, I think it is critical that you approach an interview in a relaxed state of mind and body, and also that you clear your mind of all personal feelings, thoughts and preoccupations. The whole interview should be approached almost in a state of innocence and complete receptivity, so that you can perceive without any hindrance what you encounter in your client.'

'How do you feel about work being handed on to you about a client? I'm thinking in terms of files or other background information. Do you use that in your preparation?' asked Bridget.

'No', said Hans, 'I usually just glance at them because if I were to immerse myself in the study of these documents, I should be far too thoroughly conditioned and that, I think, is absolutely detrimental to the objective, that is to say the unbiased approach to a client and to the unbiased perception of what you meet. Very often, of course, in actual fact you meet something quite different from what you have been told in advance. But I do refer to the documents after I have formed the first basic impressions. For instance, I then make up my mind whether I can agree with the diagnosis or not. But I should feel that my mind was being cluttered up with thoughts and conclusions which are anticipating results instead of organically experiencing facts, and this I would consider a fundamental failure of the whole counselling process. The counselling process should begin in a state of pure receptivity that is objectively open to all impressions as they come towards you in a purely human way and you should not think in terms of diagnostic concepts; you should experience human beings in every way as you find them.'

'So, after glancing at what you have been told about a client, you would put it all at the back of your mind and then start completely afresh, forming your own impressions?'

'Yes, I would not only put it at the back of my mind; I would put it out of my mind.'

'Could we then go on to talk about how you actually start your session Hans?'

'Yes, that depends on whether I am seeing the client for the first time, or whether I have seen her before. If I am seeing her for the first time, I try to make her comfortable, in a very informal way. I take her into the book-lined study which is deliberately furnished in a very simple way. There are no pieces of furniture which indicate a professional set-up.'

'You're expressing a very unusual concept when you say that the study is specially arranged in a way to avoid any sign of a consulting room. I get the impression that you think of counselling as a personal encounter between two people rather than as an encounter between a consultant and a patient?'

'Yes, I do', replied Hans. 'For me, counselling is fundamentally, or should be, a human encounter calculated to give the person help and guidance. I think a counsellor is in the first place a human being who is able, in terms of his experience, his humanity, his maturity, to give this help. He should certainly not give the impression of a professional psychiatrist with specialised knowledge, because the client then feels that he is not met on a human level, is not understood on a human level, that he is, to put it very bluntly, a "clinical specimen".'

'It is interesting that you should use this comparison now, because I was thinking in terms of the medical profession, and how, when you go to a psychiatrist or doctor, you are taken over, you think of yourself as being ill.'

'Yes, Bridget. The client should not feel that she is scrutinised, that she is subjected to tests, that she is being cross-examined, but that she is simply met by another human being whom she can trust, to whom she can unburden herself and who, she hopes, may be able to help. Therefore, you see, everything that indicates professionalism is deliberately avoided, while everything that indicates a quiet, orderly, warm, human situation is gently emphasised. There are books in the room which give a thoughtful atmosphere, there are flowers which I always need in order to keep cheerful. The client's seat is opposite the window and she can look onto the distant hills and let her thoughts roam freely. There must, of course, be a climate of professionalism but this should be conveyed solely through the counsellor's bearing and personality.'

'So the first stage in the actual counselling process — after the counsellor's preparation — is that the person comes and is encouraged to speak freely.'

'The very first thing perhaps is that she feels she is not coming into a professional set-up because she would rather avoid that and is probably even scared of it; but that she feels she comes into an environment which is intimate, personal, and basically free of all clinical trappings. She should experience the counsellor as an ordinary, reasonably nice, and friendly human being. Then we settle down around the fire, not with a writing desk but only a little table between us. In order to help a new client to get accustomed to the surroundings, I ask her for her name, address and date of birth, and we have a few words about some general topic.

'There are two types of people. There are, first, those who are poised to unburden themselves right away; and they are, of course, encouraged to speak, and I listen. Then there are those who are very reluctant to speak and very often want me to ask them a few questions about their general background and education, and then they get going. Much of their problem is already expressed in this general account of their background.'

'The person who is very reluctant to speak or hardly comes out with any information, you will then really have to ask?'

'Yes', said Hans, 'I give her plenty of time. Some people are very reluctant to come to the point and take a very long time to cover certain areas of their life before they disclose their problems. It's a matter of playing it by ear, and if I make a false move prematurely, that is to say if I intervene by focussing on the real problem area, which by that time I may have guessed already, she may take flight, withdraw and never come again. But if she goes on meandering and doesn't ever come to the point, then with careful timing, I ask her a leading question. But there are people who will avoid approaching a problem area even for weeks, while they cover and discuss the surrounding areas with reasonable competence, and there are cases where you must accept that, as long as you feel that the whole process of the encounter is fruitful and that the client is progressing. But there is one thing I always try to be quite certain about, and this is that the client comes of her own free will — that she is not being pushed or persuaded by friends, relations, a husband or a wife, because counselling really presupposes *the conscious will of the client to co-operate*. She cannot be persuaded to co-operate, she cannot be coerced into co-operation; it is not the counsellor's business to involve her in the counselling process with some tricks of the trade. Therefore one of my first questions, if in doubt is, "Was it your own wish to come?"'

'We could perhaps come back to this when we talk about the kind of clients you would accept or refuse; it is an important point. Why do you think *listening* is so important and what actually happens to the listener? Obviously, it will give you all the information about the history of the person, about her feelings and problems. Apart from that, what happens to the client during this listening phase?'

'Well', responded Hans, 'I think, in the first place, the client must experience that there is a person who is not only willing but keen to listen, to get to know her and to share her most intimate thoughts, feelings and experiences. That encourages her to speak out and to unburden herself. She will speak about things she probably has never spoken about before and that in itself is very therapeutic. But it is more than that. As she begins to articulate, to express these thoughts and feelings which so far have been held in, they suddenly "see the light of day" as we say. They are expressed and embodied in words, which now stand there, so to speak, in the space between the counsellor and the client; and if the client goes on articulating, she is for the first time face-to-face with her experiences, rather than being oppressed by them from within.'

'It occurs to me, as I listen to you, that one reason why people need counselling could be that in their own life, in their married life or within their circle of friends, they don't ever find the opportunity of expressing themselves, or they are never seen for what they really are.'

'Yes, that's it', Hans said. 'In a crisis situation, I always discourage confiding in friends or relatives. Quite frankly, I have hardly ever found that it will do much good. There are of course exceptional friends to whom a person can turn and unburden herself completely, but, as a rule, the relationship is too close, and people have their own ideas about the other person and about what the other person should do, so that they cannot accept her exactly as she is, without even inwardly putting any thoughts and ideas in the way.'

'Do you think any person close to the client would be too subjective perhaps and expect something of the client, whereas the counsellor has an objective relationship?'

'Yes. The counsellor has an objective relationship and he doesn't expect anything; he doesn't hope for anything. You see, he waits for the moment when he can guide the client quite objectively into the next step of creative living. I give you an example from a quite different sphere which I think is illuminating. You know that I deal a lot with children. Now children very often need coaching, and two parties are specially concerned, namely, the teacher and the parents. Again, I have never seen any good coming from either teacher or parent undertaking the coaching because the relationship is too close. The teacher as well as the parent, already expects some results from the child; he hopes for something and the child feels under pressure to produce something which it is difficult for her to produce. That situation is too close and therefore it needs a third person who comes in from outside. The child will then feel free from demands of this kind; everything is objective, and in this atmosphere of freedom and with gentle encouragement, she will do what she is able to do, and very often she will blossom.'

'It occurs to me that in a marriage relationship one partner would always be giving advice or hoping for results from which he or she can benefit. I think this is only human, isn't it?'

'Yes. Discussions of marriage relationships between partners are most complex and stressful because the situation is heavily overlaid emotionally, and the expectations, hopes, tensions and frustrations are so strong. They are therefore, very rarely fruitful.'

'Could we at this point summarise what the listening means to the client and what it means to the counsellor, Hans?'

'Well, to deal first with what listening means to the client.

The client in the first instance needs the relief of being completely herself, of being able fully to confide without reservation and to unburden herself without any inhibitions, without fearing to hurt anybody's feelings or "say something wrong". That in itself is a tremendous relief. The second benefit for the client I think, is that, as she articulates her thoughts and feelings, she becomes detached from them; for the first time she sees them as it were from a certain distance, because they have become embodied in words and they are no longer confined to her inner being. But thirdly, I think that if the counsellor listens in the right way, following the client with complete selflessness as far as he is able, identifying with her, then in a mysterious way, the client receives back from the counsellor not only what she expresses, but also her own true being. I often compare it with a living mirror.'

'You are not talking now about interpreting what a client says?' asked Bridget.

'Not at all', continued Hans. 'I'm talking about relating to her in complete inner silence. And this brings me to what listening involves for the counsellor. It may help you to understand what I mean here to share another of my favourite quotations. It is from Rudolf Steiner's book *Knowledge of the Higher Worlds*[2] and it comes in an early part of the book in the chapter called "The Stages of Initiation":

> ...Of very great importance for the development of the student is the way in which he listens to others when they speak. He must accustom himself to do this in such a way that, while listening, his inner self is absolutely silent. If someone expresses an opinion, and another listens, assent or dissent will, generally speaking, stir in the inner self of the listener. Many people, in such cases, feel themselves impelled to an expression of their assent, or, more especially, of their dissent. In the student, all such assent or dissent must be silenced. It is not imperative that he should suddenly alter his way of living, by trying to attain at all times this complete inner silence. He will

have to begin by doing so in special cases, deliberately selected by himself. Then quite slowly and by degrees, this new way of listening will creep into his habits, as of itself. The student feels it is his duty to listen, by way of practice, at certain times, to the most contradictory views, and, at the same time, entirely to bring to silence all assent, and more especially, all adverse criticism. The point is, that, in so doing, not only all purely intellectual judgement be silenced, but also all feelings of displeasure, denial or even assent. The student must at all times be particularly watchful lest such feelings, even when not on the surface, should still lurk in the innermost recess of the soul... The student can thus train himself to listen to the words of others quite selflessly, completely shutting out his own person, and his opinions and way of feeling. When he practises listening without criticism, even when a completely contradictory opinion is advanced, when the most "hopeless mistake" is committed before him, then he learns, little by little, to blend himself with the being of another and become identified with it. Then he hears through the words, into the soul of the other...

And I'll give you one example of what I mean. The other day I had a young man here who is highly intelligent and who had thought about and searched through many spheres of philosophy, occultism, psychology, magic, and so on. Now, much of what he said was very foreign to me, and personally I couldn't agree with it all, for example when he said that Christ is the God of death, for to me Christ is the God of life. But I felt very strongly that I had to keep completely silent — not only outwardly but inwardly silent — and go with him along his rather tortuous pathways of experience and thought without deserting him. After he had related to me very extensively for about an hour and a half, without me interrupting him, the whole panorama and complexity of his experience, which he himself called weird — and weird it was! — and I was wondering how he would ever find a way out of this maze of thought and illusions, he suddenly said: "But you know, now I am through it all, now I have found the way back to myself, to my true humanity, and now I feel I can find my own God." I do think that, of course, he was prepared for this, but I do also think that I was somehow in the role of obstetrician, helping him to do this, to take the final step, simply by silently being with him and mirroring back to him not only what he said to me, namely, the weirdness of his experience, but also something different which was objective, which was not yet him, *something he wanted to become.* Hence I call it a living mirror, a mirror that responds quite silently, mirroring back something of the fundamental nature of man quite unconsciously. And this is perceived by the person who talks and in an almost telepathic way he may respond.'

'Could we come back to all that later on? At this point, do you ever make an assessment of the person's situation?'

'Yes, Bridget, very much so, though I use the word assessment only when I have to give a report to someone. For myself, I call this period of listening to the client a period of *exploration and identification;* it helps me to explore her and her world in the same way that I should explore a city, by wandering about in it and getting to know exactly what it feels like, how it looks. But when I have completed this process, there are two things which I do: first, in what I call the *diagnostic interlude*, I simply ask myself a clinical question about the health of the client, namely: Is she sufficiently healthy for me to be able to expect a rational response and co-operation from her? For instance, if she is seriously ill physically, say with a very painful ulcer, I can't expect this. Similarly, if she is for example, suffering from a severe form of phobia, I can't expect it, and then I have to refer her, at least temporarily, to someone else. If, on the other hand, I feel that, although she has a certain disability, she will co-operate and can function on a rational level, I carry on.'

'Will you also assess her problem at this point? Would you say to yourself: "Now that I have entered into the life of this person, to what conclusions do I come?"'

'Yes, and this is now the next stage. After having disposed of the diagnostic issue, which is a clinical, intellectual problem, I try now to find, through living with her in her world, through this process of <u>identification</u>, the answer to the questions: <u>In what way can I help her?</u> What is missing in her life? What needs to be reshaped in her life? That may be something totally different from the problem she presented at the beginning. The young man I referred to a moment ago came with the problem that he was very shy; and so he was. He also had many intellectual and philosophical problems, as I have indicated. Now, the obvious answer would have been to help him through frequent conversations to overcome his shyness and to discuss or resolve his problems as far as possible. But after having lived inwardly with him in his world for a time — and I emphasise, I *lived* rather than *thought* about it — I felt strongly that his relationship to life, his link with life, particularly with practical work, was not established, and I felt that the most essential thing for him was to take up physical work. This process of *assimilation* defies intellectual workings out; you can think about a person's predicament, but such mere thinking will not, anyway in my case, yield any reliable results, any results where I feel "That's it". It is the old rule of sleeping on it, it's a matter of handing over a question to the deeper layers of your being, to the unconscious, which is infinitely wiser than your head. And here again I'd like to quote Rudolf Steiner. The particular passage I have in mind comes from another of his works, *Practical Training in Thought*,[3] and occurs in the part of the book in which he insists on the importance of the ability to form and retain "exact pictures" of what is presented and therefore the details of scenes and impressions. Then he goes on to say in particular:

> ...we must have the confidence that these events which in the outer world are connected with one another will also bring about connections within us. This must be done in pictures only, *while abstaining from thinking.* One must

say to oneself: "I do not yet know what the relation is; but I shall let these things grow within me and they will bring about something in me if I refrain from speculation." You will easily believe that if anyone forms exact inner images of succeeding events, at the same time *abstaining from all thinking*, something may be taking place in the invisible members of his nature.

Or, as I should put it myself, it is of the greatest importance to develop the art of visualising in feeling-soaked images. If you have lived with questions and if you have learned patiently to let them mature in the depths of your being, then solutions and answers will come from deep within, with a sense of certainty and conviction. That, of course, takes time.'

'Does a client herself ever point to the real problem in the course of the counselling sessions?'

'The other day a young man came to see me who had a study problem. He had anxieties over his studies. He was a brilliant, gifted young man, and the obvious problem was to help him to get back to his studies and master his anxiety; but in the course of the session I felt that this wasn't the right course and I said to him: "Allow yourself to dream, and if you could have your way, quite apart from the practical possibilities, what would you like to do, how would you like to shape your life?" And he said: "I should like to live in the country, in a farmhouse with other people, near a river, work on the land; or I should like to go to Russia." He was a divinity student. And when he said this, I had to tell him: "This is exactly what I think, that is exactly what you need. That's the answer."'

'Do you mean, Hans, he was removed from the source of his strength?'

'Exactly. He was getting tired because he had been pressed very prematurely, as an eighteen year old, into the life of prayer and withdrawal of a Jesuit trainee, and that deprivation was the real problem, not the study. Therefore, if a person is sufficiently clear-headed, and courageous, he may sooner or later produce a solution, or something which indicates a

THE STAGES OF COUNSELLING

solution and his real need, without me prompting, because deep down people feel what is lacking in their humanity, in their experience.'

'Could it possibly be the case that, through expressing the problems, a sort of loosening-up happens which makes it possible for a person to come up with the real issues?'

'Absolutely true, yes. I am sure it is a loosening-up. As the conscious mind is relieved, the unconscious mind, which of course contains these images of hopes and expectations which are unfulfilled, has the possibility of coming to life and therefore will produce this result. Moreover, if the counsellor is able to mirror back something like the totality of life, the totality of being human and of living, this will call out in the client a feeling of what she is lacking, and one way or another, she will indicate it; or even if she does not indicate it, she will, in most cases, respond to a suggestion — unless she is frightened, or simply unwilling to undertake the great effort and adventure of creative living. For it does need great courage, it needs effort and it needs truthfulness, and very many people are nowadays too far gone; they haven't got the courage any more, they haven't got the strength, they cannot rid themselves of old habits; and then very often they will tell me: "Yes, I know you're right; but I'm sorry, I can't do it", and they vanish.'

'Can we look again over the different stages of the counselling process we have covered so far, then?' asked Bridget.

'Yes. I think that so far we have discussed and to some extent characterised *four* distinct stages of the counselling process, namely, the *preparation*, which concerns the counsellor only, but is fundamental to the counselling process. Secondly, the process of *listening*, or as we have also called it, the stage of exploration and identification. Then, number three, the *diagnostic interlude;* and number four — and I think that this is a distinct phase — the time which the counsellor requires in order fully to *assimilate* into his unconsious mind the totality of the client's being and situation, where he hands

13

over, so to speak, the questions in his mind to the deeper layers of his being and waits for the answer to come; because there, he has far greater wisdom than he has intellectually at his disposal. So, in this sense, I think we have covered four distinct phases: 1. preparation 2. listening, exploration and identification 3. diagnostic interlude 4. assimilation (and 3 and 4 are interchangeable).'

'The assimilation will eventually culminate in some clear understanding of the person's needs, or the person's problems? But you don't think it out. My impression from the way you put it, is that you live with the problem and the answer comes up, wells up, from the deeper layers within you?'

'Yes, Bridget. I have always experienced that when I try to think and think, I become rather more uncertain than certain, while if I allow myself this time of living with it, of assimilation into the deeper layers of the mind, eventually I reach a point where I feel completely certain. I have a private expression for this, namely, that "something hits me under the belt"; I feel from deep within that I'm being almost physically gripped, I feel "That's it". I was interested to come across a Japanese proverb which at the moment I can't recall in detail but which expresses exactly this: this feeling of arriving at certainty through an unconscious process, which hits you, so to speak, below the diaphragm?'

'So it's really quite a vital process?'

'I believe that in the whole counselling process this is perhaps the most vital. We must not under-estimate how vital, how subtle, preparation is, how subtle exploration is; even the diagnostic interlude requires subtle decision-making; but the most personal phase of the counselling process, which requires the greatest patience and the confidence that life itself will give you the answer, *that the very being of the client will give you the answer and not your intellectual reasoning* — the most vital, the most subtle phase of the counselling, is what I call for want of a better word, "assimilation". It will enable the counsellor, out of the certainty which he now experiences, out of the clarity of the vision which will suddenly highlight for him certain areas that may have been indistinct or covered by a kind of shadow, to select what we may call a *target area* or several target areas. He can now make the decision to work on these; and that brings us to stage five.'

'So the process has really gone from the more unconscious layers of experience to a conscious level where you can actually turn it into concepts and select the area or the approach to the solution of the problems?'

'Precisely Bridget. It is then conceptualised, it is then made a target, it is pin-pointed; and at this point I do write down for myself, very briefly, what I call a *therapy programme*, essentially a number of *target-areas*, which I hope to be able to approach and work through with the client, as time goes on. That may take a few sessions, it may take months, that depends on the relationship as it develops and of course, particularly on the personality and the response of the client.'

'How far do you discuss this therapy programme with the client? Is it something you have at the back of your mind? How far do you disclose to a client how you see her problem, how you see her situation?'

'I have it essentially at the back of my mind, in a very tentative form. If this were too firm a structure which I tried to impose and convey too strongly, too distinctly to the client, I should stifle the therapeutic process. The therapeutic process is something which must flow freely in terms of feeling, encounter and conversation between the client and the therapist. Therefore, when a session begins, although I tentatively have at the back of my mind what I might discuss with the client, I try to feel how she is feeling, to tune in to it and give her ample opportunity to express what is foremost in her mind. This may, for example, be something which has just happened to her last week and which she has a very great need to tell me; and of course it would be a very great mistake to stop her. Or other thoughts may have occurred to her meantime. But if, as the session proceeds, I feel that her mind is more relaxed, I try to sense whether this is possibly the right moment to steer the conversation towards the target area or towards a specific objective which I have in mind.'

'Does the client to some degree share this objective with you?'

'Ideally, of course', said Hans, 'she should share it fully. This is perhaps too much to expect, but I think that it is essential that at some point at least, *she has accepted it intellectually;* namely, that she will say to me: "I think you're right, I can see the sense of what you say." If, for example, I say to a client: "I think you should do physical labour", she will agree and say, "Yes, I think that's a good idea; this is what I really need". However, it may take a very long time for this to be translated into sufficiently strong feeling and particularly sufficiently strong initiative to become reality. Or, to give you another example: the client was a young woman who was leading a very promiscuous life; she was on the one hand, enjoying it because she felt confirmed as a woman; on the other hand, she was extremely miserable about it and was unable to support a steady relationship. Now, I felt I should make it clear to her that her promiscuous life was having a destructive effect on her personality as well as on her ability to support a steady relationship and eventually enter a happy marriage; to which, intellectually, she fully agreed, she saw the point. Now, she was one of those unfortunate people whose ways of life and habits were so deeply ingrained that she could no longer do without it. This can be compared with an addiction. If you depend on a drug, you may not be able to wean yourself off it; similarly promiscuity can become an addiction. So it was with her. In the end, it was she who said, "I know you're right, but I'm sorry, I can't do it", and she went for good. You see, there are limits to what a counsellor or any human being can do. You must always keep in mind that ultimately the decision is the client's, it is she who has to make up her mind.'

'You are working with a person's motivation, you are encouraging her growth; but the person has to do the growing herself?'

'Yes, towards what I call creative living. And creative living is living which leads a person to a greater capacity to overcome difficulties and so to learning very gradually and painfully to achieve mastery over herself and her circumstances. This is how Goethe describes it in *Wilhelm Meister's Apprenticeship*:

> Probably the greatest thing that can be said to a man's credit is that he succeeds in determining circumstances to the greatest extent possible and to the least extent is subject to their determination. The whole world lies before us like a great quarry before the architect. But only he deserves this name who succeeds in using these natural blocks to give substance to an archetypal intuition with the greatest economy, purposiveness and solidity. Everything outside is only material (and I would include even the outer layer of the self in this term); but deep down in the core there is this creative power, the capacity to create what is to be, and the urge to tolerate no let-down until we have given it shape in one way or another, either outside ourselves or in our own person.
> (Quoted in *Goethe: Wisdom and Experience*, p.164).

[margin note: self mastery]

This struggle will lead the client sooner or later within the limits of her possibilities towards a truer and more complete humanity. The woman we have been discussing is miserable, she feels that life is defeating her, or rather that she has treated life the wrong way. She is, as every human being is, motivated towards growing, towards overcoming difficulties, towards turning defeat into victory, but the motivation was not strong enough, and as I said before, her strength failed her. It is a matter of strength, it is a matter of effort.'

'Could we for a moment talk about the aims and objectives of counselling, Hans? Am I right in thinking that what you have just voiced are really the aims and objectives as you see them? Would you consider the growing towards creative living as the aim? Could you enlarge on that a bit?'

'I think that this is the ideal or overall aim', continued Hans. 'We might say that the aims of counselling are two-fold.

The first is to enable the client to gain a vision of life in its completeness, in its fullness, in its reality. You have probably come across a rather famous saying of Matthew Arnold: "To see life steadily and to see it whole" (referring to Sophocles). I find this an admirable formula to describe what we all need: a vision to see life steadily and to see it whole. This is something which I try somehow to convey to the client. Her job then, and our job as human beings, is to adjust to this wholeness of life, to become steady, to unfold and to develop in such a way that we become, as far as possible, complete human beings, rather than problem-burdened fragments. Or, to put it in other words, our general aim is to become more and more of a piece with this totality and not with just part of it, to become adjusted emotionally, intellectually and spiritually. That is, of course, the ideal blueprint, and you can achieve this only partly, if you can achieve it at all. But what you might be able to achieve, and I see this as the second aim of counselling, is the establishment of *growing-points*. You will not discharge a client as a complete human being fully adjusted to the totality of life; but you will have given her an impetus to grow, you will have given her motivation, perhaps the courage to overcome difficulties, to change herself, to adapt to life in a new way; and that will be the beginning of a long process, which she will continue without you. And to achieve even this you may well have to help her to attain some more immediate and concrete objective.'

'You do not measure the way a person has gone. You are thinking in terms of sowing seeds from which future developments can happen?' asked Bridget.

'This is largely what I do. For example, I do not think that the case of the promiscuous young woman is hopeless. She has experienced and accepted a different view of life; only at this point in her life she was unable to make it a practical issue, she didn't have the strength. She will probably go through a great deal of suffering, and it is possible that the suffering will in the end bring her to a point where she will find new resources and strength so far undiscovered. But of course I should not be content with establishing only growing-points; I want to achieve practical results. For example, coming back to the young woman who should do physical labour, I want to bring her to the point where she gets herself a job, and not only that, but to the point where she gets a job and maintains it, which is a lot more. This brings us to two further stages of the counselling process.

I believe it was stage five when we opened out the target areas. Now the next stage is that we focus the client more and more directly on the *goal, on the future*. Whereas, when she came, she experienced her life fundamentally as the life which she had lived, the past, and the great difficulties and the stagnation of the present; now. As the result of work in the target area, she should become *future orientated;* because in my view people are beings made to reach out towards the future. This is what they really want: to go forward, to live and grow or, as St Paul says "forgetting what lies behind and straining forward to what lies ahead". This is a monumental saying of a tremendous man with a great mission, and we must not make the mistake of applying it to us very ordinary mortals, because we cannot all simply forget what lies behind. But essentially we can leave it behind and we should try to do better. I then hope to reach the point where I can enable the client to be more and more conscious of what lies ahead for her in various spheres of life: practical work, relationships, inner development and so on; so that the shadows of the past and the difficulties of the present become comparatively negligible, and the vision of the future lies open; that, I believe is stage six.

Stage seven supervenes when she actually *steps into her future*, makes a new life, re-shapes her outer and inner existence; in the case of the young woman, when she begins to do physical work, finds new relationships and of course, correspondingly has a new outlook and a different attitude. Now, in this process, and in this great adventure of creative living, again I feel I have to support her, because she may encounter many pitfalls, setbacks, difficulties and so on, whether it is work, or whether it is entering into a new relationship such as an engagement period or marriage.

'These, I think, are the seven stages', said Hans.

'Well, that is really a lot to take in. It is a wonderfully hopeful outlook on the abilities of human beings.'

'I think that the counsellor, however pessimistic he may be about the present situation in our society, must have a fundamental faith in human beings. I have got that through my encounters with people; they have aroused in me, in spite of difficulties and disappointments, the utmost admiration for their resourcefulness, their resilience. I find their honesty and truthfulness absolutely staggering; and whenever I encounter people who reveal themselves in utter honesty and truthfulness to me, I feel ashamed of the sham and lie which is lived in our conventional society. The situation of the counsellor and the client is, of course taken completely out of the context of ordinary social life: it is an encounter as it were on a remote island, there are only these two people there and the sky above them, and then human nature reveals itself. It has brought out in me, as I said, the utmost admiration for the strength and the truthfulness of people and their will to go forward in life. Then the spirituality which is now awakening in people, their need to understand this mysterious universe and to unite with it as far as possible, has made me feel thoroughly humble. And I have at times felt very common and ordinary, confronted with some of the young people whom I call the rare spirits. There are tremendous new possibilities emerging in human beings and I think the counsellor is in a very privileged position to recognise that. At the same time he has to recognise the appalling decline which takes place in the nature of a person who allows herself to drift and is not making the tremendous effort of creative living, reshaping her own personality, her own destiny, her own life. As some people go forward to the distant goal of humankind, others deteriorate into lying, into brutality, into disorganised ways of life. Here we reach the parting of the ways, and the counsellor's business is to help those along who try to find the way forward, who are truly future orientated.'

'Do you think I have really grasped what you said when I summarise the aims of counselling as being a matter of helping a person to develop her potential?'

'Yes, to the fullest possible extent, to develop her humanity. Of course, the human personality is fragmentary and limited, but there are always untapped resources in all of us, and I think it becomes more and more important that people, instead of becoming high-powered specialists in some fields, with a tremendous income and with a highly specialised skill and knowledge, become true persons, true human beings, who are capable of living; because living is a very great art and it has to be learned. There was even a book called *Teach Yourself to Live*. We are a very long way from really grasping that the art of living presupposes the art and the effort of becoming human and remaining human, which is again another issue. The people who neglect their humanity for the sake, for example, of their professional or intellectual progress or their money-earning capacity, almost invariably founder in life. I have met some brilliant university professors, very nice people, but totally incapable of coping with the problems of life, totally incapable of maintaining a reasonable relationship with their husbands or wives, or solving the simplest human problem. One of the fundamental faculties which I believe is to a large extent lost now and which only a true person and a reasonably complete person can recover is judgment. That sounds very simple; but judgment is in my view and experience a very rare commodity, because it develops, in a curious way, out of a fusion of feeling, intuition, and reasoning; and only a person who is reasonably complete will be able to achieve that. A person may be extremely clever in their own field, brilliantly clever; but as far as life is concerned, they may have no judgment at all.'

'Nowadays', said Bridget, 'we are called to rely more and more upon our own judgment because standards are disintegrating. The possibilities are endless, everything is changing, and we constantly have to make judgments out of our own capacity. We cannot fall back on saying: "This is the way it is done."'

'Yes, there are more and more courses about the way in which certain things have to be done. You are taught how to talk, you are taught how to communicate, you can take a course on shaping relationships, you can take a course on decision-making. In the end, you will have to take a course on which foot you should put forward first! I mean, life becomes increasingly uncertain and confused. You see, I believe much of this could be avoided if, instead of intellectually analysing these various spheres of existence, we concentrated our energies on becoming true human beings.'

'So your aim, Hans, is for a person to become a true human being, as far as it is individually possible?'

'Yes, that again may sound easy, but it is really extremely difficult and it requires courage, truthfulness and a merciless recognition of your own weaknesses. Also appreciation of your assets and the will to develop them. In order to become a true person you have to renounce certain pleasures, forego certain liberties you would like to take but shouldn't. To give you a simple example again: you simply cannot allow yourself to be involved in too much talking or gossiping, attending too many lectures or conferences and social events. There are limits. You must have periods of silence, in order to collect yourself inwardly. You have to practise restraint, control, whether it concerns food or drink, travel, exercise or relationships. Time and again you will have to weigh your inner stillness, your poise and serenity against the impact of these various active ties. You will have to establish a strict personal discipline, as it were a rule of life, self-created and self-imposed. Naturally this requires your readiness to make sacrifices, which may cause you discomfort or may even be painful. But the result will justify the sacrifice. Rudolf Steiner once said that "Creative sacrifice achieved and sustained in stillness opens up undreamt of sources of spiritual strength".'

Notes
1. Jolande Jacobi, *Jung, Psychological Reflections* (Pantheon Books Inc., New York, 1953), p.71.
2. Rudolf Steiner, *Knowledge of the Higher Worlds and Its Attainment* (Anthroposophic Press Inc., New York, 1947), pp.32-33.
3. Rudolf Steiner, *Practical Training in Thought* (Anthroposophic Press Inc., New York, 1948), p.13.

Dialogue 2: Counselling and the Archetype of the Human Dialogue

... one's not half two. It's two are halves of one:
which halves reintegrating, shall occur
no death and any quantity ...

                                            E.E. Cummings

'I was extremely interested to read the transcript of the conversation you had with your friend Bridget, the social worker', said I to Hans at the beginning of the morning's conversation. 'This particular series of dialogues between us began when I asked you some time ago what was involved in psychotherapy. You then said, if I may sum up your reply, that four things were required: an all-round knowledge of human beings arising from the widest possible experience of people, life, art and religion; the possession on the part of the counsellor of a personality formed by a deliberate spiritual training; a basic attitude, that of one human being as a whole meeting another human being as a whole in a spirit of highly-disciplined listening and respect; and a basic skill in dealing with people. You then went on to deal principally with this last aspect, explaining how a counselling relationship would typically unfold in seven stages, in much the same way as you had already done, unbeknown to me, with Bridget. And what I now see, after having been able to read the transcript of your conversation with her, is that you were able to give me such a clear and profound account not only because you had already responded to a similar request from Bridget but because before this you had spent years — over twenty years — exploring and practising all this intuitively in your work as a paediatrician and counsellor with children and adults. In other words, your practice came well before your reflection.'

'Yes', Hans replied. 'These seven stages simply emerged in the discussion with Bridget. As I talked with her, I began to realise that there is a certain organic sequence of stages. As our conversation proceeded, I discovered that I do instinctively go from one to the next and that a certain process, a dynamism, is there, and this dynamic can then be sub-divided into these seven stages: ①preparation, ②listening and exploration, ③ the diagnostic interlude, ④assimilation, ⑤ the selection of a target area or areas, ⑥helping the client to focus on the future, ⑦supporting the client as she steps out into this future. I was rather surprised by this at first, and then I was encouraged by discovering that David Stafford-Clark had also described a dynamic principle underlying the therapeutic encounter, albeit in a different way. In his view, insight therapy, as he calls it in *Psychiatry for Students*[1] develops in three essential phases: Receiving, Assimilating, Intervening. Therefore I did not start with Stafford-Clark, but I was subsequently glad to find that his was an independent variant of the method I have gradually evolved.'

'And it is this seven-stage dynamic that you have since reproduced for me, with this difference, that when you did so, you added various refinements of what you had previously said to Bridget. And the chief refinement, as I understand it, was that the concept of preparation for any individual counselling session was much richer. On the one hand, by the time you expressed your reflection on your practice to me, you had come to see more clearly that the preparation — your stage one — was really the preparation of the whole personality of the counsellor, in particular through a sustained spiritual discipline. Strictly speaking, therefore, one should think of the spiritual training of the counsellor not as something lying as it were alongside or parallel to the practice of counselling in its seven stages but as something penetrating the very substance of the counsellor's personality or activity. But, it seems to me, this has so many implications that I should like to discuss it with you on another occasion.'

'I should be delighted to do so', Hans replied. 'But may I say in the meantime that when I first spoke with you about the whole complex of factors involved in psychotherapy, I did indeed distinguish, on the one hand, the basic attitude of listening, which is crucial in the process of counselling, and on the other hand, the humanity as well as the spirituality of the counsellor, whereas now I should stress how all these elements interpenetrate each other. The spiritual training is not simply a specific training in spiritual skills and achievements but presupposes the counsellor's total humanity. It is this that must form the basis of his spiritual development, otherwise he would become a sort of dehydrated saint, which is a lamentable condition. And in this connection, we thought of the great examples of St. Augustine and St. Francis of Assisi who first lived fully human lives and then transmuted and refined them into spiritual energy and experience. In modern times we have the example of Thomas Merton who was also very much a man of the world before he submitted himself to the monastic cell.'

'There are many others', I added, 'for example, Charles de Foucauld, Martin Luther King and Dorothy Day who died only recently.'

'And, of course, one of the greatest examples, if not the greatest of all, is the Buddha.'

'So all that is a big subject, Hans, and I very much look forward to exploring it with you another day. To return, however, to the other aspect of the refinement of what you had said to Bridget in your subsequent re-exploration of the subject with me, you insisted that the most important single factor in counselling is the personality of the counsellor, so that the real preparation for any particular counselling session is the whole life that the counsellor brings to any such session.'

'Yes', said Hans, 'and it is perhaps here that I have really moved on in my thinking since I last spoke on this subject even with you. The seven stages which I explained to Bridget and then again to you represent the way I have gradually come to articulate what I should like to call <u>the dynamic of a therapeutic encounter</u>. But what has become clear to me only recently is that this seven-stage dynamic is basic *not only* to the therapeutic encounter *but also* to the human encounter as this manifests itself in the *Gespräch*. And by *Gespräch* I denote any meaningful conversation, a truly human dialogue, where people raise fundamental questions, exchange basic impressions, and where they both grope for some kind of direction, for some kind of, if not ultimate solution, at least some provisionally valid approach to these questions. And I think that if you scrutinise these seven stages, you will see that they also apply, though perhaps in a slightly modified way, to the process and dynamism, the organic dynamism, of an ordinary *Gespräch*, provided only that this is meaningful.

And that seems to me to be quite important. For example, I have discovered that when I am due to have a *Gespräch* with a friend, I have to go into this kind of <u>preparatory stage of silence and recollection</u>, exactly as I do with a client. To take another example: You may say, "Well, what about the diagnostic interlude? Surely you don't make a diagnosis when you meet one of your friends?" No, of course I don't make a diagnosis. But you see, in order to be sensitive to the needs of a person, you have to assess — in inverted commas — "diagnostically" what kind of condition this person is in, what you can say to her, what will be helpful or significant, how much she can take, and so on. You see, in this sense, a kind of "diagnosis", something comparable to a diagnosis, will come into it.

So we have here something quite fundamental, and I think it is fundamental in the sense that, as I now see things, the seven-stage process works not only in the therapeutic encounter but in the truly human encounter, the *Gespräch* as such. And in this respect it is different from Stafford-Clark's scheme since he applies it only to the therapeutic encounter. Then I should like to make one more point. But is that alright so far Marcus?'

'Yes, yes. I understand very well', I replied. 'It is as if your practice of counselling had come long before your reflection on it, but also as if, once you had begun to reflect on this practice with Bridget and then with me, the dynamic of your practice had continued, but now in a different mode. The same dynamic which eventually prolonged your practice into reflection has now been at work in the process of reflection itself, so that what began as an articulation of the practice of the *counselling relationship* has worked even freer to become the articulation of *any* true and deep human relationship, as manifested in the *Gespräch*. What you have recently come to, then, is a deepening and a widening of the significance of the sevenfold dynamic?'

'Precisely', said Hans. 'It now has a wider social significance. It is as such that it has a profoundly human significance. You see, once you have absorbed these attitudes and allowed them to become instinctive, then, whenever you have a human encounter, you will somehow go through these seven stages of preparation, exploration, assimilation and so forth.

'There is, however, a difficult question here. I have been asked: "If that is so, how do the various therapies come in? I mean, what about Freud, what about Jung, what about behaviour therapy and so on?" This is a very important question. If the sevenfold process has a basically human significance, where do particular therapeutic methods, as distinct from the general therapeutic encounter, come in?

Now, I think the answer, as far as I can see, is this: you remember that we spoke of a target area which has to be selected (our stage 5). And then we said that we have to work through this target area (our stage 6). Now I think that it is here, when we have selected a target area, that we have to make up our mind what therapeutic method, if any, we are to use. Right? For example, if you have a person who has a neurosis, a claustrophobia, and he can't go out or be in a closed room, you've got to do something about this, and after you have cleared other target areas you want to concentrate on this. The question then is: how do you do it? You see, you can decide on an analytical method, or you can decide on dream interpretation, or on suggestion, or simply on the "talking" therapy. You can also decide on conditioning therapy. You can, for instance, say that for this particular person, it is best to take her out in a car with you. *In this way, I think, specific therapeutic methods or techniques can be inserted into the complete process at this juncture and are built into the whole structure of the human encounter. Therefore the structure as such, I think, remains unchanged and is, as it were, archetypal.*'

'That is very interesting. Because that answers a question I have been very much considering within myself. You see, I am acquainted with several therapeutic methods, but more and more I'm convinced of their relativity and therefore of the need to adjust and to choose the exact method for each person. I have been dealing with three people recently to whom I instinctively just listened as totally as possible, and without having conceptualised it in the way you have, I think I came to something like a diagnostic interlude, when I asked myself: what does this particular person need? And it does seem to vary, so that to use one method only is to put people in a procrustean bed.'

'Absolutely', said Hans with enthusiasm. 'You see, the upshot of it all is that what I am talking about is not a specific therapeutic method, just one more added to the great number that already exist. No, these stages express the archetypal pattern of the therapeutic and human encounter as such, and this is basic and therefore unalterable. And into this has to be built, and can be built, any, but any, therapeutic method or technique. *Therefore this type of counselling or Gesprächstherapie has no quarrel with any other psychological or analytic method. It recognises all of them as far as they are valid and free of error. So it is also capable of and open to using them, but with discrimination, and it is not committed to any one specifically.* And as you indicated, the methods of therapy can be as unlimited as the possibilities of life itself. But the therapy must be specifically selected. You see, any human activity and human experience can ultimately, if rightly placed, work as therapy. At the same time, they each have their limitations, and so can complement each other. <u>I do, however, believe that the most fundamental and ultimately most powerful therapy is the therapy of the human encounter as such, where the very being of the therapist heals</u>. Of course, we're at the very beginning of experiences of this kind, and of such possibilities. I think that it would, therefore, be a fatal mistake in the training of therapists and psychiatrists to underestimate the importance of the maturity and the spirituality of the personality which is conveyed to the client, and to concentrate the training only on the technicalities of a method or of a school of thought or the clinical aspect, whatever it may be.

May I take it still a stage further? You see, more and more people who have all sorts of spiritual experiences, whether through meditation or spontaneously, are now coming in touch not only with priests but with analysts and psychiatrists. And psychiatrists who are ignorant of the spiritual dimension of human nature and the kind of spiritual experience people are capable of having, react to them — and I have two particular cases in mind — as if such people were simply suffering from aberrations. And this just won't work. Because events of this kind will simply explode into our, in this respect, complacent society. It just won't work for a psychiatrist to say, "Oh, well, this is a depressed and deluded person" because they are very often not depressed or half-mad. All the more important therefore that we deepen our experience in this human and spiritual realm in order to be able to face what is coming.'

'This explosion of the spiritual?' I asked.

'Yes. But that's only by the way. It's at a tangent to what we were discussing, namely the relationship of this basic human encounter as embodied in these stages to specific therapeutic techniques, whether psychiatric, analytic or other techniques or methods of healing, from the crudely physical to the

COUNSELLING AND THE ARCHETYPE OF HUMAN DIALOGUE

spiritual — the whole range.'

'That may indeed be something of a digression, Hans', I said, 'but it does follow on from what you were saying about the inner development of your thinking on the subject of the deeper significance of the process of the therapeutic encounter. To return however, to the main point, I find this latter notion fascinating; and at the deepest level I am captivated by it. At another level, however, I feel certain difficulties about this latest stage of your thinking.

Before I attempt to express these difficulties to you however, may I recapitulate what we have discussed so far? When I asked you in what proved to be the first in this series of discussions, what was involved in psychotherapy, you said that in your opinion there are four main things: first, the widest possible experience of life and people; secondly, a sustained spiritual discipline; thirdly, a basic attitude of one human being seeking to listen to and respond to another human being; and, fourthly, a developed skill in gradually eliciting the other's potential for growth and managing his own destiny. It was primarily with this latter skill that you dealt in your discussion with Bridget, whereas it was with the general presuppositions that you dealt in your discussion with me. Now, with hindsight, I can see that there was, as I mentioned before, an inner dynamic to your own life, practice and thinking, so that your thinking seemed to be a continuation of your practice, and your latest thinking a continuation of both. I can further see that in the latest stage of your thinking, as you have expressed it to me today, you have penetrated the deepest meaning of the therapeutic encounter and thereby uncovered the *structure of any inter-personal communications*, into which any form of therapy can be fitted — the inner structure, therefore, as you put it, of the archetypal human encounter *tout court*, as this is then manifested in the *Gespräch*. This conclusion therefore seems to have the singular force of a certain inevitability; it is like some pure distillate — and not only of your own prolonged experience but of a far larger, more universally human experience of which your particular experience is therefore like an alembic.

For all that, however, with my analytic self I still have these nagging doubts. So what I should like to do now, Hans, partly for the sake of the clarification of the ideas in my own mind and partly for the sake of truth and completeness, is to go over the seven stages and to check whether we can in fact transpose the description of the encounter between counsellor and client into a description of the encounter between one human being and another. For, if your thesis is valid, we can now analyse the truly human encounter in the same way as you have analysed the encounter between counsellor and client, so that every stage of the therapeutic encounter should correspond one by one, in its own way, with an ordinary but deep conversation — such, for instance, as the one we're having now. For presumably this discussion obeys the same law, to the extent that it is a true *Gespräch*?'

'Yes, indeed', Hans agreed.

'Well' I continued, 'the first stage — if I make a mistake, you'll correct me, won't you? — is that a client tries to explain herself, and you made a distinction between the presenting and the real problem.'

'No, not quite', Hans interrupted. 'The first stage is really the stage of preparation. Now this applies to the visit of a friend as well as to a session with a client. So here I visualise somebody coming who I know will want to discuss something of personal importance. Quite briefly, I withdraw into this room about ten or fifteen minutes before. Then the friend or the client arrives, and, assuming I know her, I try to keep perfectly still. I quiet my mind so that I know I shall be quite receptive. I do not *think* about her but *visualise* her, so that I can get a feeling of the kind of world she lives in, the feeling of the atmosphere which is peculiarly her own. That is the preparation, right? And that applies to visiting friends as well as to clients. Then stage two is simply the stage of observing, listening, exploring, with the main emphasis on listening. Now the friend will tell me something about what she's coming for, what she wants to discuss. Apart from listening, I make myself open in exactly the same way as with the client, I try to explore her special situation at this moment in her life. That is to say, I'll ask certain questions in order to be able to get as rounded an impression as possible of her situation, her relationships, the kind of life she leads, for example.'

'You're talking about a *Gespräch* between friends now? Not a therapeutic encounter?', I asked.

'It's exactly the same', Hans replied.

'So presumably, between two people who are similarly minded, the reverse could happen? I mean, she could also explore you? To the extent that you're on the same wavelength, there might be reciprocity?'

'Yes, that's perfectly true', Hans agreed.

'Isn't there therefore, a certain assymetry between the situation of the counseller and client and that of friend and friend? As between friends there's absolute equality, isn't there?', I asked.

'Strictly as between friend and friend, yes I agree', answered Hans, 'but perhaps I'm biased in a certain way. I must admit that it happens so rarely in my life — the process of reciprocity — that I'm conditioned...'

'Exactly, that's what I mean', I interjected. 'What I detect is that the model of counsellor and client is still so dominant in your life and therefore in your thinking that you haven't really worked the application of your insight right through to do justice to the relationship of two equals. And what I wonder is what happens when two people are really equal, whether it's two friends, as, say, in our situation (I hope!), or as between husband and wife, where neither is playing the role of father or mother, if you like of superior, where they're wrestling equally with each other and with some common problem. Then perhaps the model breaks down to a certain extent, doesn't it?'

'I don't know, I'm not at all sure', said Hans.

'But surely you do have to alter the model somewhat in this particular instance', I said, 'because the relationship of counseller and client is really on the basis of superior and inferior, of one who has something to give and of another who has to ask, whereas in the case of true friends, it is a common search. There's a dependency in one case, which is absent in the other, isn't there?'

'Yes, but I think that "superior" and "inferior" are terms...', Hans demurred.

'They're not good terms', I agreed.

'No, they're not terms I should be inclined to use', Hans continued. 'But I think, as far as I can judge it now, that the answer to your question is not that the model breaks down, but that the two participants explore and function so to speak simultaneously, according to the same basic pattern. For instance, they would have to listen to each other, observe each other in order really to understand and to get somewhere. The usual breakdown and the loss of meaning in conversation has its root in the fact that this very thing doesn't happen. Either the whole thing falls apart or it becomes one-sided.'

'Well, Hans, I'm very glad that you have now explicitly allowed for the element of reciprocity. The trouble is that, by doing so, you have made rather a difficulty for yourself, as it seems to me. The problem arises as follows. The intuition you have recently come to is that the therapeutic encounter is only a variant of what you call the archetypal human encounter, and that an analysis of the therapeutic encounter is therefore substantially an analysis of the archetypal human encounter. But you have come to your sevenfold analysis through your experience of the therapeutic encounter. The question, therefore, is whether there is really an equivalent of each of your seven stages in a simply human *Gespräch* once one allows for the element of reciprocity which exists between equal friends and which does not exist between counsellor and client. In other words, can we restate your sevenfold analysis in such a way that it does justice to the mutuality of an ordinary but true dialogue? So what we need to do now is to resume the attempt, but now systematically, to check that a *Gespräch* does indeed unfold through your seven phases as much as the therapeutic process does.'

'Yes, yes Marcus. You see, deep down, I'm convinced that it is so. I've not been challenged to articulate it so clearly before. But just let me try, and we'll see how far we get. So, again starting at the beginning: Stage one, I prepare myself, by sitting quietly, because I want to be ready for the *Gespräch*, and not full of my own thoughts. Stage two: my friend comes. Now when the friend has come, I watch, listen, observe, and try to find out what her life-situation and her state of mind are, exactly as I do — of course, in a modified form — with a client. Now, as I said before, then we come to the diagnostic interlude, Stage three. Here again you might say, "The thing doesn't work", But I believe that in every basic human encounter you have to assess what your friend's mood is, what her general state of health is, whether she is tired or fresh, how much she can take, what you will say to her, how you will say it. In that sense it is a variant of the diagnostic interlude.'

'Except that we now have to add that it is reciprocal. Ideally the friend should do the same for you?', I interjected.

'Yes.'

'There should be a mutual sensitivity, so that neither forces anything on the other beyond his or her capacity.'

'Yes. It's very interesting that it's you who make this point', Hans said, 'because it usually happens in one direction in my case so that I'm hardly aware of this mutuality — though I must say that my friends are very much aware whether I'm tired or not. So in this sense you're quite right, it's reciprocal. So then, we come to Stage four, the stage of assimilation. Of course in every *Gespräch*, as in every encounter with a client, this process can happen very rapidly. Ideally it is a process which should be allowed to proceed and mature slowly. I mean that, after you have gained an impression of the personality and of the world of relationships of this person, you should live with these images and assimilate them slowly. But very often conditions force you to act very quickly, and you select, or you are "hit" by, certain significant images or it may be only a gesture. And the same applies to the encounter with your friend. **Here too you have** to assimilate, usually very quickly, unless you feel you need time, in which case you should say so, if it is a very important talk. You assimilate, almost half consciously, a certain range of impressions and images which you feel are essential for this person, and to this you will respond.'

'I'm just thinking, Hans, that you seem in the very way you're describing things to have slipped back into talking from the point of view of a counsellor. And I'm always trying to visualise a situation where you're *both* clients, if you like, where you're both equal. So that the process is reciprocal, and then, it seems to me, it isn't just a question of one person entering into the feeling world and images of the other but of both entering into the feeling world of each other. And perhaps more than that, it's a question of trying to enter into and slowly construct a *common* world of feelings and images, isn't it? Because, as you said at the beginning, in any human *Gespräch*, you don't really know where you're going, you're groping for something together.'

'Yes, I agree, Marcus. But the essential thing is that even if you put it like that, which I accept, it would still mean that what happens in the therapeutic encounter had a parallel in the meaningful and mutually helpful human encounter of the *Gespräch* where two people want to find each other with a feeling of gain in understanding, not only of each other but of themselves and of life.'

'Yes, I can accept that Hans. Once again the assimilation that takes place is mutual. That's the major modification to make.'

'Yes, you've made me aware of a completely new dimension and aspect of the matter, which I wasn't aware of, namely, that the process can happen simultaneously in two directions. And then it's all the more valid and valuable. And quite clearly, if we take Stage six, the working through...'

'What about Stage five, the selection of the target area?' I interrupted. 'What's the equivalent of that in a *Gespräch*?'

'Well, it's the target area that is psychologically or

practically the most essential thing in a *Gespräch*. In other words, you don't woffle, you don't drift. You have a directed, a purposeful conversation, you want to go somewhere, and that you can do only if you follow a certain direction.'

'Would you say it's a question of agreeing upon an issue?'

'Yes exactly, it's a question of agreeing on an issue in the sense that either your friend or you yourself move towards an issue, and then you both feel that it's the right one. And if you feel, as you move in a certain direction, that you're going in the wrong direction, you redirect yourself. So much for the target area. Then you begin to work through that in order to arrive at a conclusion that will give some assurance or comfort or a feeling of fresh vitality. This would be Stage six. And finally, you see, Stage seven, guiding the client into a new pattern of life, translated into terms of a purely human *Gespräch*, becomes the feeling which we sum up by saying at the conclusion of a conversation with a friend, "That was a good talk". What do we mean by that? We mean either that we go out into life and know better how to handle certain situations, how to think about certain problems, or even if this doesn't apply, we go back refreshed, with a new zest for life, and with a sense that we have left behind the trivialities, concentrated on something worthwhile and therefore have gained in vitality.'

'Yes, I can see that Hans. Now it seems to me that two things have emerged from our attempt to translate the analysis of the therapeutic encounter between counsellor and client into an analysis of basic human dialogue. First, I think that you and I have both seen more clearly that we have to be very aware of the difference between the two situations, and therefore have to modify the description of the *Gespräch* to take account of the vital element of reciprocity which I think you're always inclined *not* to do. The other thing that has emerged, I think, at least to my mind is this: it is much clearer that when one has translated the model from one situation to another and has allowed for the reciprocity, one sees that there is in fact much more reciprocity in the original situation of counsellor and client than I at least had thought. You see what I mean Hans?'

'I know exactly what you mean.'

'Which is interesting, it seems to me, because I think that one's general image of the relationship of counsellor and client *is* one of dependency and so on, whereas what our conclusion makes clearer is that the process between counsellor and client is fundamentally at the level of two human beings struggling with each other at a task in which *both* have to learn — which, I think, you indicated at one point, and that's partly why you rejected my terms "inferior" and "superior". In other words, there's feedback.'

'Yes', replied Hans. 'I must say — and I'm not saying this to exonerate myself — that I never had the feeling, consciously (perhaps I had it unconsciously to some extent), of some superiority. The expression I always use with my clients is: "We have to work together." It's a question of a *common* working through of problems, of questions, and I'm very much aware of the enormous enrichment of my life that comes from my being permitted to do this. So although I was not conscious that the process was reciprocal in the sense which you have now made explicit, and which is probably more so in the case of a consciously conducted *Gespräch* between friends, I always felt that the inflow of experience, the encounter with destiny, the entry into a wider life which came to me from my clients as well as from my friends was something that enriches and sustains me. I feel particularly privileged to be able to enter into the thinking of young people because they bring ideas, impulses and inclinations which are quite different from anything I've experienced before. For example, their concern with events in Africa, Asia, India was totally unknown to us when we were young.'

'I quite agree.'

'The impulses of helpfulness, compassion, participation were unknown to us, not because we were bad or stupid people but because our life and our world were very narrow, very restricted. And if you read a book like Stefan Zweig's *The*

COUNSELLING AND THE ARCHETYPE OF HUMAN DIALOGUE

World of Yesterday, the first few chapters, then you will get an admirable description of this restricted, dusty, twilight atmosphere, of really being cut off from the totality of life. And in this sense, you see, I experience a tremendous inflow.'

'Yes, I completely agree with you Hans. And to be more conscious of this is important in at least two respects. First of all, in regard to one's own attitude, which is therefore much more one of humility. But even more importantly, one is perhaps more conscious of trying to communicate this sense to the other person in a counselling situation. For I have certainly found that so often people put me on a pedestal and say, at least in extreme cases, "But I'm giving you nothing". This is very bad for their self-esteem and, you know — I think of one person in particular — to the extent that I'm aware that she's giving me something, I can in principle help her self-esteem. But it's the last thing they think when they feel bad or rejected, and capable of giving nothing. I think that it could be important to try to communicate this sense that, as you say, we're trying to work through something together, that we counsellors are receiving something, that we're privileged.'

'It's absolutely true, Marcus. You see, as you're talking, I become conscious of the fact that in former years, as distinct from the present, people often said this to me. And I can't tell you, nor do I know, why it has changed — probably because my basic feelings have changed, probably also because the difference between a priest and a doctor is very great: a priest is very much more an object and a person to be revered. A doctor, you see, or a therapist, if he tunes-in in the right way, will, I think, be able to — "project" is again a bad word, but you know what I mean — will come across to the other person as a fellow human being, and he can then indicate, primarily, of course, in his silent inner attitude of listening and receiving, but also, occasionally, in a more explicit way, his appreciation of what he's allowed to listen to. This reciprocal relationship can be established and gently emphasised. But that is in contrast to what some therapists think, in terms of life as well as in terms of a *Gespräch*. Reciprocity, that is a fundamental thing. And the more the client becomes aware of it, and the more she feels deep down that the counsellor is just someone who shares things with her as a person who has experienced his own difficulties, his own troubles, which he has tried to solve, and that by speaking to him the client gives him something which the counsellor receives as a gift, the more the therapeutic encounter will gain, and the results will of course, improve. So shall we leave it there?'

'I think you've made your case, Hans!'

'Well, you put me on my mettle!'

Notes

1. David Stafford-Clark, *Psychiatry for Students* 5th edn. (London, 1979).

Dialogue 3: Relationship and Solitude

> *Looking back over the course of life from birth, we can detect a continuous ebb and flow between intimate intermingling with other people on the one hand, and self-contained, even solitary, thought and action on the other .... It seems that growth can only come through an interplay betweew sociability and solitude.*
> Eric Rayner *Human Development*

'I've been thinking a great deal about what you said in our two previous discussions, Hans, and allowing it to turn my experiences and thoughts over and over, like a plough with the earth in the autumn. I don't know whether I've been more fascinated by your analysis of the process of counselling into seven stages or by your subsequent deepening of the significance of this process so as to see it as one, but privileged example of the human dialogue as such. As a result of this pondering however, I've come up with a problem which, from one point of view represents a stop, but which, from another point of view, can be the starting-point of yet further insight, and which I should therefore very much like to discuss with you. I can broach the problem I have in mind like this. You have, if I remember rightly, at least once quoted one of Rilke's lovely sayings to the effect that relationship is a matter of two solitudes greeting, touching and protecting each other, haven't you?'

'Yes', replied Hans, 'it is another of my favourite sayings, I quote it quite often.'

'Well now, Hans', I continued, 'I first came across this particular saying myself indirectly, via a beautiful book of memoirs written by Lawrence Whistler, entitled *The Initials in the Heart*. He was the glass engraver, married to a promising young actress who died in giving birth to their second child, and he wrote this book some years later in order to achieve some tranquility by celebrating what was obviously a rare and quite special relationship. And towards the end of the book he quotes this saying of Rilke, but added something critical: "This appealed to our romantic side, and she quoted it, sensing and believing also that love can go further than that. The solitude is not sealed, somehow it is penetrable." Now what was important to his wife and to himself in recalling this comment on Rilke's saying was what he called the "penetrability" of people to each other, and this is also the way in which this saying of Rilke is immediately relevant to our discussion to date, in so far as all these reflections deal with the relational side of our lives. My problem, however, is that there *is* also this other side to our lives, the fact that Rilke referred to when he said that what greeted, touched and protected each other, the subjects of the relationship, were two *solitudes*. Isn't there ultimately within us what you yourself have well-termed an island where we are alone with ourselves? Isn't there, therefore, an ineluctable solitude, that solitude from and within which we face death, so that we can even, as the earlier Heidegger said, be described as beings for death? But, if this is the case, then, so my thoughts have gone so far. Another way of describing what life is about is that it consists in a polarity between, on the one hand, the real need for other people, the need to reach out to them, to become as "penetrable" as possible to them, in ways that may be infinitely variable, such as we have been discussing so far, and on the other hand, this inevitable and final solitude. Thus even in a life-long relationship, there is a continuous inter-play between these poles of relationship and solitude. Now that's as far as my own thinking has gone, but in so far as it's valid, it's the element of solitude that sets up the polarity which I should like to go on to grapple with. Do you see?'

'Yes indeed, Marcus, and I think that you've already gone very far. May I remind you of one of the first things you said when we met, and this is that what attracted you to enter the Order was this basic movement between activity and withdrawing into contemplation. And I think it is probably one of the basic laws of living altogether, even one of the basic laws of life in the biological and physiological sense, that we need to return to our own centre. It is like sleeping in regard to wakefulness, so that in the end we desire sleep in order to be awake again. Similarly you have the same kind of basic law of going inward, taking in and then pouring out operative in breathing.'

'In the heart?', I asked.

'Yes, in the breathing itself, systole and diastole. So there is no question of this not being true. Loneliness can never be anything one-sided, in one direction, such that you return to yourself so to speak once and for all.'

'I'm glad that you corroborate my view, Hans, but your use of the word "loneliness" introduces another note, and brings me back to my problem, especially as loneliness is where the problem of solitude becomes more practical, more applied and more concerned with therapy. Even I have found that quite a lot of my work is concerned with trying to reconcile people to their loneliness. However, one way in which I have tried to come to terms with this myself — for myself and for other people — is to see loneliness as being something very distinct from solitude. On such a view, loneliness is an unhappy state, but probably a transitional state, almost an ordeal you have to go through, as part of your grappling with solitude, as a way through to solitude. I should therefore, distinguish very sharply between loneliness and solitude, and I think that I remember your saying that the Austrian philosopher and theologian Lotz has written a book to this effect, hasn't he? That loneliness is the ordeal, the purgation for, almost the initiation into solitude?'

'Yes, he has', replied Hans. 'He has written a wonderful

book about solitude, and he does indeed distinguish between loneliness and solitude. I believe the terms he uses in German are *Vereinsamung*, which is the equivalent of loneliness, and *Einsamkeit*.'

'That's an ordinary German word, isn't it?' I asked.

'Oh yes. And this *Einsamkeit* is creative solitude.'

'It is. In this solitude you're very much in touch, you're in touch with all manner of things, therefore implicitly with everything else.'

'Exactly', continued Hans. 'It's the artist's, the mystic's solitude. Because once you have got through to this solitude, broken through to your true centre, which is the essential implication of the word, you are no longer alone, because in some mysterious way your whole being widens and begins to make contact with, begins to identify not only with creatures but with creation, with the creative world altogether. In something I've read, I no longer know where, this state is described as consisting in an identification with the trees, with the souls of trees, with the storms, with the grass, and of course with all living things. It depends, of course, on the intensity of this stage, it can be comparatively narrow, and it can be extremely wide and expansive. But here again you have the same basic law, and basic rhythm. Once you have achieved this journey inwards to the very end, you are already on the journey outward, and a greater journey outward than you have ever undertaken before, than you can ever undertake in ordinary life — I mean in the life of a purely physical condition, where you are confined.'

'I quite agree, and I'm sure that is so,' I said, 'because I think I've glimpsed it. It's only a glimpse, if only because it's also a progressive thing, it's a rhythm, it's part of the rhythm of life and of the individual, and it's a rhythm which deepens, doesn't it, and which extends throughout the system and personality as one grows older.'

'Yes exactly, Marcus. You see, as you grow older, quite naturally even your physical possibilities of expanding outwards become much more limited. For example, you cannot walk so far or so fast, you cannot exert your body so much, and more and more the people who surrounded you, your friends, either are somewhere else or are dead. But the more the outer world contracts, the more — ideally, at least — your inner world can and should expand, provided of course, you have not developed a habit of clinging to the outer structure of life. You must be prepared for the move, and you must be on the way as far as this journey inwards is concerned. And then there are simply no limits to the scope and to the newness of your experience.'

'I can see that, Hans, though I'm obviously not at that stage myself. It seems to me that at an earlier phase of life, say middle age, I think that there is a possibility of a slightly different emphasis, and this is that to the extent that you can get in touch with your inner centre, your contemplative withdrawal is — again ideally, and for some — not only very compatible with an increased activity but at a certain point occurs in the very midst of activity, so that the rhythm becomes much more subtle, it is interiorised. You talked about this communion with the trees, and so on, and about the experience of going into the country for relaxation and getting away from it all. This is an everyday version of the pantheistic, Wordsworthian sort of experience, but it seems to me that this is in itself only symbolic, that the natural, stable, continuing and self-renewing world of nature is in itself a symbol of the creative principle. And I think that ideally one could be in touch with that creative principle of the universe, something vaster than oneself, the origin of one's own and every other person's origins, in the midst of bustle and the city. I think that this contact is extremely difficult to sustain, and that, practically speaking, one may need these periods of physical withdrawal. But I also think that there comes a point where activity and contemplation are almost fused, because one has broken through. One needs to sleep, one needs to withdraw, the rhythm of life is the same and yet it expresses itself differently. To the outsider this person is almost ceaselessly active and energetic, and yet at the same time he is deeply contemplative and is only active because he is contemplative.'

'Yes, I think that is profoundly true, Marcus, and I think it has a very important bearing on the work which we try to do. As you say, you can remain in touch with the centre, at least once you have reached it; this is a pre-condition in bustle and activity. But I think it is absolutely essential that, once you have touched it, you consciously re-establish the centre in any human encounter, whatever your previous activities were. So you have these two dimensions when you are opposite another person who presents you with a problem: on the one hand, you withdraw into the centre of silent openness, silent listening, you are in a way entirely contemplative, on the other hand, you are entirely turned outwards, to receive the other.'

'This is that dynamic relaxation to which you referred before?', I asked.

'This is dynamic relaxation. And I think that in ordinary life, you also ideally need this balance, or fusion of these two elements, in order to cope with life. And in actual fact, the more you have established a centre, free of memories, concepts, and the like, in an impersonal way...'

'A very dispossessed, unpossessive way?' I interrupted.

'Yes, in a dispossessed, an unpossessive way; and the more you have established this, this kind of room, like a holy of holies ...'

'Like Rilke's *Weltinnenraum*, the world's inner space?', I suggested.

'Yes, indeed, then the more the other person or experience can enter.'

'I must say I absolutely agree with all that, Hans. You're describing, in your own idiom, the inwardness of the schema, the abstract schema of what John Macmurray in his idiom referred to as the rhythm of withdrawal and return. And I think it is also what the Hebrew psalmist meant when he referred to the man who goes out and comes in. It's a very frequent description of the human predicament and condition, so that the classical Hebrew often refers to men who come in and who go out. It represents a very simple and particular way of hitting off the same rhythm, which through this very particularity is in the end nothing less than the rhythm of the universe itself. At the same time, all that we've said, with the various qualifications we've put in, means to say that this abstract schema of withdrawal and return can in fact take very many different concrete forms. It no doubt needs to be sustained by physical withdrawal, at least in the period of training, of initiation, and perhaps always to some extent, since as physical, mortal creatures we need these periods of acted-out withdrawal and return. But, granted that, the abstract schema seems to be able to take very many different forms, according to one's temperament and one's age and phase of life.'

'Absolutely, yes. And although, as you say, it can take ever so many individual forms according to age, disposition, temperament, circumstances, conditions of life, it must first of all be *established*. It must also be *maintained*, and in my experience it requires an enormous amount of perseverance, patience and tenacity. For this reason therefore, it has something of the character of a discipline.'

'It has a spiritual reference, you mean, Hans, it is a spiritual discipline?'

'Yes', Hans went on. 'But it is a discipline of great practical and therapeutic importance. Most, if not all the people I meet get into a state of crisis or distress because they have not learned to fight their way back into, not loneliness, but what we have now referred to as creative solitude.'

'That's exactly one of my practical difficulties in therapeutic counselling work. I'm thinking of two or three people I'm dealing with at the moment, and if I reflect on it, I now realise that what I'm trying to do is to enable them to enter into their own solitude. Yet the drag of dependence and of activism and of compulsion to be connected with other people in different ways is so strong in such cases that you have to be very patient, and very, very gentle. And it may be very difficult in regard to such people to indicate the possibility that they have to find a systematic way of continuing to find their solitude. The most I have been able to do with two of the people I have in mind is to indicate to them that the answer is within. The next step would then be for them gradually to realise that there is some form of life particularly appropriate to them in which they can express and consolidate this. Very few people, as you say, I think, can do this, because once they are over the crisis they almost inevitably relapse.'

'Yes, that is absolutely true, Marcus. I've recently had the case of a very fine woman who is completely identified with and absorbed and overwhelmed by an environment which is not a very genuine environment for her, and as a result she is constantly being pulled away from her own centre. I've tried various things, but she is almost always pulled away again. And I feel now with her and with very many people, that what we have to do with such people is not simply to try to help them with ways to solve their problems but to teach them an inner discipline, which is again a spiritual thing. For example, we have to show them how to achieve a certain measure of detachment. When you mention the word detachment to a person, it sounds quite wonderful but it also sounds very strange. They wonder what it's about, and even if they understand what it is, they do not know how to achieve it. This is why my own thinking has rather gone beyond counselling as a form of helping people to deal with personal problems to counselling as a form of helping people establish a disciplined inner way of life, where they can achieve detachment, where they can achieve creative solitude. And that's a different matter altogether.'

'Yes, that again echoes my own experience very exactly Hans, and in a quite particular sort of way in connection with the two people I'm thinking about in so far as they are both women. They've made great progress, they're much more self-possessed, they're much more able to live with themselves, much more free of infantile fantasies and dependencies. Nevertheless they've both got an almost *idée fixe* about having a man. Now I feel that what is fundamentally in question here is some extremely important need to relate, but also in so far as this is expressed in terms of *having* to have a man in their lives this very need constitutes a block.'

'Yes, I follow you, Marcus, and can I say something to that very briefly? Generally speaking, then, I have yet to see a woman who does not need to have a man in her life, but the essential thing in my opinion is that for many women it is not absolutely necessary and sometimes not even desirable to have a man in terms of a lover or a husband, but a man who represents the guiding, manly, spiritual element. It may be a priest, it may be a doctor, and you must know from your experience how women can come and fasten on to the therapist or the priest because he is a man. Now there are two aspects in such a case. On the one hand, her emotions, her erotic, her sexual feelings will tend to flow towards him, but woe to him if he confuses matters, then he is a fallen idol. On the other hand, it is a fact that the life of a woman can — to a very great extent, not fully, of course — be fulfilled by a kind of relationship to a spiritual guide, a man to whom she looks up. It must be a man, because if there is no man, some theories say she will again become mannish, and that's a very bad thing.'

'She becomes what Jung would call the animus-ridden woman?', I asked.

'Yes, under some circumstances she could become absolutely indigestible, aggressive, self-righteous.'

'So, Hans, the important thing for a therapist in such a situation is first of all to be quite clear himself so that he can as far as possible gradually communicate the distinction between himself as a man and as an archetypal figure. And, of course, this very way of formulating the question is very androcentric and so immediately raises the further, correlative question as to what a man needs in regard to a woman. But that's another subject in itself and we haven't time to go into that today.'

'No Marcus, indeed not. But may I just dot an "i" in regard to that first question? A man who deals with a woman should not, in my experience and thinking, deny that he is a man.'

'No, he can't become disincarnate, he is a person, a real

human being, and therefore a sexed being.'

'Yes, Marcus, and I make a point of telling women, whenever I can truthfully do so, that they are very nice, or attractive or beautiful women, or whatever may apply. However, the fact that the therapist is able to control inappropriate immediate responses and, moreover, to indicate a different and even a higher level is something that people are really waiting for, they are still waiting for it.'

'I have to go now Hans, but may I just say before I do that to me the upshot of our discussion this morning is that true dialogue presupposes solitude, which turns out to be a spiritual matter, that reflection on the nature of dialogue leads on to the need to consider as it were the spirituality of counselling, and that we really need, at some stage, to undertake such a discussion together.'

'I should indeed very much like to do that at some time, Marcus. I'll gather my thoughts around this topic and look forward to that.'

Dialogue 4: The Stages of the Spiritual Path

Every step forward, as well as providing pleasure and new opportunities, means leaving something behind.
Isca Salzberger-Wittenberg
Psycho-analytic Insight and Relationships

'Well, Hans', I said this particular morning, 'we must have been discussing matters that are very close to our hearts on and off over some five years, and in that time you have explained to me your ideas, your evolving ideas, on the stages of counselling. A little bit further in our acquaintance you developed your ideas about the counselling session as a privileged example of the archetype of the human *Gespräch*. We've also discussed the subject of relationship and solitude, and that of woman and man, and in both discussions we've found ourselves uncovering a spiritual dimension. But what we have not done is to record together a dialogue on the spiritual path, on the stages of spiritual growth, and I know that this is an extremely important thing for you, in its own right but also in its relationship to counselling. So I should be very grateful if today you could recapitulate your ideas on the spiritual path as such, independently of the counselling, as it were. You understand? Then if I may, I shall just come in with questions or requests for clarification, as may be, alright?'

'Yes, as you say, quite some time has passed since we began discussing all these things,' Hans replied, 'and I'm inclined to forget what I've said before. So you may find that what I try to say today will be different in many ways, but not in any fundamental way.

Now, I think I'd better start with a statement about what we might call the essential structure of the spiritual path. And I believe that nobody has stated it more clearly than the great teacher, the great yogi, who was, so many believe, the greatest teacher of the spiritual path, namely, the Buddha. And I encountered this particular formula about the spiritual path and its structure in the so-called, "death-gospel" of the Buddha, that is to say, the narrative of the events of the Buddha's life as he in his wandering with his monks approached death. Now at this time, by way of a supreme testament and message to his monks, he repeated over and over again one formula, the formula about the being and structure of the spiritual path. Naturally, apart from the formula, many other details are added, for it is of course enveloped in the events of his life during the last few months. But I should like to read you this because I have never found anything else quite as revealing as this. He says:

> And so the holy one spoke to his disciples in rich detail about the essence of holy truth, indicating to them over and over again: This is ethical discipline, this is meditative recollection, this is true higher knowledge. It is only if ethical discipline supports and refines it that meditation is fruitful and blessed; it is only if meditation supports and refines it that knowledge is fruitful and blessed; it is only if such knowledge penetrates and refines it that the spirit can become free ...

'Where did you come across this particular formulation?'
'This is a translation by Professor Hermann Beckh who was a Sanscrit scholar and in my opinion a very great one, who translated the writings of the Buddha in a most beautiful and poetic way. You'll find this passage in his book *Der Hingang des Vollendeten*[1] (*The Passing of the Perfected One*).'
'I'm not acquainted with the statement, testament, in that form.'
'Well, Marcus, it is to me one of the profoundest

clearest statements ever made on the spiritual life, and Professor Beckh, who later became a priest in the Christian Community, based his book *Buddha und seine Lehre (Buddha and his Teaching)* — which I think is one of the most remarkable ever written on the Buddha, with the profoundest understanding of the master and his teaching — just on this formula. Now, if you approach it with, if you like, an analytical — a mildly analytical! — attitude you can see that four stages are mentioned, namely, first, the *sittliche Selbsterziehung*, or, as we put it in a previous conversation, character training. It is really training of the whole personality, it is not only the training of your thought, but of your emotions, your feelings, your will, your attitude to life altogether.'

'A life of personal discipline?'

'Yes, a life of personal discipline, life in relation to others, and so on. It goes into the smallest details of personal conduct, for instance, even into the details of how you should move, how you should speak, how you should be silent, how you should sit down, get up, even how you should perform your bodily functions. It is a kind of enlightened awareness of everything you do, without, of course, the overtones and stresses of self-consciousness. It is the total co-ordination of the human being and the co-ordination of his relationship to the world.'

'Body, spirit and relationship?', I asked.

'Exactly, Marcus, everything. Now this is No 1, and of course this is extremely far-reaching and will permeate and penetrate the whole of your day. You can then speak, as very many spiritual teachers have spoken, about — I say it again first in German: *"Der Alltag als Uebung"* — everyday life as exercise. Everyday life itself becomes an arena of exercise and moral training for you. And he says that, without this, meditation cannot be *ertragreich*, fruitful, productive and *segensvoll*, beneficial, full of blessing, because it needs the well-structured foundation of discipline and control.'

'The soil?'

'Yes, the soil', Hans continued, 'in order to approach, to

enter into the sphere of thought or pondering. He calls it *Sinnen*, a very beautiful word — the German equivalent of "pondering". You need this character-training in order to maintain yourself in this sphere of thought and pondering, without being thrown into chaos, fantasising or whatever it may be, holding fast to the same clarity, the same control there as you have in ordinary life.

So we go from *moralische Selbsterziehung* or character training into the sphere of meditation. This is realm two. As we enter more and more deeply into the life of personal discipline and moral training, it is the general experience that we gradually begin to feel at home in the realm of meditation. I say "general experience" advisedly because we are here not discussing primarily Buddhist meditation. That would be a wrong assumption. No, the Buddhist way is simply one classical, though almost pre-eminent, form of the archetypal spiritual path which, as such, is present in one or other form in all classical traditions of the spiritual path, including the Hindu one, and also the Western one. It is only a matter of difference of terminology.'

'It is a particular way of expressing a universal possibility of experience, with universal stages?'

'Quite so, Marcus, and the universal stages are these four. So we come to meditation. What happens is that you slowly penetrate the content of your meditation. This content may be greatly varied. It is very varied for me: it may be a sentence or a scene from the New Testament, primarily St John's gospel, because that is the gospel of the Word, or it may be something out of the *Bhagavad Gita,* or out of the discourses of the Buddha, or perhaps a great poem. The less sensory the content the better, of course, because the more it'll help you to become liberated from your body and from your intellect. And as you thus become more and more liberated from body and intellect and penetrate deeply into what you are meditating, the border-line between you and the object of your meditation begins to dwindle, it begins to vanish and you become submerged in it. And what usually happens (not by any means every time) is that in the end your mind begins to rest, to focus, on one word — say the word "holiness" or "joy", while the other words, as you increasingly relinquish rational consciousness, begin you might say to melt away, dissolve. So you focus in the end on this one word. And then even this begins to melt away and only a kind of atmosphere, an awareness of this word remains. Can you imagine what I mean?'

'And this is stage three', I asked.

'We are now approaching stage three, yes.'

'What does the Buddha call that?'

'Stage three he calls *Erkenntnis*, intuitive knowledge, yes? Now we have reached a stage where the rational discursive consciousness has faded away, and only the essence, as it were, the awareness, if you like a taste of what you have meditated on, has remained.'

'I think that this is what St Thomas Aquinas called the *simplex intuitus veritatis*, the simple intuition of truth.'

'Yes, Marcus, now we come to that. And at this stage, you have to be able to hold you mind completely still or do what Jakob Böhme said you have to do when he was asked, "How can I experience God?" namely, "Put yourself out of the way". And this applies particularly here. Then, to the extent that you can do this very difficult thing of putting yourself completely out of the way, then you will enter this next stage, and perhaps have, however slightly, some experience of intuitive knowledge. Now the great question is what is meant by intuitive knowledge?'

'This is now realm three?' I asked again.

'This is realm three, *Erkenntnis*. For the Buddha this was perfectly clear: he perceived very clearly his own former lives; he was able to follow the destiny of beings as they go through the cycle of rebirth; he described super-sensible beings and found the great truth concerning suffering and the overcoming of suffering; super-sensible powers of hearing and seeing enabled him to know what was far beyond ordinary human perception and knowledge. In this way the super-sensible world opened up for him. Now I think that for ordinary mortals it is as if one were standing on a beach, and one felt, perhaps very faintly, felt and heard the sound of waves surging towards one, and knew that one was standing on the border of a different world. And what this different world conveys is that there is something beyond the material which very, very gently begins to speak to you; it begins to *sound* to you and it begins to *light* up for you, and it has *being* and it has *movement*. There is one specially wonderful expression of this which I've loved for a long time, in Thomas à Kempis. Characteristically his *Imitation of Christ* is also in four parts, and with the passage I have in mind we are at the beginning of Part III, so we're standing again at exactly the same point we've reached in our present discussion. And what Thomas à Kempis says is:

> Let me hear what God is saying within me. Blessed are the ears which take in the sounding of God as he approaches, and which perceive nothing of the noise of this world.

Now this wording — we may say the gentle sounding, murmuring, of a super-sensible world — is wonderfully expressive, and in so-called spontaneous, *super-sensible,* mystical experiences, this particular fact of the experience of *sound* is very often emphasised. The translation I've got goes like this: "Blessed are the ears that catch the breath of the whisper of God, and give no heed to the whispering of this world." Beautiful isn't it?

Now, Marcus, this is one characteristic aspect of such an experience: you hear something that strikes you as an intimation of what is beyond the natural world. But you can also experience it in the form of certain more clearly defined sounds, which therefore seem to be inspired sounds, and they will be reminiscent of music; or you can experience such sounding in the form of more definite words, which seem to be equally inspired; they may even form themselves into poetry. Therefore this world has also been called the world of inspiration.'

THE STAGES OF THE SPIRITUAL PATH

'It's the world of what have been called the *Urworte*, the primordial sounds, of the sounds before they articulate themselves in particular ways, into the great poetry of the world, or the Scriptures — primordial sound?'

'Exactly, Marcus. It has also been called the *Weltensprache*, I mean the archetypal sound-langugage of the world. Now the great poet, in a moment of inspiration, or the great musician, like Mozart, is entered into by this world, or enters into this world. For this reason geniuses, like Mozart, were always felt to be people who didn't belong to the earth, but lived on a different level of consciousness — albeit without being aware of it. Even the Buddha describes how one can at this stage hear heavenly music. But the essential feature for him is that in this world knowledge, *Erkenntnis*, is to be found intuitively. Again I repeat, while his *Erkenntnis*, his knowledge was exceedingly clear and definite, what we ordinary mortals can expect is an awareness, an intuition, in various ways, of a world which is beyond the material world, but perhaps occasionally more. Our intuition may even reach further: at certain moments we may be granted a sudden insight, a spontaneous understanding of something the intellect had never been able to grasp. Right? So we can enter the fourth stage. Now we must have the strength even to leave *this* world behind and enter — this is particularly difficult, the most difficult part of it — the world of complete stillness, where our being and our own perceptions, even what we have discerned at stage three, are so subdued that we are ready to encounter something that is ultimately beyond words and beyond description. It has the character of "mystical silence" (*silentium mysticum*) and through it we may experience something like an encounter with "a presence" which may or may not reveal its nature. What one encounters at this level one can't describe, because the moment one begins to describe it, one falsifies it. It is beyond description, beyond explanation. It is an encounter with something which you feel utterly and which in every way transcends your ordinary comprehension, and yet you experience it as a reality.'

'It sounds to me, Hans, rather like what St Ignatius of

Antioch, at the end of the first century AD, called the mystery of silence — the mystery of silence that cries out for expression. So behind the primordial sound that lies behind articulate speech is the primordial silence?'

'Yes, Marcus, that is very well put: it's a primordial silence, and it is this, as far as one can put it in human terms, which I think the human heart and the human spirit long to achieve, namely, stillness. You learn to surmount the various areas of, well, unrest, stress and almost disintegration, until you come to a sphere where you can rest in complete silence, in complete stillness.'

'By passing over these various thresholds?'

'Yes, by passing over these various thresholds. And the mystics have described all this in various ways. Of course, it depends largely on the individual personality.'

'And culture?'

'And culture. I believe that Aquinas described it as an almost death-like stage: you have died into something higher, and died certainly to yourself and to the world. In this connection, I often recall an expression of Rilke, who was very aware of the tragic nature of the human condition. He spoke of people as "*wir, die Zerfallenden*, we who disintegrate". In everything and at every moment we are in danger of disintegrating, in our thoughts, in our feelings, in our very bodies, but the moment we have achieved the crossing of the various thresholds into what you call so well primordial silence, then disintegration is behind us.'

'Well, if I may come in here, Hans, I'd like to say that this is wholly illuminating, and from very many points of view. Because we've spoken about the subject quite a number of times, directly or indirectly, and I know that it's something very dear to your heart. But what is new to me is your starting from this quotation from the Buddha. I don't remember your ever having done so before with me. And I dare say that you've chosen it because it expresses with unexampled succinctness the essential content but also the, as you say, structure, the dynamics, if you like of the spiritual life, the stages of the spiritual path which can be schematically and analytically divided into these four: the character training, the meditation, this intuitive awareness and then finally the ...'

'Liberation'.

'Liberation into a meeting, into a sense of the transcendent *other* of some sort, is that right? Now one of the reasons why I find this very enriching is because, when you have spoken about this subject before, you've done it in terms of the more Western tradition and the corresponding scheme of the *via purgativa*, the *via illuminativa* and the *via unitiva*. We have already agreed this morning that the value of this particular statement of the Buddha is that it is particular in expression but universal in scope. So it's not surprising to find the essential content re-expressed in different terms, in different traditions, in different cultures. But I wonder whether you would like to say a bit more about its re-expression in this Western mode, Hans?'

'Yes, Marcus, well first of all, I particularly like your word "dynamic", because I think that the whole discussion of the spiritual path should be based on the fact and the acceptance of the fact that it is something which is the spiritual equivalent of an organic dynamism. Just as there is an organic necessity to pass through certain stages, for example, in the assimilation of food (chewing, digesting, resorption and so on), or certain stages of muscular activity in order to move and to climb, so we also have to move as it were organically along the spiritual path, in these four stages, if we take it really seriously and are determined to reach our goal. Then we are simply being carried from one stage into the next — provided we have the staying power. Therefore, you see, it is perfectly inevitable that though the terminology may change, the actual dynamics will never change. I firmly believe that if we want the truth about it, we must keep to the archetypal or classical tradition.'

'Because it is founded on human nature?'

'Because it is founded on human nature, and something you can change as little as you can change the fact that you have to breathe in and out if you want to breathe normally.'

'Or that normally you pass through certain developmental stages as part of becoming more and more fully human?' I asked.

'Exactly Marcus, through youth, middle age, life generally.'

'And that each stage is divided by what the anthropologists might call a *rite de passage*, a rite of passage — precisely a death and a rebirth into the next stage?'

'Yes, I think that it is particularly important to realise this, because there is a danger and also a certain temptation of, to put it very naively, getting stuck at certain stages. And it requires great effort, concentration and awareness to go beyond that stage, and particularly, as I mentioned, to enter ultimately into that primordial silence.'

'Again Hans, I suppose that this is the eqivalent of what the psycho-analysts would call "being fixated", so that the whole business of therapy, especially psycho-analytic therapy, is to release people from being "fixated", from being stuck, in order that they can resume the spontaneous dynamic growth that belongs to them as human beings, what Winnicott called the "maturational process". That's what you're saying?'

'Exactly, that's what I'm saying. You see, it is in this respect also highly characteristic and significant that it is called a *path*: a path is there to walk along, and you may imagine it as a mountain path which leads upwards.

Then, as far as the comparison of the Western and Eastern traditions is concerned, I see no difficulty here at all. Quite clearly the *via purgativa* is the equivalent of the character training, it is the purifying of your ordinary human nature, isn't it? Then, as far as I know, in the Western tradition, the words meditation and contemplation also enter, don't they? Now if we move on through meditation to contemplation, then contemplation designates the stage when ordinary discursive consciousness begins to fade away and you are on the threshold of something else, having left behind the discursive consciousness of what is technically stage two.'

'Can I just pause there, Hans', I interjected, 'because I now see the solution to a difficulty I've had whenever you've talked about the Western way of articulating the spiritual path. For, on the one hand, you have faithfully reported the Western tradition to say that there are *three* aspects or parts of the spiritual life: the *via purgativa*, the *via illuminativa* and the *via unitiva* — three, whereas on other occasions, on the other hand, you have talked, as you have again talked today, of *four* stages. Now, in view of what you have just said, we can resolve this little intellectual puzzle by saying that the three Western *viae* or ways express the successively dominant characteristics of the experience of the growing spiritual life rather than the successive stages of awareness but that they do correspond to modes of prayer and therefore to stages of awareness, and that as such the *via illuminativa* can be sub-divided to include *both* the stage of meditation *and* the stage of contemplation. Therefore the stage of meditation in the Western sense corresponds to the Buddha's meditation, whereas contemplation in the Western sense would then, presumably, correspond to his *Erkenntnis*, intuitive knowledge?'

'Well, I've experienced it differently', responded Hans.

'Ah', I said.

'You see, the very word "illumination" indicates that you are, well, suddenly illuminated, that you see something, and to me this is an experience which very much belongs to the sphere of stage three, to intuitive knowledge, where you suddenly see truth, literally see something which you haven't so far seen, maybe in a spontaneously arising image or symbol. Meditation and contemplation represent stages of approach to the state of illumination which I believe is identical with stage three, the stage of *Erkenntnis*, of intuitive knowledge.'

'This may be just a question of words Hans. I think I should tend to think of contemplation in the sense in which St Thomas talks about it — in terms of *simplex intuitus veritatis*. For him simple intuition (and he deliberately uses the word *intuitus*, intuition, not *ratio*, the discursive activity of the mind, as I've indicated to you before) is the essence of contemplation, and then I think it would be the equivalent of your illumination, not merely an approach to it.'

'Absolutely Marcus, yes. You see, it's very difficult to equate the terminology exactly because different people and different teachers have attached slightly varying meanings to different terms. So I don't think there is any real difficulty. Clearly, what in the Buddha's terminology is called liberation, or what you call entering into the primordial silence, or into the transcendent other, is akin to the *unio mystica*. So it is exactly the same path, it is bound to be the same path. And when you read — I read this book quite a bit and although it is too large and over-written, it is a classic of its kind — Evelyn Underhill's *Mysticism*, you see that a quite amazing amount of super-sensible knowledge has entered the minds of the mystics on the way to the *unio mystica*, which is the ultimate aim. So it is one and the same path. There is another book which I much appreciate and which has come out fairly recently. Admittedly it concentrates primarily on the Eastern tradition, but by no means only, and it is called *The Varieties of Meditative Experience* by D. Goleman, obviously deriving its title from William James' *The Varieties of Religious Experience*. And the essential message of the book is again that, although the *terminology* differs, the basic *dynamics* are the same.'

'Well, as I say, what is new for me in today's discussion, Hans, is your placing the topic of the spiritual path within the context of that peculiarly condensed saying of the Buddha. I can also see that it has been present to you for a long time but I haven't been aware of it being so explicitly part of your learning and life. Then there's one other thing I'd like to hear you commenting on. In all this exposition, you've spoken primarily in terms of knowledge, and only once, I think, have you used the term "heart" which I take to stand for the more affective side. And as I understand the subject of prayer and meditation in the Western tradition, prayer is essentially a matter ultimately of the *heart*. If you take a classical formulation of the tradition such as that of St Francis de Sales in his instructions to beginners on how to pray, you'll find he is very concerned about the preparation — not only the remote preparation of daily life, as you interpreted the Buddha to be saying, but also the more immediate preparation of putting yourself in the presence of God, of the use of the imagination (what St Ignatius of Loyola calls the "composition of place"), of the gradual stilling of the powers of the body and the interior powers of the imagination, and even of the intellect, the reason. And for him all this preparation is in the interest of, and is directed towards what I call the *kindling of the heart*. You see that, whether or not prayer ultimately grows — is given to grow — into the higher reaches of illumination or even union, it is essentially a matter of the heart.'

'Yes. Can I say something to that?' Hans asked.

'Yes.'

'Well Marcus, the first thing is by way of a personal remark: that through my destiny, or perhaps, through my constitutionally more contemplative disposition, I was more drawn to and also taught about meditation than about prayer in the spiritual path. But I believe that apart from my contemplative inclination, I am essentially a feeling person. Apart from these personal remarks, however, I should say that if you want to enter a meditative content, your essential guide, the essential force which you use, is feeling. The moment you begin to use intellect, you are lost because you dissociate yourself from the content of your meditation. So from the start you must immerse yourself through your feelings in what you meditate. You must attend, for instance, not so much to what the words mean but to how they sound, and if they don't touch your heart and your feelings, you will get nowhere. And this of course, permeates the whole way upwards. But further, equally important and perhaps even more so, is that when you encounter this presence, this otherness, which you may do at the end of the path, it will not just remain there but it will enter you. It will begin to permeate you, and Ignatius of Loyola and other people too, used a wonderful comparison, namely, eating. It is something which you can drink, or which wants to be drunk and to be eaten by you. It simply begins to descend into you. That is the experience. You see right away the relationship with communion. It is, spiritually speaking, communion. And here, of course, the most important phase of this feeding, of this nourishment, is that it fills and nourishes the heart and gives you in this sphere nourishment and strength.'

'So you would agree that at every stage it is the heart which is primary?'

'Absolutely.'

'That the training is essentially a training of the heart, of the feelings, of the affectivity; that the meditation, even the contemplation, is with a view to the stilling of the heart. That the higher stage, the listening, is a listening with the heart?'

'Exactly, Marcus.'

'And that the *unio*, if it is given to one, any union, of any quality, of any explicitness, is a union, as it has been said, of the heart to the heart, *cor ad cor*? You'd agree with that?'

'Absolutely. It's again, of course, not for nothing the Buddha's teaching has been called "*die Lehre von Liebe und Mitleid* — the teaching about love and compassion." I don't need to tell you anything about the Christian concept of any meditation. But perhaps it's a good moment, if you like, to remind ourselves of that lovely summary which I've quoted to you before.'

'The one about the *Umarmung*, the embrace, you mean?'

'Yes, Marcus, may I read it out to you in its entirety, because it depicts this element of sublime love and union so beautifully. It comes from the *Upanishads*.[2]

> Just as a man, closely embraced by his loving wife, knows nothing without, nothing within, so does this "person", closely embraced by the Self that consists of wisdom (*prājña*) know nothing without, nothing within. That is his [true] form in which [all] his desires are fulfilled, in which Self [alone] is his desire, in which he has no desire, no sorrow.
>
> These ... states of being (*loka*) are no longer states of being, gods are no longer gods ... an ascetic no longer an ascetic. He is not following by good, not followed by evil;

for then he will have passed beyond all sorrow of the heart.*

So, you see, even here we have the element of surrendering and giving love, of the highest order.'

'I think that's particularly beautiful, and very relevant to the whole series of discussions, because not only does it sum up the inner dynamic of the path we've been talking about this morning, that thrust or élan towards union which, therefore, when it is achieved, as it were dissolves all the forms of separation there are — between the ego and the greater self, between inner and outer, between the self and the other: that is the mystery, the ultimately ineffable mystery of the *unio mystica* — but it makes the transition to the heart again, as we were saying; it emphasises the heart, the warmth of love rather then the light of knowledge. But even more than that, I think, what is so fascinating is that it does so in terms of the basic human experience of the love of man and woman. At the same time, it transforms that. It expresses itself in terms of that basic experience but it takes it into a higher realm, and so it really draws together practically all the themes we have talked about in this series: the theme of being with another, the real quality and meaning of the depths of such an experience; the experience of solitude as distinct from loneliness; the relationship between a man and a woman; and all this it seems to subsume and draw upwards in this beautiful expression about the *innigste Umarmung*, the innermost embrace.'

'Exactly', said Hans.

'Very beautiful indeed.'

'One might say, in a very banal way, this is really what life is all about. If there is any answer to man's predicament and to the multitude of predicaments, then the answer's there.'

'It's a question once again of allowing the implications and depths of ordinary life and ordinary encounters to be touched and explored and followed through with persistence — and ardour, very great ardour, what the Hindus call *tapas*, energy, fiery energy.'

'The ardour: I'm glad you mentioned that Marcus, because

anything lukewarm will not do. This is perhaps again a matter of training and habit in the best sense of the word, that habit that becomes part of you, second nature. So that in the end you pursue this path with the ardour, the longing of a lover, in the highest sense of this word. If you haven't got that, you will not get there. Certainly not with the interest simply of somebody who wants to know.'

'And perhaps with the word "lover" we are once again at the full, and glowing centre of all the traditions: the tradition of the *Symposium* and of Plato in the West, the tradition of the *Bhagavad Gita* in the East, and so on. I should like to say that here we are at the glowing centre, the burning core, not so much of the material world, not even of the spiritual world, but of the world that is patient of being spiritualised, the one *cosmos*.'

'Yes, indeed', said Hans, and so closed this morning's discussion.

Notes

1. Verlag Urachhaus, Stuttgart, 2nd Edn., 1960.
2. *Brihadāranyaka Upanishad*, 4,3. 21-22, quoted in Udo Reiter, *Meditation-Wege zum Selbst* (Mosaik Verlag, Munich, 1976), p.47.

* The translation of this passage is contained in R.C. Zaehner *Hindu Scriptures* (pp 67-8, Everyman Library, London, 1966).

It could be noted that Zaehner translates the Sanskrit text in terms of a man *being* embraced by his wife and then by the Self, whereas the translator into the German text originally used by Dr. Schauder, translates his text in terms of what could be taken as *his* embrac*ing* his wife and then the knowing Self – a difference between passive and active from the man's point of view. Now apart from the uncertainty as to whether the genitive in the German translation is subjective or objective, and apart from the question of the text translated by Reiter and Zaehner respectively, two interesting problems lie behind these technicalities. Even if the English translation envisages the individual subject *being* embraced and the German envisages him embracing, the very complementarity of the translations brings out something which the perhaps deliberate ambiguity of the German also brings out in any case, namely, that there is a *mutual* embrace or implication and therefore a unification between the individual mortal and the divine principle. At the same time this very complementarity, as well as the contrast between the persistence of the two subjects of the unification and the unification intended, both nicely leave open the large philosophical question whether the unification involved is to be understood in terms of what Radhakrishnan has called pure or modified monism (*Indian Philosophy*, London, George Allen and Unwin, 2nd Edn., 1929, I, pp.31-34). For, as has been very acutely observed, there can be non-dualism without monism, so that the undoubted principle of *Advaita*, a-dualism, is open to two very different interpretations: in terms of the dissolution of one principle into the other, like the proverbial drop in the ocean or the camphor in the flame, or in terms of the abiding co-existence of both man and God. The critical question is whether those who were formerly two attain a union of fusion or a union in distinction. The latter, is, I believe, the fundamental Christian position, but is it also the Hindu position? Is it one possible interpretation of the Hindu position, or is it excluded by it? See on this subject Michael Simpson 'Hinduism and Christianity' in *The Tablet* 30th August 1980, pp. 842-3.

Dialogue 5: Stages of Counselling in Relation to Stages of the Spiritual Path

As 'twixt two equall Armies, Fate
  Suspends uncertaine victorie,
Our soules, (which to advance their state,
  Were gone out,) hung 'twixt her, and mee.
And whil'st our soules negotiate there,
  Wee like sepulchral statues lay ...

When love, with another so
  Interinanimates two soules,
That abler soule, which thence doth flow,
  Defects of loneliness controules.

John Donne The Extasie

'I'm very glad that you've come to keep our usual appointment, Marcus', began Hans this particular morning, 'even though you've got a touch of laryngitis. I'm sorry about your indisposition, but I'd like — if I may say so without appearing to be unfeeling — to take advantage of your relative voicelessness to tell you about a certain experience I had recently when I was working with a client. For this experience has a bearing on two of the major topics we've discussed together so far, namely, the stages of counselling and the stages of the spiritual path, in so far as it revealed to me something of the relationship of the spiritual life to the actual event of counselling.

Now you will recall that in a previous conversation, we defined the four basic stages of the spiritual path, namely, 1) first, a moral training or the *via purgativa*, a character training, as I called it; secondly (2), the stage of meditation, which then proceeds into the third (3) stage of contemplation or illumination or intuitive knowledge, the stage at which we transcend thinking and perceive truth intuitively; and fourthly (4), the stage of liberation, of union, where we are able to enter something which is completely beyond our ordinary self. This may be our own higher self, it may be something of a divine nature, or in ordinary life, the very existence of another being with whom we then become intuitively identified.

So far, and in this way then, we have been thinking about the spiritual path as a path of human development and purification, as a way of transcending our lower self, of transformation and perfection. However, the experience which I want to describe to you today adds a completely new dimension to this matter. For what I learned in it was that if we are living constantly in the dynamic, so to speak, of this life and proceeding through these stages, if we are walking forward and upward on this path, then even in ordinary life, and particularly in the counselling situation, we will, in relation to our clients, develop certain perceptions which would otherwise be denied to us. I mean that perceptions which I believe are extremely important and helpful would not occur to us in the same way.

This is a bald statement of my discovery, but to put you in the picture, I'd like to take a few steps back and say that I had to prepare for a counselling session with someone who is a friend of mine. He had come from a foreign country and I knew in advance that he had led a life which was very disappointing to me. He had developed relationships, multiple relationships, with women, among them with the wife of his best friend. He had rather lost his way and got involved in a number of very questionable intellectual and spiritual activities. I therefore approached this encounter with considerable apprehension, and I knew that I could function properly only if I was able to overcome this apprehension or any possible resentment or disappointment I might feel. It therefore needed a more than usually intense effort of preparation to get ready for this session. Now you know my idea of preparing by achieving a state of inner stillness or what I have in another context called a state of innocence, in which one frees oneself as far as possible from all prejudices, personal preoccupations, thoughts and feelings, and achieves a state of inner stillness which can perhaps best be likened to the stillness of a lake on a windless sunny day: you can look through the surface of the lake right into the clear depths whilst clouds that glide through the sky are mirrored in the surface. That is, of course, a poetic image, a classical image, and I make no claims to have achieved this stillness completely, but on this occasion I tried to be completely calm and I think I did to some extent achieve that state. Now, quite clearly, this is the stage that corresponds to the first stage of the spiritual life, the stage of character training or *via purgativa*.

The next thing was that I became aware that I was listening in a kind of meditative attitude. I'm sure I had done this before but now I was conscious of doing so. Now what does it mean to listen in a meditative attitude? I think it means that you subdue your intellect, you make this effort of subduing your conscious intellectual mind which works by searching for sharply defined impressions and looking for signs and symptoms, is constantly aware of concepts, and is inclined right away to draw conclusions, to make judgments and so on. All this needs to be subdued. I'm not suggesting that it should completely vanish from your mind, because here and there you will probably have to use your conscious mind. But, generally speaking, in order to open yourself up to taking in the full reality of what comes towards you as an experience, you will have to do that.

I could put it like this: to vary a phrase of Rudolf Steiner I have previously quoted to you, namely: "You must learn to think whilst abstaining from thinking", you must here learn to *listen whilst abstaining from thinking*, and then the inner state of the person whom you meet will gradually begin to light up. Images — significant images — will begin to develop, begin to become more intense and will as it were come towards you.

You will not search for them; they will come towards you and will eventually impress themselves on your mind — they may be images strictly so called, or certain words, certain gestures. As you listen and observe, you will have an experience comparable with the experience of observing colours and shapes, of listening to sounds and tunes, and also comparable with experiencing objects and the world of objects through the senses of touch, taste, even of smell. So that when you have fully absorbed or taken in such an experience, you are filled with impressions which have a life of their own, filled with a vital, *soul-experience*, which penetrates right into your very organism. You have taken it in, in the same way as you take in something which you eat or drink. The experience will, therefore, have a palpable reality which you will not be able to question — as little as you question the experience of being out in nature and seeing trees, stones, smelling the air, experiencing the sunshine.

Now this experience of immersing yourself, of being filled with impressions of that kind has an obvious affinity with the activity of meditation. Therefore I think is is justifiable to call it an attitude of *meditative listening* and observing. And the more you have schooled yourself in meditation, where it is fundamental not only to subdue your intellect and the activities of your brain but to transcend them, the easier you will find it to listen and observe in this attitude.

The next stage of the spiritiual path, as you know, is the stage of so-called illumination or intuitive knowledge. And it was after I had thoroughly immersed myself in the personality, presentation and problems of my friend in this attitude of meditative listening that I became particularly conscious that something *happened* to me which I had not experienced with such intensity before. After I had heard the experiences which this person, my friend, related to me — and it was a very complex story, and a story of many conflicts — he asked me a question, for he had to make a decision. Now what I experienced was that I did not have to think about it but could immediately give him an answer which I instinctively felt to be the right one. It offered itself to me, so to speak, as naturally as breathing does. I'm not saying, and I don't want to say, that this was a particularly difficult question. I'm quite sure that I or any other person would have been able to answer this question after giving it a little thought. But what I do want to say — this was the experience that alerted me — is that in actual fact I didn't think at all about it consciously. The answer presented itself convincingly to me and with equal conviction to the other person. At that moment I experienced a transition from the stage of meditative listening and observing to something akin to and comparable with intuitive knowledge.

Then the experience went further, and I felt as our session continued, that my thoughts about his conflict situation and the answer I had given, as well as all the experiences which he had related to me, began as it were to vanish. More and more I felt *him* and his state of being as he was. I felt so to speak identified with him in an — perhaps this is the right word — existential way. I suddenly knew what it was and how it was to be him at that moment. There were no thoughts about him. The whole conflict and all the experiences had dissolved but I felt him. And the feeling I had was of being stressed and strained, so to speak, in various ways, with forces pulling powerfully from the periphery in various directions, and of the centre more and more weakening. And I believe that essentially this was his problem: that he had lost contact with his centre, his essential inner self which had begun so to speak to weaken or perhaps even to disintegrate. Now I believe that this experience of identification is nothing but an equivalent of the experience of union, the last stage of the spiritual life where the person identifies with, enters into, something which is not himself but another being, another reality which he begins now to know and more than know, to identify with.

I think that these few remarks will make it sufficiently clear that the spiritual life is not only a great training ground for the purification and development of one's own personality, but also the training ground for enabling one to have certain perceptions during the counselling session and to relate to a client in a way which would otherwise not be possible, at least with the same clarity, certainly, the same insight. Anybody who begins to think about it will, I believe, readily be able to relate the so-called seven stages of the counselling process to the four stages of the path. They interlink, and as the counselling process continues, so the developing stages of consciousness of the path help one to understand and move the counselling process forward again, as in a spiral. They are in fact interacting constantly. We become aware of this, and if we live the counselling encounter through in this way, then we realise that the counselling process and the stages of the path are one interlinked, integrated whole. They belong together — perhaps this is an adequate comparison — as breathing and the heart-beat belong together.

In conclusion, Marcus, I should like to say that just as the counselling process in its various stages manifests the archetype of the *Gespräch*, the dialogue, so the spiritual life as I have now discussed it can manifest and does manifest in real life the archetype of true relatedness and deeper mutual understanding.'

'Well, Hans', I said, when we were able to meet again the next time, 'I think that your new insight is indeed something of a breakthrough. I'm captivated by it, and in a way I'm glad that I could not speak last time since you were as a result able to express your thoughts in a single flow. But now that I am able to respond and, in addition, have had time to think over what you said the last time, I should like to say that you've aroused my critical as well as my creative spirit. You've enabled me to glimpse certain connections I've never glimpsed before. But I'd like to deal first with what I call the critical part of my reflections. So may I say that, stimulating as your most recent thinking is, it does pose something of an intellectual problem for me, in so far as I do *not* see exactly how the seven stages of the counselling process relate to, fit in with, the four stages of the spiritual development. I realise that you did suggest something of the way these respective stages matched up with each other, but I must admit that at least to my — over? — logical mind this correlation seemed to be at once too vague and too forced.'

'Well', rejoined Hans, 'let me try to meet your query — though you realise that this purely logical and abstract thinking is not really my line! Starting then, with the first stage of the counselling process, the stage of preparation, this is a matter of clearing one's mind of all intruding thoughts, feelings, conceptions, which presupposes a training in character that is the subject-matter of the first stage of the spiritual life. The second stage of counselling is the state of listening, primarily of listening but also, of course, to some extent, of exploring. And here the meditative attitude which I have described in relation to the second stage of the spiritual life comes into play, although occasionally it may be interrupted by a very conscious attempt to question and to explore. So we come to the third stage of counselling, the stage of assimilation, of inwardly absorbing what we have heard, and this is even more markedly correlated with the meditative attitude. (And I should like to remind you that the stage of assimilation and the stage of the diagnostic interlude are inter-changeable).

From there we move on to the next stage, the fourth, the stage of the diagnostic interlude. Quite clearly this has something to do with the act of knowing. We must consciously make a diagnosis, but we all know that the diagnosis can be a very, very subtle matter and even for the most professional mind it is often overlaid with a great deal of uncertainty. Even at the strictly psychological level, many psychiatrists, for example, will in all sincerity make very different diagnoses. Besides which, I personally, as you know, try to take into account a person's physical constitution and cosmological position as well as his biography and development. In all these circumstances, therefore, our intuitive knowledge will be a most valuable guide in sorting out our uncertainties in this sphere, helping us to make the right diagnosis.

So we proceed to stage five in the sequence of counselling, the selection of the target area. Again this to some extent must be a conscious act but it is ultimately as subtle as, or even more subtle than, becoming clear about the diagnosis. And once again our intuitive feelings, our intuitive knowledge, that which arises from within with a sense of certainty apart from and beyond any conscious thought, will be a precious instrument. Therefore this is again related to the area of intuitive knowledge.

The next stage, stage six, consists in working through the target area with the client. Quite obviously this is already in a much more marked degree than at the previous stages a matter of the relationship of the therapist to the client. He must guide her, and the more clearly he feels what kind of person the client is — feels her very being, the more he feels identified with her — the more certainty he will have, the more assurance he will have to guide her. At this stage, therefore, we have what I believe is a significant transition from the realm of intuitive knowledge to the realm of identification. And this pertains even more to the last stage, stage seven of the counselling process, when the client has lived through the essential stages and phases of the therapeutic process and has now reached the point of adjusting to life, of finding a foothold in life again, of discovering new insights, new attitudes, new values, which will help her to start again. Here, quite clearly, the more we shall have exercised our capacity to identify with her, to feel her as she is, beyond all thoughts and concepts, the more we will be able to guide, to help, to support.

So you see, Marcus, that is the way I see the two schemes — of the counselling process and of the spiritual life — fitting together. Is that clearer? But let me just add this. I've again spoken about a scheme. I do however, want to insist that ultimately this is abstract, whereas the whole process of counselling is a living process in a constant flux. Nothing is fixed, and if an abstract scheme such as I have outlined intrudes, and particularly if it intrudes permanently, it drives the very life out of this living encounter between two human beings. Any scheme — this one included — is nothing but the bare, dry bones, it *is* a structure, and this structure must sink into the very depths of our being, where it belongs, just to give us a kind of foundation, a kind of supportive foundation on which the edifice of the creative action must be built. You can therefore compare it with the scheme and structure which a creative musician has to learn when he or she learns the technique of composition. If they *are* creative artists, all this will sink into the very depths of their being, and from there it will support the creation of a work of art. It is basically exactly the same in counselling: we need the structure in order to have the foundation, because we are always in danger of losing shape in our thoughts, in our approach, in our attitude, in our whole being. As I've mentioned already, Rilke once spoke of people as *die Zerfallenden*, those liable to fall apart. We can indeed slowly, imperceptibly disintegrate, and the structure, once it is acquired and deeply sunk into the foundation of our being, will help us not to disintegrate. But apart from that, the encounter must be an act of creation, adjusted to the uniqueness of the situation and to the uniqueness of the individual. So what we must realise above all is that in such an encounter we are creating something, and creating something out of what is in flux, as life in the cosmos is in flux. I think yet once again of Goethe's lines; for Goethe, life is a matter of "forming and transforming on the part of the eternal mind that eternally sustains us". And, with that caution, do you understand how in my thinking the two "schemes" fit together?'

'With my feeling and intuitive being, Hans', I replied, 'I find all this wholly fascinating and real, and yet, with my critical being, I must admit to still having certain doubts. My thoughts are still a little too turbulent at the moment for me quite to be able to work them through, but trying to frame them as best I can, I feel on the one hand, that in the reformulation of your case to meet my query you were not quite true to your own initial intuition, but that, on the other hand, you are saying something extremely valuable which could be reformulated and, in the reformulation, be seen to be something different from and, *therefore*, also something even more profound than you seem to be saying immediately.'

'Possibly', said Hans, a little doubtfully.

'You see, Hans, to take the negative part of my response to you first, I think that my question about the exact manner of inter-relation between the stages of counselling and the stages of spiritual development and its accompanying degrees of consciousness goes to the heart of your thesis *as* you propound it. What I want to say about this inter-relationship is parallel to what I said about the previous inter-relationship you sought to establish between the stages of counselling and the stages of an ordinary but true dialogue, a *Gespräch*, between friends who as such enjoy equality. Do you remember how, when I sought to test whether there was a point-by-point correlation between the two sorts of exchanges, we got a bit unstuck? You had to labour to establish a point-by-point correspondence then, didn't you, just as in my opinion you had to labour just now to establish the details of the correlation between the stages of counselling and the stages of the spiritual life.'

'Yes. Can I interrupt you for a moment?', asked Hans.

'Of course', I replied.

'It's exactly as you say, Marcus. Your question put me in an awkward position. Left to myself, I should not have continued beyond that preliminary exposition of my new insight. To me that was enough, you know, and beyond that I had to some extent, as you rightly said, to strain intellectually, which is not really my nature at all. The essential thing for me was what I call the organic inter-linking of these two processes, and if I have to pick out one idea from all the rather laboured statements and attempts to state the nature of the inter-linking which followed later, it is the fact that in my experience we are here ultimately involved in *an act of creation*. And you may remember that this is what Jung said. I didn't say it because Jung had said it, but I was extremely glad when I found that he did say it. It's akin to the creative act of the artist, because you see, the changes which take place can be so rapid and so surprising that you have to be completely adaptable, so to say, in a state of creativity, adjusting to what comes towards you, understanding it, and taking it a step further, although you may be totally unprepared for it. And what I am saying is that this state of creativity can only be achieved through two things: on the one hand, by allowing the purely structural elements of the counselling process to sink into the subconscious or even unconscious, and on the other hand, by following and living in the spiritual path daily, for then ideally, at least, you should have contact with something — I overstate it now, please — with something like an inflowing spirit, you know, which will keep you going and enable you to overcome the obstacles, to untie the knots, to recover from surprises, without being completely thrown. In other words, the process will flow, it will be alive, this is essentially what I meant.'

'Yes, I understand that very well, Hans, but you see what I'm concerned with is really to see more precisely what it is you're saying. I think that this insight into the inter-action between the two processes of counselling and the spiritual life is a most important one. In fact it's because it is so important that it's worth trying to disengage its nature as clearly as possible. I see further that what you're trying to do is to articulate very consciously something that goes on more or less unconsciously in any good act of communication, at any level. And I suspect that some such process goes on not only in the case of counselling but in the case of the musicians whom you have quoted to me before, or even, I suppose, in the act of sexual love-making.'

'Absolutely', concurred Hans.

'There seems to be a common element in all such acts of communication. And I think that it is extremely important to try to express, define, formulate what it is that is going on because this is, I believe, largely unexplored territory — not the *fact* of what is going on, but what is *said* to be going on, and I think that you have expressed a great deal of what's going on, very, very well. But I should really like to go back to concentrating on two aspects of this, yes? On the one hand, critically, on what stage of the counselling process corresponds to what stage of the spiritual life; on the other hand, more constructively, on drawing out some of the implications of a more exact statement of your insight a little further. So I wish to take your thesis both backwards and forwards.'

'Yes, please do. Continue', said Hans.

'Well, then, I'm thinking aloud, Hans. But, especially in the last bit, where you were trying once again to link the seven stages of counselling more precisely, point-by-point, to the four stages of spiritual development and consciousness; I had certain misgivings, and I can perhaps make them clear by summarising your argument in the form of a simple chart. The seven stages of the organic process of counselling seem in your mind to be correlative to the four stages of the organic process of spiritual growth in the following fashion:

Stages of counselling	*Stages of the spiritual life*
can be correlated with	
1. Preparation	1. Character training
2. Listening and exploring 3. Assimilation	2. Meditation
4. Diagnostic interlude 5. Selection of target area(s)	3. Intuitive knowledge
6. Working through the target area(s) with client 7. Helping client through into new life	4. Identification

Would you agree to this diagrammatic way of recapitulating your thinking, Hans?'

'Yes, though subject to the reservation about the essentially creative nature of both processes, in themselves and in their interaction, that I have already expressed.'

'I accept that, Hans, but if you in your turn accept my summary, then it seems to me that on the negative and critical side of my response to you, this summary throws three difficulties into relief. In the first place, I'm not happy about your correlating the stage of assimilation to meditation, since the task of assimilation above all would seem to me to call for the deepest degree of awareness which you call intuitive knowledge, even identification. Then secondly, I agree that it is again at this stage of assimilation that the what I shall now call discursive intellect most needs to be subdued in favour of the intuitive, almost subconscious, intellect, and yet, even on your own account, this same discursive intellect needs to be brought back into play for the purpose of the "diagnosis" (Stage 4), let alone for the purpose of the selection of the target area(s) (your Stage 5).'

'May I interrupt you for a moment on this last point, Marcus? You are, of course, quite right to say that the more conscious mind partly re-emerges at these stages of the counselling process. But I tried to allow for this by saying that at the stages of the "diagnostic interlude" and of the selection of the target area(s) (and the subsequent stages too for that matter) "intuitive knowledge" is not the only function but one that aids the conscious function: the intuitive intellect as it were backs up the conscious mind.'

'Yes, I understand now', I replied, 'but that still leaves me with my third and main difficulty here. You speak so well about the need to identify with the other that you seem, at least to me, to fail to do justice to the fact that the counsellor nevertheless *also* remains himself. For the fact that the counsellor remains himself is essential to his being able to work through the target area(s) with his client and to help her to establish herself in her new life, the final stages of the counselling process. You see, what interests me is not only the nature of the interaction between the two people, including the possibility of identification, but the very fact that there are two people for there to be an interaction at all, who themselves therefore also remain themselves.

And here I want to go on to the second, more constructive part of my embryonic reflection on your thesis, and that is: What is the most accurate, the best, the most adequate way of describing what is going on? You talk in terms of becoming the other, very finely and intuitively becoming the other, almost at the expense of, to the loss of, oneself. But in fact one does not disappear, as is proved by the fact that one re-emerges, and it is essential that one does so. So what precisely is going on? It is an identification with the other *without the loss of the self*. In fact one's continuing to be there and to be oneself, albeit in reserve, as it were, is vital for the other person. And this is so not only for the obvious reason that being an articulator, assessor, target-finder and guide presupposes the counsellor simply being there first as an experienced and distinct other. It is also for the more fundamental reason that this is a condition of opening up to the client the possibility of her going out of her own world by entering another's, initially here the counsellor's, which, I now think, is the way in which the real alchemy of encounter works.'

'Aha', Hans nodded. 'Go on.'

'I've been thinking a little more about all this myself. And, to expand what I mean by the metaphor of alchemy, I think that it operates by way of a reciprocal movement. On the one hand, the counsellor, through the sort of indentification you began by evoking, can progressively enter into the world of his client, can, by a receptive, humble, even self-emptying way — "getting himself out of the way," as you've said before — allow the client to guide his empathy into the very feel and contours of her being, literally to feel his way into that other world, *and yet remain radically himself*, so that the counsellor is still *himself, only in another position*. At the same time, this very process, which is more non-verbal than verbal and thus communicates itself before the counsellor says or does very much, is not merely something that emanates from the counsellor to the client, it is also an implicit overture, an invitation to the client to respond in kind, it is a model, if you like. As well as being an initiative, it is an offer. Thus, on the other hand, the client is shown the possibility of her *in her turn* moving into another's world and thereby leaving the fixed exclusiveness of her own alone.

By moving into her world and then back into his own, to and fro, the counsellor demonstrates that identity does not consist in being identified rigidly with one world or another, but, on the contrary, in this active potency to move in and out of different worlds and positions, to take up and put down different points of view, to let different world-views jossle, conflict with and enrich each other — like the author or the audience of a play. The counsellor enacts but also demonstrates the capacity to hold other, many, even conflicting as well as complementary points of view within one containing and sustaining identity, and thereby invites the client to reconsider, reframe, re-jig, re-organise and correct, in any case to move out of and enlarge her own world. In more psycho-analytic language, the client can learn to introject the model of the counsellor, take in this potency and capacity. In return for the counsellor exercising the active potency — Keats' now well-known "negative capability", if you like — of entering the client's world, while remaining himself, the client can learn the knack of entering another's world while remaining *her*self and thus, by learning in this way to take in another's world, move more and more flexibly out of her identification with her own alone.

Counselling, therefore it seems to me, is thus intrinsically the possibility of an *exchange of identifications*, in which the counsellor proffers such a process so as to enable the client to enter into and continue it, more or less completing the circle of exchange. But, if this is in any way true, then it means that two being present is of the very essence of the matter, so that talk of dissolution of the self or anything that suggests this, is strictly inaccurate.'

'But I didn't say that the counsellor somehow dissolves', protested Hans.

'No, you didn't, not quite, but I think you very much underemphasised yourself, because you were so concerned with becoming the other — "I felt her", "I felt ... identified with her", "I suddenly knew what it was and how it was to be her at the moment", subject to all her stresses and strains as if they were your own, you said.'

'May I interrupt here for a moment, Marcus? I do follow you, and I don't want to interrupt for long, because you have, with great subtlety and perceptiveness, taken the analysis much further than I have or could have done, because you know, I haven't that sort of mind. But once you put it like that to me, I see that you are quite right. Even when I say I identify and speak of total assimilation, I do retain my sense of self, there are two of us.'

'But, Hans, think that this is very important for the accuracy of the description of what's going on. Because I think that if one didn't insist on this one could all too easily slip into an Eastern type of sense of the dissolution of the self. And this is where I think that the second, more constructive part of my incipient critique of your thesis really comes in.

You see, what I'm saying is that there are two present all the time, interacting in an extraordinarily sensitive and subtle way. But I wonder whether that's all there is to it, and whether the very perception of this fact doesn't carry us further. What I'm feeling towards, Hans, is something suggested by a term that came to me as we were discussing the interpenetration of the spiritual life and the stages of counselling. You see, you began by speaking about the counsellor's *identification* with the client. I was thereby drawn on to canvas the idea of the identification beginning to work *the other way too* — by the client catching enough of the empathic energy of the counsellor to begin identifying with him. In this way I arrived at the idea of the encounter as an *exchange of identifications*. And it must have been this that set the bells of association ringing.

For we are now talking about the dialogue in terms of a *reciprocal* process of identification between two human beings. Yet once we begin to think about the relationship between human beings in this way, I am reminded of the fact that the Fathers of the early Church, if I understand them aright, had a sense of just such an interplay of reciprocal identifications in abiding distinctness — but not so much as between human beings as *within the Trinity itself*. They summed this up by the term *perichoresis* in Greek and *circumincessio* in Latin, *perichoresis* literally meaning the proceeding around each other in a kind of intimate dance, and *circumincessio* literally meaning a going round and into each other within a circle of communication.

So, having arrived at the idea that we can think of the relationship of two human beings in terms of an exchange of identifications, I have been reminded that the Greek and Latin Fathers suggested that there is some comparable sort of exchange of identifications within the Trinity itself. But I can have associated my latest characterisation of the human experience with a characterisation of the inner life of the Trinity only in virtue of some implicit hunch that the human experience is somehow a transposition or version of the divine, just as the notion of *perichoresis* or *circumincessio* as pertaining to the Godhead must have owed much of its excitement and persuasive power to the human resonance it was obscurely felt to have.

The idea now is, therefore, that this exchange of identifications operates, not only at the human, but at the divine level and, moreover, that this is because of some *mysterious correlation between the divine and the human reciprocity*. And since the teasing out of what is involved in this correlation promises to shed further light on the nature of this exchange of identifications, I feel propelled to investigate this correlation just a little more — if I may?'

'Please do go on, Marcus', said Hans, 'for although I have to admit that I am finding your pursuit taxing, I am also quite riveted by it.'

'You are encouraging, Hans. Well, then, the idea that is surfacing is that there is some analogous exchange of identifications operating at two levels: at the level of two human beings and at that of the persons of the Trinity. But, if this is so, then we can further think of the interaction of the two levels as working in two directions.

On the one hand, working from down upwards, we can start from the sort of apprehension of the play of cross-identifications between two human beings at which we have arrived so far and then *extrapolate* this to the level of the interplay between the persons of the Trinity. In this case, the human process of interelationship becomes the foot of a ladder up to what we can then see as its most pre-eminent form, the interelationship of the persons of the Trinity: it is when you take the human experience and then prolong and intensify it that you end up with the divine experience.

On the other hand, once we have arrived at such a full and final notion of the inner life of the Trinity, we can then also look at it from up downwards and say that the life of the Trinity consists essentially in an empathy between Father and Son so vibrant that it is itself a person, and therefore in an intensely intimate interplay and dance of cross-identifications in nevertheless abiding distinctness. Moreover this divine exchange of identifications is charged with such a prodigal and irrepressible urge to communicate itself that it cannot be kept for itself alone. And this is why the inner essence of human encounter is an off-shoot of the divine encounter and consists likewise in an exchange of identifications in intactness, although it is this only derivatively and writ small: it is when you take the divine experience and miniaturise and refract it that you descend down the scale to find human experience. And we begin to see more clearly too why the patristic term about the Trinity did have such human resonance: the human experience was an echo of the divine. In this light, at least two things follow.

First, if we want to assert simultaneously the empathy involved in counselling and the retention of self-identity as well as the subtle inter-deployment of these two aspects, I wonder whether it is not, paradoxically, this initially theological term, *perichoresis/circumincessio*, that provides the best way to hit off the features of the encounter between human beings that we have progressively uncovered.

In the second place, the use of this term not only thus

expresses as no other term does for me, the dialectic of cross-identifications in distinctness inherent in any true dialogue between two human beings on the model of the inner life of the Trinity. This description also suggests the hovering of the actuality of that Trinity around and within the dialogue of the human couple. This term, therefore, also articulates and confirms, even amplifies, any glimmering we may have had of the presence to the two of some third thing, a sense, not only of the other, but of the Other, with a capital "O". This would accordingly provide a larger background for the sense which you have yourself expressed that even when one is apparently alone, practising as best one can, in all humility, the spiritual life in a strict sense, there is an "inflowing of the Spirit".'

'I couldn't agree more', Hans interposed. 'That's very beautiful, what you say about the *perichoresis* — is that the right word?'

'Yes.'

'This is what I felt, Marcus, but could not formulate like that. It's what I, perhaps very inadequately, implied with the quotation from Goethe. For in what he refers to as *Gestaltung, Umgestaltung*, you have the element of movement, of flux, therefore of finding and losing, everything that you have indicated in your term *perichoresis* and your talk of the "dance", almost the cosmic dance, contained therein. But what you have also indicated — I am most grateful for this too — is something else that I have been conscious of in a penumbral way and then become centrally aware of as you challenged me, and this is that the Other with a capital "O" is present. But then, even here, Goethe can be said to have pointed the way, in so far as, after the *Gestaltung, Umgestaltung*, he goes on to mention what can be taken to refer to that influx in the living spirit which comes from above, therefore from the Other. And there you have it all, only I could never in my life have expressed it like that by myself. So here again, as far as our own relationship is concerned, we are, if I may say so, acting out the *Urphänomen*, the proto-phenomenon that we two function at different levels; I function at the level of simple experience, whilst you function at a more analytic level. The difference as well as the mutual responsiveness is amazing, but quite frankly, I don't think that there is any contradiction between us in all this.'

'No, Hans, there's not', I agreed.

'You have just refined and expressed what I had said in a much more, well, spiritualised form and thereby immensely enriched the whole thing, that's what it is.'

'Well, Hans, that's a very generous way of talking about an exchange in which I persist in thinking you have in fact had the really seminal ideas. But, emboldened by your remarks, may I now just dot a few "i's" and cross a few "t's"? I think that through struggling with your ideas — or perhaps I should say, through entering more intensely into your struggle with your own ideas — I can now see a little more clearly how I should reformulate this major insight of yours. The apparently negative part of my criticism of your thesis is very much subordinate to the more positive part of it, namely, the reformulation of your insight in such a way as to enable us to see further implications of it. I think that what I'm trying to say is that I certainly want to affirm your central insight about what you call the inter-linking of the stages of the counselling process with the stages of spiritual development, since it is most valuable, but I also want to locate them more precisely in relation to each other, if at all possible, and so be able to take your insight further. For if I'm right in thinking that the different stages of awareness are interfused with different stages of any true communication more variously and more subtly than you seemed to state in the reformulation of your initial insight, then I think that we can restate my own central idea of the *perichoresis* — which is a reformulation of your central idea! — in another way. We can say, can't we, that precisely because there is this *perichoresis*, this alternating response and successive interaction of two people in the sustaining presence of the Other, a Third, in the *Umwelt*, in this enveloping ambience, if you like, of the *ewigen Sinn*, eternal meaning and its *ewige Unterhaltung*, its eternal upholding, then the different stages of spiritual development represent various aspects or levels of the circling or spiralling of communication. They represent as it were the rising and falling, of the conscious self of now one, now the other, as well as of the reasoning self as distinct from the intuitive self of one *within* himself, so that there is — it's very difficult to describe — something like a wave motion, there's a rhythm, an undulation and a rhythm of alternation and balancing, yes, of some dance between the two, but also of some dance *within* each one.'

'Yes, very beautiful, Marcus', said Hans. 'And again you used a cosmis image; you used the image of flux, of motion, of the tide, of *Gestaltung, Umgestaltung* formation and transformation again. So here I want to come back to what for me is the essential thing from a practical point of view. So far we have been thinking — *I* have been thinking — that there is a counselling process on the one hand and there is a spiritual life on the other, so that you can be a good counsellor — or you can try to be a good counsellor — in one part of your life, and in another part of your life you can go along the spiritual path in order to become a well balanced and perhaps a slightly more spiritual human being. But I had never before experienced with such immediacy that there is a complete interaction. In other words, if somebody wants to be a counsellor in the sense we have been discussing, then there is really so intimate an interplay between the processes of counselling and the spiritual life that it is necessary *not only* to give a counsellor, say, a training analysis, which is very good, or supervision over a period of time, *but also* to give him a spiritual training — and not only a spiritual training in order to make him a better, a more balanced, a more orientated person in himself, but also to give him the possibility of being *a better counsellor* who will function in the very counselling situation with much greater perceptiveness, and with much better judgment. That is my main point.'

'Yes, I quite agree with that, Hans, and I think that it is for this reason that I should again slightly reformulate one of your other important statements, namely that the spiritual life can become the manifestation of the archetype of true relationship. I think that I should put it slightly differently and start by recurring to another reference of yours to Goethe. According to you, Goethe speaks of humankind being *der dialogische Mensch* — a creature capable of and constituted by dialogue. *Gespräch* or dialogue is the archetype of which counselling is one expression because human beings in their innermost beings are dialogical beings. It's because humanity is a *dialogischer Mensch* that human beings carry on dialogues.'

'May I say "should be"?', said Hans.

'Well, should be and therefore in some profound sense by nature is, a being of dialogue. In his or her innermost being, he or she is capable of dialogue, however overgrown or stunted this capacity may be. And it follows that the tearing, the losing of the centre which you began by speaking about can then be defined as an impairment of this innermost nature. What, then, is the innermost nature of this *Gespräch*, this dialogue? Let's take this a bit further. Well, the *Gespräch* is with a human partner in dialogue and so has an evident human dimension. But we have also begun to glimpse that every true dialogue seems in its depths also to declare a third thing, aura or person, and to have another dimension, the dimension of the Other. Concurrently with this, not only have we seen between us that the goal of the spiritual life is union with the Other, we have also glimpsed that this union in principle liberates us for deeper communion with other human beings. The very discipline of the spiritual life is therefore also about our fellow human beings, the human dimension. The dialogue is thus explicitly a human phenomenon and yet also has an implicit reference to something other, the Other, just as the spiritual life is explicitly about the Other and yet also has an implicit reference to fellow human beings. It seems to me, therefore, that the human dialogue (whether in its ordinary form or in its intensified form as counselling) is as it were the becoming explicit, the showing forth of the implicitly human element of the spiritual life, just as the spiritual life is the becoming explicit, the showing forth of the implicitly divine element in the human dialogue. Put in a slightly different way, where the dialogue makes evident the human aspect of the triadic relationship of, shall we say now, I — thou — Thou/we, the practice of the so-called spiritual life make evident the divine aspect of the triadic relationship. In this perspective, then, dialogue and spirituality become as it were the two faces of the same reality, the one the more overtly human face, the other the more overtly spiritual face; or the outwardness and the inwardness of the same thing. So I conclude with you that the process of counselling and of the spiritual life are indeed indissolubly united, but I do so in a somewhat different way from you. Do you see?'

'I do indeed', responded Hans warmly, 'and I quite agree with that way of seeing it too. In that regard, I should just like to add something which has recently come to me. I was reading the gospel of St. John again not so long ago and there I came upon that passage where Jesus is reported as saying — "He who receives the one I have sent also receives me, and he who receives me ..." Now as I read this, it occurred to me that this expressed exactly what happens at a sort of mystical — is that the right word? — level in a *Gespräch*. You take into yourself somebody whom destiny, life itself has sent you, but the moment you do that, you take on the Other, you follow me? We are back to what you just said. In other words, if you think of the *Gespräch*, the listening, as an interiorisation or assimilation, then the moment you truly and devotedly and humbly and lovingly do that, then you take into yourself, you accept, you receive someone who has been sent to you, and by doing so, Him who has sent that person. Do you follow me? Does that relate?'

'Yes, indeed', I replied, 'it's the same trinity, if you like.'

'Yes, the same trinity', Hans confirmed.

'It's the mystery of the inter-relationship between one's fellow-beings and God: God is in the other and yet is more than the other, he is other than the other.'

'Yes. And when I came across this passage, it occurred to

me to say to a friend who came up to see me and asked: "What is a *Gespräch*, a dialogue?", "Well, in the first place it is a mystery".'

'I don't think there's any more to say', I said. 'Or else there's still so much to say. Besides, it's almost time for me to go.'

'Shall we switch off then?', Hans asked.

Dialogue 6: Counselling and Creativity

Some four hundred years ago, there lived in India a poet-saint called Rajjab. When it was known that Rajjab had received his 'illumination', men from far and near came to him and asked: 'What is it that you see? What is it that you hear?' He answered: 'I see the eternal play of life. I hear heavenly voices singing, "Give form to the yet unformed, speak out and express."

K.M. Sen *Hinduism*[1]

'We've already discussed a great deal together, Hans', I began this particular morning. 'You'll remember how we first met professionally but soon discovered that we shared so much simply as people, let alone as counsellors. So we began to meet fairly regularly, and our association grew into friendship. In the process we also soon realised that for all our sharing we came to our experiences from our respective starting-points as counsellor and priest as well as from different backgrounds and that this made for a rich contrast and complementarity. So we've already explored our agreement but also raised a number of important issues between us. Inevitably, however, we've left a lot undiscussed. I can glimpse a few of the further topics I should like to talk over with you, and there's one of quite central importance in particular that I'd like to take up with you again. I therefore wonder whether you'd care to start another series of conversations on subjects of mutual concern?'

'I should not just care to continue our previous dialogues, Marcus, I should be delighted to do so. These meetings have become very important to me. You're well aware that we've been having these conversations for many years now. When we started, I was already approaching old age, and now I'm experiencing it fully. In these circumstances I have to say that our talks have been a veritable life-line for me. You see, I've always lived on the level of intimate experience which, however, I tried to deepen through a feeling that's possibly akin to artistic feeling. But I'm not naturally articulate. I've never written anything – except a few poems – I've never given a lecture. You, on the other hand, have a gift for thinking, your profession is to speak, and you bring your extensive knowledge of philosophy and theology to bear on anything you discuss. As a result when I'm with you and am – happily! – exposed to your highly trained and searching mind, my thoughts, instead of floating like clouds, begin to condense. I'm very grateful.'

'You're very kind, Hans. I hope you appreciate how even the very contrast of our sensibility nourishes me too. But let's get down to work. I've already indicated that the first question I'd like to pursue with you arises out of our previous discussions and it happens to be the very one you have yourself already touched upon in your reference to "artistic feeling". For at the outset of our previous meetings you had explained that for you the typical process of counselling unfolds in seven stages: the stages of preparation, listening and exploration, assimilation, "diagnostic interlude", selection of target area(s), working through the target areas with the client and finally, helping the client into a new life. Now that was very illuminating, but what I've wondered more and more on reflection is whether the very precision of this articulation of the seven stages could not distract us from the essential thing that keeps the whole process moving along. We could fail to see the wood for the trees.

Let me put it like this. I realise that these ideas evolved in a highly personal way, and yet I cannot help relating them to the ideas of others. You yourself led the way by comparing your sevenfold scheme with the threefold scheme of Stafford-Clark:

Receiving; Assimilating; Intervening. And mentally I made the further comparison with the similar threefold scheme of Carkhuff and Egan: Ventilation and Exploration; Understanding; Positive Action. My real interest in bringing together these different universes of discourse, therefore, is to try to put my finger on what is distinctive about your own approach. The surface comparison between your sevenfold scheme and others' threefold scheme is a useful device for beginning to do this. And I've begun to feel that what you were really talking about is a driving force that is embodied in the sevenfold process, but that can too easily be lost sight of in the details of this process. And this is something that you referred to in our previous discussions when you occasionally called the whole process "creative" without spelling this out further.

Am I right Hans, in thinking there is something on these lines that is for you the essence of the sevenfold scheme?'

'You know Marcus, you have almost uncannily homed in on one of my own further reflections on our previous *Gespräche*, conversations. So I'm particularly pleased to try to explain my thoughts on what you have quite rightly perceived is the true driving-force of the counselling process.

I should like to begin by saying that in one sense there's nothing sacrosanct about the number seven. In fact my own sevenfold rhythm could be reduced to a threefold rhythm, the first three stages being concerned with *taking in*, the last three with *giving out*, and the fourth one serving as a point of balance. It would be like breathing in and breathing out, punctuated by a pause and turn. But these are only so many different ways of ordering something which I first experienced as a continuous flow. As I told you before, I practised my particular approach long before I reflected on its process, let alone before discovering that Stafford-Clark had worked out a substantially similar scheme. And I should be quite happy to see them as independent variants of each other.

What I do want to say is that I first lived the experience of counselling and, further, that I lived it as a *human* experience, the experience of two human beings meeting with, engaged with, each other. And perhaps the most important thing of all, as I now realise more clearly, is that all along I've felt and imagined as well as thought of any such real involvement in depth with another human being as a *creative* process. What goes on in a counsellor is for me more like what happens in the composition of a work of art or a piece of music than anything else. It may be a little far-fetched to say that the counsellor is like a creative artist in relation to the client, so let me give a preliminary indication of what I mean.

A serene open-mindedness and objectivity enables the counsellor to absorb a multitude of impressions from his client which come to him unsought in the most varied form, from the most subtle, almost imperceptible, to the most obvious ones. But he will not speculate about them. He will let them sink into the depths of his being, so that they mature there, undisturbed by the interference of his intellect, until in the end they have achieved an organic unity and coherence, a life and being of their own, and reveal their nature and meaning in their own idiom. Understanding and insight into the being of the client and her needs will now dawn on the counsellor, in the same way as artists or poets, patient of innumerable subtle impressions, will in the fulness of time be the mouthpiece of the work of art which has matured within themselves, revealing an, as yet, undiscovered truth and not an arbitrary construction of their intellect. And this is no doubt one reason why I insist that a counsellor should be thoroughly versed in works of art as well as in the ways of the world – I was probably speaking out of the passionate interest I had in frequenting musical concerts in Vienna as a student when I could no longer stand the mechanistic approach to medical studies!

It's this way of looking at counselling that accounts above all, I now think, for anything that's distinctive about my own approach. I also realise more sharply that it's in the *stages of preparation* and then of assimilation that all this is concentrated and comes to expression most of all. You will recall my saying that it's in my opinion critical that a counsellor allows himself time to prepare for the visit of the client, time in which to collect himself and transcend his ordinary intellectual and everyday consciousness. He seeks to tune his whole being to the state of mind which will be necessary for listening to the client. I quoted Steiner's words about thinking "while abstaining from thinking". Essentially the same idea is captured in two further quotations, one from the West and one from the East. Would you be interested in hearing them?'

'I should indeed,' I replied.

'Well, the first is from Carl-Gustav Heyer who, as you may know, was a pupil of Jung, albeit a very independent-minded one. It's an extract from a lecture to his own students which my wife Lisl and I translated into English:

> Then I did something which, according to my experience, is always to be recommended whenever one is faced with a phenomenon and finds that one has got stuck. Allow me, for the sake of brevity, to put it this way: I did not focus on it, did not look at it energetically, but instead I "blinked". Why just that? In the course of scientific training with its basic attitude, its discoveries, theories and practices, we are accustomed to placing certain facts which have been established into the full light. The gaze of the scientist, whether engaged in research or in practical work, focuses on them. And the more such a scientific tendency is perfected, the brighter these things will get, the darker, however, other things will become, with the result that they will move more and more into the shadow. But if you wish to perceive something which is in the shadow – you know this from walks in the night, from groping through cellars – then you cannot find your orientation by focusing sharply, but by looking through half-closed eyes. For thus those over-bright things which with their dazzling light hide others, are dimmed. That's the sort of thing I mean to describe when I say I "blinked" at the phenomenon. I could also say: I have allowed it to affect me; or: I have

behaved in accordance with the old Indian proverb which says: "When someone says to you that he has searched and found, then don't believe him; but the man who tells you that he has not searched, yet found, him you may believe."

This sounds pretty paradoxical to our Western ears and attitudes. I can, however, assure you that in the psychological realms which we will have to deal with, we shall have to acknowledge time and again that *one finds much less through active searching than through allowing things to work on one*, to make their impact on one: through *"blinking"*.

Let me go into this still more specifically, because this passive attitude – as I have said already – plays such a significant part in psychotherapeutic work; and because, when coming to it from clinical medicine we are used to an utterly different attitude. The psychological process has, to a much higher degree than the somatic process, the character of uniqueness. After all, pneumonia and leg fracture again and again produce a very similar picture and will also to a great extent require similar treatment. In the realm of the physical, human lives are organised in a very similar manner. Therefore in the physical realm, once a few points of reference are established, we may expect to find a diagnosis with some certainty and also to pursue this diagnosis. The position is quite different and much more complicated as soon as the life of the soul is concerned. There the great difference between human beings, according to their inborn qualities, their previous history, their character, becomes obvious and demands full consideration. Certainly I do also know some psychotherapists who have told me proudly (and, as it seemed to me, in a somewhat bored way) that, after having talked with a patient for five minutes, they already had a clear picture of him; for it was always the same thing anyway ... The same thing? Yes: namely the pattern F, the pattern belonging to some school, to which that therapist had sworn his allegiance and into the framework and conceptual system of which school he had accustomed himself to compress the whole wide variety of life. I may frankly confess to you that I have not yet achieved that sort of pride (nor the boredom connected with it!). Certainly afterwards, after one has seen the whole dramatic event of a human life move past, with all its scenes so rich in colour and full of personages, when one has experienced it again and again, ever anew and always differently – then one will be able and also permitted to classify: here is an hysterical mechanism, there are inferiority anxieties; this is infantile and that is disturbed according to such and such a concept. But if I apply the pattern too early, then I believe I know, and yet in fact I know nothing. For it does not matter for the true understanding and the treatment of a person that I can spell out his diagnosis, but that I learn and, more important still, that he senses it: that his present, highly individual psychological situation is being understood. There it is a question of listening to fine nuances, of being able to be surprised and full of wonder! For it is not what I already know that will necessarily offer me the key to the room of his inner being in order to open up his secret – since the realms and the possibilities of psychological processes are as wide as the world and greater than the sphere of experience of even the most expert individual, it will very often be a matter of sensing and unravelling things which have so far remained unknown, unexplored. Anyone who lets his inquiring eye be blinded and restricted by anticipatory concepts of some doctrine, by preconceived notions, will certainly always find his expectations subjectively confirmed; but whether he will also objectively do justice to the facts, that is an entirely different matter. Therefore we must, in psychotherapeutic work, "blink" very often, so as not on any account to be blinded and diverted by the brightly-lit concepts in the mind of the doctor (*and* in the mind of the client) away from those often more significant events which have their secret life in the background , in the shadow.²

I find this quite magnificent and profound, and that is why I have allowed myself to quote it at length. The most significant thing, however, is that he sums up the state of mind and preparedness he advocates in the apparently humble word "blinking": the deliberate dimming down of our ordinary, everyday intellectual consciousness. The other quotation is from an essay about the Indian sage Krishnamurti written by A. Bancroft in her book *Twentieth Century Mystics and Sages*.

> He always returns to the same point: that we must die to our conditioning, die to the known past, in order that we can become fully aware of the present which is unknown. This is a dying which can take place moment by moment, he says ... We are afraid to contemplate the Emptiness which might be seen if we ceased to cling. Essentially we cling to the known, which we call life, and are afraid of the unknown.
> "So the problem," says Krishnamurti, "is to free the mind from the known, from all the things it has gathered, acquired, experienced, so that it is made *innocent* and can therefore understand that which is death, the unknowable."³

You see that the basic endeavour is to achieve a state of innocence in order to understand, which is what I try to do. The key-word, therefore, is "innocent". The connection with "blinking" is obvious.'

'Yes, indeed Hans', I answered, 'and that is precisely the point I want to take up. But before I do take it up under its main aspect, I should just like to say that I find these quotations as pertinent as they are striking but also that they seem to me to point to a potential state of mind which people keep rediscovering. I began to be aware of this when I read a paper by two psychiatrists, Clancy D. Mackenzie and Lance S. Wright which forms an appendix to *The Silva Mind Control Method* by José Silva and Philip Miele.[4] May I therefore return the compliment and proffer you a quotation?'

'Yes, please do', replied Hans.

'I should perhaps preface the quotation by telling you, in case you don't already know, that José Silva is a Texan with no formal education who first discovered within himself – and then over the years developed and finally published to millions, in the manner of an all-American success story – a method of tapping the deepest layers of the mind called the Alpha level, so as to harness them to the use of the conscious mind, referred to as the Beta level. And as I understand it, it is the combination of these two levels, if you like the passivity of the unconscious and the activity of the conscious mind, that warranted the name of "dynamic meditation". His method is measurable by EEG machines and as such takes its place among those many explorations, at once scientific and meditative, which are drawn upon by, say, William Johnston in his *Silent Music*. So here is the quotation from the above-mentioned paper:

> The entire course consists of techniques for using the mind in beneficial ways. After experiencing this ourselves and witnessing many others using it, we have no doubt about the superior ability of the mind to function when the person is using specific techniques in an alert relaxed state. It is similar to the state Sigmund Freud described in his paper on listening; like the state Brahms went into for creating his compositions, or the state Thomas Edison described for arriving at new ideas.[5]

I might add that the state of mind indicated here also seems to be the same as that hit off by one of Freud's most original followers, Wilfred Bion, in his own marvellously teasing phrase "without memory or desire".

Now I think it is interesting to connect all these people from East and West because it suggests, to me at least, that we are dealing with a potentially universal human faculty that is periodically realised only to be lost, time and time again. In other words, we are talking about part of people's birth-right as human beings, and the very fact that it has to be recovered from being lost makes the term you derive from Krishnamurti doubly appropriate: "a state of innocence". It's as if the attainment or recovery of this state of mind were part of the mystery of regaining a more general state of innocence. It seems to be of the order of coming to see "those angel faces smile, which I have loved long since, and lost awhile", as Cardinal Newman put it, or, in the suggestive terminology of Zen Buddhism, of recovering the face one had before one was born, albeit now with effort.

The point, however, is not so much that it requires a sustained habit of will to let drop what one has learned and is inclined to bring to the new situation by way of preconception. The main point is rather that once one has acquired such a fresh receptivity of mind, one can and indeed must *also* use any knowledge one may have. After all, Hans, do you not yourself, in fact, allow for these more consciously reflective processes, when you refer to the "diagnostic interlude" and the selection of, and working through, target areas?

I think it's important to see the process as a whole and so better grasp the due and reciprocal role of each part in that whole. There is indeed the effort towards openness, which you are emphasising, but isn't there also the labourious, tangled business of discursive search, trial and error, the passive but also the active, the unconscious but also the conscious? So don't we have to acknowledge *both* the necessary innocence, self-emptying, the deconditioning, which you're talking about, and *also* the ability to use what one has learned in order to structure what one is now taking in, albeit from a new point of view which is appropriate to the present occasion? Do you see?'

'I do take your point, Marcus. You're concerned, as so

often, with seeing things as a whole – as I've said before in another context: "seeing things steadily and seeing them whole". I should, however, like to say in my own defence that I did allow for what you call the more conscious and discursive elements, as you've admitted. I just didn't correlate them as explicitly as you have now done. What I wanted to do above all was to bring out the importance of the first process since it is, to my mind, insufficiently appreciated. In fact I should go so far as to say that the second process you've just talked about – the conscious and discursive – will be more or less sterile unless it's preceded by the first process I'm stressing. It's *this process which for me is at the heart of counselling*, and I'm very concerned that it should be properly understood.

The so-called seven stages of counselling should certainly not be taken as a sort of holy cow on account of their relationship to the number seven. Nor should they be taken as just another "method". For me it's a matter of a basic law of life and, more specifically, a basic and inescapable law of *creativity*, rooted in the soil of the "state of innocence". And it's perhaps for this reason that the essence of what I mean has been expressed by creative artists. In particular I have two artists in mind, a poet and a painter.

You may well know the justly celebrated *Letters to a Young Poet* which Rainer Maria Rilke wrote to an aspiring poet. I'll translate the lines I'm thinking of from the German original:

> It is all a matter of carrying things to full term and then giving birth. *To allow every impression and every germ of a feeling to come to fullness deep within oneself, in the dark and in the unconscious, below the reach of words and of one's own understanding, and to await the hour of the delivery of a new clarity with humility and patience: this is the only way to live creatively, whether from the point of view of understanding or of production ...*
> Patience is all, *Geduld ist alles*.[6]

And there is a fascinating convergent statement about the painter Matisse:

It is told of Henri Matisse that he gazed at an object which he intended to paint for weeks, for months on end until the spirit within him began to stir and drove him powerfully to bring it to expression. He surrendered himself so completely to such attention that he lost himself more and more in the object. The result of all this was that it was not his ego or his own ideas which painted the object but the object which painted itself through him as its tool. Such works of art are then not just copies, like photographs, they are filled with the very essence of the object.[7]

And for me both these statements have been summed up by somebody who was not an artist in the strict sense of that word but who was, in my opinion, a highly creative presonality. I refer once again to Steiner, who in *Die Welt der Sinne und die Welt des Geistes* wrote as follows (and again I translate myself):

We should let things themselves speak, hold ourselves more and more passively towards things and allow things to reveal their secrets. We would save a great deal of trouble it we refrained from judgements and let things declare their secrets ...
Surrender is the attitude of mind according to which one does not want to extract truth from within oneself but expects to gain it from the revelation which streams from things and waits until one is ripe to receive it in this or that particular way.[8]

Do you see, Marcus? The dynamism of this law, as these three creative people have so well expressed it, is that if we are to live through experience in depth and to make it fruitful, we must absorb the totality of the impressions, the crude as well as the subtle ones inherent in the experience, slowly and patiently. They must be allowed to mature, to ripen in the depths of the soul until they begin, from deep within, to speak their own language, in the way that, as Matisse says of his own medium, the painting begins to paint itself. Only then will the questions within the experience, or, in our case, within the encounter of client and counsellor, lead us gradually to the right responses, attitudes and answers.

That this law of creativity applies universally came home to me with particular force when I was reading a biography of Max Reinhardt, the producer, by Leonhard Fiedler. This is what the author says – I translate from the German:

> One of the characteristics of the producer, however paradoxical it may seem, is *the capacity to stand back and to take in impressions*: "It doesn't do any harm to listen and that way ideas come." The art of attending to, recognising and grasping the kernel of individual performances, to cultivate them and then to integrate them into the harmony of a production is Reinhardt's most frequently reported and most admired quality.[9]

Not only does this quotation show a striking parallel to the creative act of counselling, but this is further highlighted by the fact that Reinhardt was famous for keeping largely silent during rehearsals, predominantly listening, never ostentatiously directing or advising, but occasionally getting up quietly and whispering something into the ear of his actor.

What is more, from all this we can also see more clearly that the counsellor will not be able to make the constantly renewed act of will to clear his mind of preoccupations and preconceptions, except as part of a sustained effort to purify and transcend himself, which is essentially what I mean by a spiritual life. The operation of the inescapable law of creativity, as I have sought to indicate it, must be made secure by a discipline of a spiritual order. To put it simply, nothing merely subjective or arbitrary must be allowed to intrude.'

'I can completely accept what you're saying, Hans, and I'm glad that you talk about effort and renewal of effort, because this helps to explain a paradox I've experienced. To put it personally, I have sometimes noticed that people seem to absorb a sense of recollection from me and the very room in which I habitually work even when I am, myself, conscious of not much else than distress, tumult and darkness within myself. It's as if we were capable of living at different levels simultaneously and could retain recollection at the deepest level and communicate it from there whatever else is going on inside, *provided* only that there was that serious and strenuous spiritual effort of self-transcendence which you insist on, so that it's from one's deepest desire that one communicates.'

'Yes, Marcus, I'm talking about something which is hard won and only gradually won, the progressive product of a struggle rather than of anything naturally inherited or induced in the process of nurturing, and I accept completely that we live at different levels. We can, therefore, communicate more than we seem to have at certain given moments. I once had striking personal confirmation of this in the shape of a letter from a young woman I had been seeing and who then wrote to me from abroad. She wrote, amongst other things – I translate from the German: "I don't expect a reply from you, but if you could occasionally include me in your peace and stillness, I should be most grateful." And essentially the same sentiment is expressed in a more universal way by Goethe in his *Iphigenie in Tauris*. Iphigenie is the priestess and she speaks of those troubled by confusion, distress and guilt:

> If the heavenly beings destine one of the earth-born to many confusions and mean him to experience violent swings from joy to pain and from pain to joy, they also make sure that, near the town or in some remote place, help is available in the hours of need – *a serene friend*. O Gods, bless our Pylades and all he undertakes! He is the arm of youth in battle, the piercing eye of venerable age in assembly: for *his soul is still. He retains the sacred, inexhaustible good of peace* and from its depths he offers help and counsel to the bewildered and the driven.

It will not escape you Marcus, that the peace which is in

It will not escape you, Marcus, that the peace which is in question is not only personal peace, something at least striven for by the individual, but a peace which comes from elsewhere, beyond ourselves, and that it comes not so much from what we do but from what we are and are given.'

'So what you're bringing out, Hans, is the idea that peace can be transmitted from one person to another, caught by one from another. But can't we take this a little further and say that creativity too can and needs to be communicated to the other? For what you've been talking about so far is the way in which a veritably creative process of assimilation and maturing akin to gestation takes place – or should take place – within the *counsellor*. But the counsellor is there in order to help the client so that his processes must be made to serve the client, and this in turn suggests the thought that the creative process should at least in some measure spread to the client in a sort of healthy contagion *so that the client too, slowly learns to live from her own deeper resources.* Don't we have to say that the creative attitude you've been indicating, in principle, becomes a joint and shared process?'

'Indeed we do, Marcus, and what's involved is summed up for me in a little incident in the life of Fritz Busch, the conductor. For it's like the relationship between an orchestra and the conductor. Every conductor, you will know, has to beat time, but it's the difference between the sound achieved by the great conductor, often with just a few gestures or glances, and the lesser one, with a great deal of exertion, which convinces me that there is an almost telepathic relationship between orchestra and conductor, from the word go, and this works both ways. Thus, in the incident I'm thinking about, Fritz Busch was rehearsing the overture to *Figaro* at Glyndebourne when the violinists lifted their instruments and he said: "Already too loud." You see, the tiniest gesture, the very mood spoke between them.'

'I appreciate the example, and you know, in the face of so many of your ideas which derive part of their potency from being so condensed and suggestive, I sometimes feel a little guilty about exposing them to the clumsy touch of my own analytic mind. But as long as we can appreciate the complementarity of each other's mentalities, we can I hope, proceed with mutual enrichment.'

'I certainly feel that', Hans rejoined.

'Well then, Hans, if that's so, may I take the thrust of our exploration a little further yet, on lines you've already suggested.

Where we began was your insistence that counselling is a creative process, more like a work of art than anything else. You went on to explain that this creativity is concentrated in the stages of preparation and then of assimilation in so far as this consists in a state of mind which can variously be called receptive, unconditioned, innocent.'

'Yes, Marcus, my point is that this willed and disciplined abstention from thinking is *the precondition* for allowing the other's being and situation to mature within him in the way in which a creative artist allows the work of art to live a life of its own.'

'Just so, Hans. We then agreed that the "state of innocence" was less a matter of achievement than of striving on the part of the counsellor and that it was precisely in this respect that he could emit a certain peace. And from there I went on to suggest that creativity too could be communicated in a similar way. So we're saying that the being of the counsellor is more important than any doing of his, even that any such more active involvement must be anchored in his being; and that he can sometimes emit a greater peace than he himself feels at the time; and finally that the, as it were, alchemy of change in the client consists in large part in the catching of this creativity. But in saying all this, aren't we pointing to some further truth?

You see, when you showed me Udo Reiter's book and the passage about Matisse I noticed a few further lines down the same page that the author quoted Matisse himself – may I have the book back for a moment:

> Art begins in real earnest when one no longer understands what one is doing and what one can do and yet

detects a power within oneself which grows stronger the more one resists it. One therefore has to keep oneself completely clear, pure and innocent for it.

Now Matisse's own mention of a "power" working in and through the artist and the author's complementary talk of the artist being a "Werkzeug", a tool or instrument, suggest that there is something beyond the individual being creative from his or her own resources alone. Matisse comes to stand in the line of Socrates who spoke of being inspired by a *daemon*, some inbreathing from outside. But this means in turn that where another is progressively gathered into such a process of creativity, there is something beyond both of them. So aren't we saying in effect that the process of the *Gespräch*, the dialogue, could be redescribed as an invitation by the counsellor to the client to join in the process more and more as an equal partner and therefore as the communication of the effort of self-transcendence from one person to the other until both are acting together in such a way that they are also receiving some common thing together, which is therefore greater than either? Could we even say that they can come in the joint service of some common thing? In other words the counsellor seems, not so much to impart, as to mediate, not so much to give as to initiate into some larger process. Aren't we revealed to be not so much even agents of transformation, as vehicles – along the lines on which Mozart, despite, and in his very humanity, was seen at last by his rival Salieri to be a relayer of the silent "music of the spheres", truly *amadeus*, cherished by God?

And the point of venturing to draw out your insights in this way is that it brings us full circle and enables us to see at a deeper level why counselling is what you have for long seen and said it is: a creative process. We begin to grasp how it can be seen to be part of a cosmic process. Here I'm reminded of the almost final words of Esther Harding in *The Way of All Women* – which incidentally also relates the process of counselling back to ordinary life:

In every act of sexual intercourse, the woman implicitly accepts her role as servant in the Temple of Life ...

In the recognition that man does not live for himself alone even in his most individual and personal acts – not even in his relation to the one person in all the world whom he loves – in this recognition the truly religious spirit is born. The most precious things of life do not belong to us personally. In our most intimate acts, our most secret moments, we are *lived* by Life. Again and again we are reminded that in the daily contact with one we love our little personal egos must be surpassed; only so *can we take our place in the stream of life and submit ourselves to that suprapersonal value* which alone can give significance and dignity to the individual. For when two people experience each other unmasked – in stark reality – emotional energy which has had its counterpart in the past only in religious experience is in modern times released and made available for human development.[10]

'You know, Marcus, I'd never seen it quite like this, and yet I have for some time now been dimly aware of some of the cosmic associations of my sevenfold scheme.'

'Yes, Hans, what we seem to have stumbled on is the intuition that – at its deepest and best – the counselling process is a reproduction at the inter-personal level of the creative process on the world level. This is why it's better spoken of as process transcending the narrowly personal, and since the world's evolutionary process is directed and so goal-seeking and future-orientated, isn't this also the reason why you have also long seen that the counselling process must be future-orientated? So perhaps we ought to take up this theme and develop it along these lines?'

'I should love to do so', said Hans, 'but on another occasion, please.'

'Very good, I'll hold you to that.'

Notes
1. p.13.
2. *Der Organismus der Seele*, Ch.1, p.11. The italics are added.
3. p.76. The italics are added.
4. 1980.
5. p.172.
6. *Briefe an einen Jungen Dichter*, p.19. The italics are added.
7. U. Reiter Meditation – *Wege zum Selbst*, p.45.
8. pp.32 and 34.
9. *Max Reinhardt*, p.38. The italics are added.
10. pp.275 and 276. The italics are added.

Dialogue 7: Backwards and Forwards

But how is it
That this lives in thy mind? What seeest thou else
In the dark backward and abysm of time?
                    Shakespeare *The Tempest* Act I Scene 2

If you can look into the seeds of time,
And say which grain will grow and which will not,
Speak then to me, who neither beg nor fear
Your favours nor your hate.
                    Shakespeare *Macbeth* Act I Scene 3

'I'd like to take up where we left off last time, Hans. We were exploring your conviction that counselling should be seen, above all, as a creative process and we ended up by agreeing that it was ultimately creative because it was part of the larger creative process of the cosmos. We concluded with the thought that these greater processes were directed, and so future-oriented, that the counselling process should, therefore, as a reflection of them, share the same feature. I know that this is something else you are quite convinced of. I realise that you are essentially right, and yet I cannot shake off certain perplexities. It is not just that a great deal of therapy seems to be concerned with interrogating the past in order to reassess and reconstruct it, that there has been talk of controlled regression and, even more recently, a great interest in re-birthing and the primal scream. There seems to be a feeling about in at least some therapeutic circles that if only we can return to the origin of our ills, we can begin to imagine and feel an alternative.

In this connection I think it is significant, not only of the tendency in pychoanalysis and its derivations, but of its popularisation that an interview with Donald Winnicott should have been published almost twenty years ago now in the *Observer* Sunday Colour Supplement. The interviewer put an objection: "How do you *know* a baby feels like that about the breast? It can't tell you, it doesn't remember later." He said: "When you get badly disturbed patients under analysis they don't just tell you things, they actually *become* what they've been – they sit there and mess themselves and cry, they suck milk off your fingers." I said, "But these people are not normal people – how much can that tell you about normal babies?" After a bit, he said, "It's the most wonderful thing – they begin to show you *how it could have gone right*".[1]

Now personally I find that these last few words have the simplicity and the ring of truth of so much of Winnicott's writings, though the credit of the real pioneer must once again go to Freud. At the same time, your stress on future-orientation also feels right, and I associate this tendency with, apart from yourself, Professor Eugene Heimler, who, interestingly enough, is also a Jew. Perhaps the contrast between Freud and Heimler represents a polarity in the Jewish psyche. Be that as it may, Eugene Heimler, as you may know, belongs to that band of survivors from the holocaust of Auschwitz and Belsen who made of it a crucible of creativity and deep insight into human nature, people like Bruno Bettelheim and Victor Frankl. And one of Heimler's main convictions is that people need to be helped to work towards the future and that it is the success in coping with the present that sets in train a new feel and view about the past, not the other way round.

My problem, therefore, is whether the counsellor should work on the past or the future, go backwards or forwards; if you like, whether Freud or Heimler is right.'

'Once again, Marcus, you've touched one of the nerves of

my thinking, because I am quite convinced, as you say, that the main business of the counsellor is to open up the client to the future. I can sum up my meaning in terms of an experience which has come to be a significant image for me.'

'Part of your personal mythology?'

'Yes, Marcus, part of my personal mythology. Well, you know that I used to love walking down towards Crammond. In this way I observed that the little harbour was usually clogged with various bits of debris and that the River Almond which opened out into it at that point was usually too sluggish to move any of that junk. Every now and then, however, the river would gain power and sweep away a great deal of all this deposit from the past out into the sea. Not that everything would of course be removed in this way. It might be driven into the bed of the river, but in any case it was not an obstruction any more. It was this fact of nature that became an image for me of the way in which life can become obstructed but also renewed. If we can only help people to release the energies of life that are directed to the future, most of the blockages in the way will simply be swept away.

Now I realise that such release of energies and drive towards the future represents a *second* phase after what I should call a more quiescent and introspective phase. Nobody can make the effort of release who is totally wrapped up with her past and she needs a lot of patient care to be freed of her emotional burdens and her sense of guilt and failure. This initial phase is no doubt what corresponds to the analytic process as you have evoked it in your references to Winnicott and Freud. Only I don't call this phase analytic, because, quite frankly, I've never experienced it in this way.

In the first place, the very term "analytic" sounds too mechanistic, suggesting as it does to me chemical analysis and search for something specific, some flaw.

Why else do I find the analytic approach unhelpful? I was puzzled about this, and I've come up with a tentative answer. It seems to me now that such an approach was quite appropriate in Freud's age, for it was a repressive age in which so much was driven underground. I know it, because I experienced it, I was there, I knew about the family situation and about little Jewish boys sleeping with their mothers and the Oedipus conflict, and so on. But so much has changed since then. Our age is not repressive. On the contrary, we have, in sexual matters, found a new freedom. A freedom we can't yet control. Young people are marvellously free and are aspiring souls, and yet they flounder because they don't have discipline and insight. So when I deal with young people, as I've been doing for a long time now, I don't need to unearth what's been buried – it's all out in the open. What I experience is a mass of shadows, guilt and failure, and above all error, misjudgement. It is significant that in the teaching of the Buddha, who, after all, knew human beings very well, the source of all ills was the failure to comprehend reality as it is. So what I have to do is to help people to see things as they actually are – as Goethe puts it in a beautiful little poem, "sich ins Richte denken", to think oneself into the right outlook.

So what I do is doubtless no easier that what analysts do, but it is different in character. I do not search for the deep-seated unconscious block, because for most people *it isn't there*, but I do need to clear away all sorts of mistaken notions, wrong judgement, errors. But once we have cleared these away and people can begin to emerge from the twilight guilt-ridden zone with a measure of self-respect, we can begin to work on releasing the river of life, energy.

Here I should like to bring to your attention two quotations which made a great impression on me. The first is taken from Prabhavananda and Isherwood's account of the teaching of Patanjali, the classical exponent of the yoga system, in their book *How to Know God – The Yoga Aphorisms of Patanjali*. They begin by quoting the third aphorism in Book IV of the Yoga Sutras themselves, on liberation, and then add their own comment:

> Good or bad deeds are not the direct causes of the transformation. They act only as breakers of the obsta-

cles to natural evolution; just as a farmer breaks down the obstacles in a water course, so that water flows through by its own nature.

Here Patanjali explains the Hindu theory of evolution of species by means of an illustration from agriculture. The farmer who irrigates one of his fields from a reservoir does not have to fetch the water. The water is there already. All the farmer has to do is to open a sluice gate or break down a dam, and the water flows into the field by the natural force of gravity.

The "water" is the force of evolution which, according to Patanjali, each one of us carries within ourselves, only waiting to be released from the "reservoir". By our acts we "open the sluice gate", the water runs down into the field, the field bears its crop and is thereby transformed ... "All progress and power are already in every man," says Vivekenanda. "Perfection is in every man's nature, only it is barred in and prevented from taking its proper course. If anyone can take the bar off, in rushes nature."[2]

Of course the therapist himself can't take the bar off, the client has to do that: "You can take the horse to water, but you can't make it drink." The therapist can, however, alert the client to the existence of the bar.

So humanity is by nature future-oriented and must – and wants – to go forwards. At the same time people can make this effort only once they have been liberated to say Yes to this effort.

My second quotation is from Goethe. You will know that he was a universal human being, but he went through very great crises and struggles and experienced much illness. The secret of his survival was "tätig sein", to be active, so that a general statement of his outlook is really autobiographical. This is what he says in *Wilhelm Meister*:

> To heal psychic ailments that we have contracted through misfortune or faults of our own, the understand-

ing avails nothing, reason little, time much, but resolute activity everything.³

I don't go all the way with Goethe here. I do think that understanding can avail, but I do agree with this emphasis on activity. So we're back to setting a person in motion directly towards a goal, being motivated to lead what Victor Frankl, the "logotherapist", calls a "life of meaning".'

'You've said a great deal there already, Hans, I'm particularly captivated by the way you've given your humdrum experience of the River Almond a quite archetypal significance by associating it with Patanjali's river of Nature. What you're saying is that the therapist's essential function is to enable the release of this stream of life by raising the sluice-gate or removing the obstacle in the way of its natural flow. At the same time you've indicated that the release of the stream of life is the second phase of a process which has to begin with what you call a more "quiescent and introspective phase" and which you say corresponds to Freud's analytic work. It's at this point that I'd like to come in, because the very juxtaposing of your emphasis on the future with Freud's delving into the past leaves my initial problem intact: Should the therapist and client go forwards or backwards and, if in some sense both, then how and in what proportion? Do you see my puzzle?'

'I do, Marcus, and I'm not sure that I can resolve it at present. I wonder, however, whether it would help it I illustrated what I've said rather generally with a few concrete cases?'

'That could be very useful, Hans. Please go ahead.'

'Well, then, my first case is taken from the significantly entitled *New Pathways in Psychology: Maslow and the Post-Freudian Revolution* by Colin Wilson, who had a personal contact with Maslow and wrote this book after the latter's death. The essential theme of the book, as you may know, is that the first, and certainly the second generation after Freud began to turn away from preoccupation with the past towards a greater attention to the future and incidentally, in this respect rejoined Jung in one of his major concerns.'

'You know, I had thought that this revolution, as you call it, had already started with Karen Horney in America, Hans?'

'That may be, Marcus, I just don't know. All I do know is that any prior tendency in that direction became more pronounced and explicit with Maslow. So here, in the first of the cases as presented by Colin Wilson, in a paper called "The Need to Know and the Fear of Knowing", is the way Maslow describes one of his crucial cases:

> "Around 1938, a college girl patient presented herself complaining vaguely of insomnia, lack of appetite, disturbed menstruation, sexual frigidity, and a general malaise which soon turned into a complaint of boredom with life and an inability to enjoy *anything* ... As she went on talking, she seemed puzzled. She had graduated about a year ago and by a fantastic stroke of luck – this was the depression, remember – she had immediately got a job, and what a job! Fifty dollars a week! She was taking care of her whole unemployed family with the money and was the envy of all her friends. But what was the job? She worked as a sub-personnel manager in a chewing-gum factory. After some hours of talking, it became more and more clear that she felt she was wasting her life. She had been a brilliant student of psychology and was very happy and successful in college, but her family's financial situation made it impossible for her to go on into graduate studies. She was greatly drawn to intellectual work, not altogether consciously at first because she felt she *ought* to feel fortunate with her job and the money it brought her. Half-consciously then she saw a whole lifetime of greyness stretching out ahead of her. I suggested that she might be feeling profoundly frustrated and angry simply because she was not being her own very intellectual self, that she was not using her intelligence and her talent for psychology and that this might well be a major reason for her boredom with life and her body's

boredom with the normal pleasures of life. Any talent, any capacity, I thought, was also a motivation, a need, an impulse. With this she agreed, and I suggested that she could continue her graduate studies at night after her work. She became more alive, more happy and zestful, and most of her physical symptoms had disappeared at my last contact with her."

It is significant that Maslow, although trained as a Freudian, did not try to get back into the subject's childhood and find out whether she experienced penis-envy of her brothers or a desire to murder her mother and marry her father. He followed his instinct – his feeling that creativeness and the desire for a *meaningful existence* are as important as any subconscious sexual drives.[4]

Now I personally find the facts so simple that you would have to be a fool not to leave aside the subsidiary symptoms – the boredom, insomnia, sexuality etc. – and not go straight for the central thing in the present. The case does, however, make the essential point.'

'It's a paradigm of Maslow's approach?' I asked.

'Yes, Marcus, he worked with the concept of *meaning*, much as Victor Frankl did, although his own preferred term is self-actualisation, which sums up his notion of humankind being a forward-moving, growing, developing, integrating personality. It is this characteristic which dominates everything else, because for him – as also for me, if I may say so – this represents humanity's basic impulse, although it can, of course, be dammed up, as Patanjali had already observed.

So we come to my own two cases.

The first case is that of what I call the "Irish girl". She was referred to me by the Samaritans, and turned out to be typically Irish, blue-eyed, black-haired. She was married to an Egyptian doctor. The problem was that of a total breakdown of the marriage at every level. I saw her and she was miserable. The next thing I did was to see her husband – I feel that one can't solve any marriage problem without dealing with both partners, simply because one can't rely on the description of somebody emotionally distressed. He turned out to be a gentle, sweet-natured and talented man, who couldn't understand what was the matter. When I saw the Irish girl again, I discovered that she had trained as a nurse but was now sitting at home and had become what I call a "captive wife". After some discussion she ventured to mention that she would like to study medicine, but this seemed to be too far-fetched and adventurous. I saw the husband again, and he said it was fine by him, provided it was practically possible. Well, it was possible, and from that moment the whole thing resolved itself like magic. They left the country, and they wrote to me at Christmas saying that she had started her medical career and they were very happy. So that's a simple case of breaking out of captivity into freedom.

The next case was not quite so simple. It involved a young homosexual man who worked in a factory. What initially bothered him was his sexual isolation but what came over above all was his total cultural deprivation, a veritable dehydration and emptiness of life. To cut a long story short, I discovered that he liked music, and he developed an interest in opera. He became so enthusiastic that whenever the opera came to town he was the first in the queue for tickets at the box office. From then on, the whole feel of his life changed. He began to have a glow, an enthusiasum. He didn't cease to be a homosexual, but he felt that there was something in his life, something to look forward to, something which could develop, and he became able to talk with women by way of a simple human exchange. The total concentration on his homosexuality was dissipated, simply by virtue of the fact that he had discovered opera. Then things gained momentum and he developed other interests as well.'

'He found a goal?'

'Yes, and self-respect.

The final case is strictly not my own but one of Bridget's, which I discussed with her. Again a marriage was in crisis.

The man was highly intelligent and in a good position, and the woman was very simple, almost mentally-handicapped; she could hardly cope with her domestic situation. In addition their one son was deaf. The whole situation was very confined. She could give her husband little enough, sexually, culturally, humanly, but he was attached to her and they got on surprisingly well, except in one respect. He had one great wish, namely that she should perform erotic dances – which is fairly common after all. But how on earth could a woman who was so handicapped and helpless oblige? You could as easily imagine an elephant dancing as this poor woman.'

'A complete impasse?'

'An impasse. What to do? So Bridget came to discuss the situation with me. I asked her whether there was anything the woman could do. It appeared that there was *one* thing she could and liked to do, which was to make dresses, but even that she did very badly. Well, perhaps she could learn to make them a little better? So Bridget arranged for her to have dress-making lessons, and I suggested that the woman should make it really purposeful and aspire to make beautiful dresses. She was enthusiastic. It gave her endless pleasure to be able to make something beautiful for herself.'

'But did she learn to perform the erotic dances?'

'The long and the short of the story is that she *was* able to perform erotic dances for her husband, and I when I last asked Bridget about her, she said "Oh, she's come a long way since then – she's branching out".'

'These cases do illustrate your thesis very well, Hans,' I said, 'and it is very appealing. Yet I have to say that questions remain in my own mind. In the first place, I doubt whether our age is as different from Freud's as you make out. I personally find in my work both as priest and as counsellor that a lot of us are still riddled with guilt and fear and repression, especially in matters sexual, and that those brought up in the Protestant and Catholic traditions suffer only variants of essentially similar hang-ups.

At a more theoretical level my impression of even the

psychoanalytic tradition of therapy is, on the one hand, that psychoanalysts are essentially as concerned with the present and the future as you are, and on the other hand, that the attention they give to origins and development, to what Melanie Klein well called "the roots of adult life in infancy",[5] is justifiable.

More personally, I should say that I have through my own analysis moved from an apparent preoccupation with the past to emerge to a conception of a very subtle interaction between past, present and future. In this conception we are, in therapy as in life, always concerned with coping with the present and with blockages to such coping here and now. We therefore attend to the past only in so far as the problems in the present prove to be versions or reactivations of maladjustments, traumas, displacements, circumventions, compensations, distortions, what have you, in a past in which one gradually discovers that "it could have gone right", it could have been otherwise, as Winnicott so succinctly put it. This is surely because we forget nothing, everything is there, so that coming back to what appears to be the origin in the past is in fact coming to a point of choice and growth in one's *present* resources. Birth is a metaphor of rebeginning *now*.

My initial problem, therefore, still remains. Only I should, in view of what you have said, now put the problem a little differently: Let us grant the importance of releasing people into the future, as you stress; let us grant further also the therapeutic value of becoming aware of where difficulties in the present began, especially in view of your admission that the phase of moving into the future is preceded by a "more quiescent and introspective" phase – then what is the relative weight of these two phases, how do they interconnect?'

'You do press me, Marcus, don't you? But it's probably good for me. And since you do, I must say that I abhor "method" as a preconceived pattern of approach to interpreting the infinitely varying manifestations of life, as I hope I've made clear before. Incidentally, I'm encouraged in this aversion to "method" by discovering that I share it with none other than Jung. He said: "The doctor and observer must be free from every formula to allow the living reality to work upon him in its entire lawless richness ... It is therefore wise of the physician to renounce all premature assumptions ... When it comes to things like these, everything depends on the man and little or nothing on method."[6]

However, by saying this I don't wish to be taken for a kind of dreamer drifting on the waves of what one might benevolently call "imagination". I trust that by now I've made it sufficiently clear that, although I dislike any so-called "method", yet I am totally committed to identifying, in a disciplined way, with the processes of growing, unfolding and forward-moving life, as it expresses itself in the seven stages of counselling, on the lines we have discussed in our previous series of conversations. Naturally, no single element should be made sacrosanct. That would be lapsing into dogmatism. Therefore, if I have any method at all, it is based on the trust that, if I fully submit to this discipline and if I am able to exercise restraint and patience, then life itself will guide me – it may be forwards, it may be backwards, to use your terminology – and will eventually, in the fullness of time, give me the answers. If this sounds rather like poetic language to you and reminds you of a process of fulfilment, like waiting patiently for the fruit to ripen or like gestation, then, yes, you are right: the analogy is valid.

Thus I believe passionately in releasing the river of life into the future, and yet I do recognise that there are times when you have to go back. Then you may get the sense of what I call *ungelebtes Leben*, unlived life, from a client, a life or a period of life which has not been lived through. Let me give you an illustration. I was seeing a fine, happily married mother of five children, a woman of forty-two, for the first time. Prior to seeing me she had gone through a period of extreme anxiety. I took her biography, as I usually do. She had done her nurse's training, started nursing and then married at twenty-six, one event following the other in very quick succession. I lived with this story, as I always do, without any particular idea of the outcome, without brooding, just letting the events follow each other within me. In this way I gradually began to feel that something was missing from her life, that she had not had the opportunity for freedom and experience which I have found young people need in order to discover life and the world and so themselves. So, towards the end of the next session, I told her that I had the impression that her life had gone rather rapidly, and asked her whether she felt she had missed out on anything. She said easily enough that she had not, then she suddenly became thoughtful and said: "Now that you mention it, I remember that just before I married I had the strong feeling that I ought to take a year out, but I didn't and I felt I should have done." That was it. You see, you can only be future-oriented if your past is in order, if you have lived through the phases you need to live through – which, of course, varies from one individual to another.'

'That's all I need to hear you say, Hans. And now that you have made the essential concession I felt was necessary, you've made it in a marvellously telling phrase: *"unlived life"*. In two words you sum up the reason for what you call the initial "quiescent and introspective" phase and for a great deal of the work of psychoanalysts. It's to the extent that we all, to a greater or lesser extent, have parts of our life outstanding, still due to be lived, as it were, that we need to put them in order, as you put it, before being able to move on. It's like an advancing army that leaves pockets of resistance behind it needing to be mopped up; the question is when and how it is to do so.'

'Yes, Marcus, the question is how one is to rectify such a situation. In the case I mentioned the ideal solution would have been for the woman to go to Paris to bask in the arts which she loved so much, feeling "This is me", for the six or even twelve months she should have had almost twenty years earlier. But how could she do this now with five children? What was more feasible was to go for one month. That would be a compromise. You see, to my mind, there are ideal solutions, compromise solutions and there are token solutions.'

'You think that somebody who discovers this "unlived life" like this must live it through, act it out in some way, do you, Hans? Wouldn't it be enough simply to recognise the need, realise it and face it internally alone?'

'Perhaps, Marcus, once again there is no general answer, but only a series of individual answers. What my experience has convinced me of is that, if a person has a burning need, it becomes part of their destiny to face it, and sometimes at least the very fact that they have expressed the need and realised the problem may resolve it. They may be able to go back to ordinary life and say: "I can carry on now." In any case the question is whether the accumulation of unlived life has been mentally, psychologically discharged or not.'

'By so fully and vividly allowing for this as it were debt from the past – perhaps the ontological *Schuld*, guilt/debt of Heidegger – you have allayed my misgiving about the one-sidedness of an exclusive concentration on the future.

At the same time I hope you will not think me captious to put to you another difficulty that has come to me as you were speaking. I want not so much to test you as to draw out further implications of what you are saying. Let me put my new difficulty like this. You speak fairly consistently of the counsellor listening, exploring, understanding, correcting errors and misjudgements, *knowing*, whereas I'm more and more convinced from the experience of myself as well as of others, that change, release, action is a matter of *feeling* much more than of *knowing*. More and more often I've had people echo my own question: "Yes, I understand, but what am I to *do*?" Once again this problem is not confined to us. Even such usually clear-headed summarisers of the heritage of Freud as Sandler, Dare and Holder in their admirably succint and informative book *The Patient and the Analyst*[7] flounder when they seek to sort out the concept of "insight"[8]. Is it a matter of cognition or of affect, or somehow both? "The major problem in the psychoanalytic literature following Freud appears to lie in the need to define the qualities which distinguish 'true' or 'emotional' insight on the one hand and purely intellectual insight on the other."[9]'

'Yes, that's a very fair question, Marcus. I should like to begin to try to respond by saying that the interchange between therapist and client is for the therapist a matter of *knowing*, perceiving clearly where the client has got bogged down, what prevents her from seeing reality as it is. The client for her part will then gradually *feel* different.'

'The therapist's effort to understand will somehow communicate itself to the client in terms of feeling? Is that what you're saying, Hans?'

'Yes, it will, so to speak, deposit itself in the client in the form of feeling. It's not so much that she'll think that she's wrong in this or that way, it's rather that she'll feel different, which is an existential thing. These things are very subtle and difficult to analyse. I come back to saying with Jung that the process is like a work of art: there is an infinite number of ways of composing a symphony or painting a picture. The particular emphasis must vary from case to case. I'm dealing, for instance, at the moment with a young fellow who feels that he's a failure. This is at the most a partial truth. For my part, I have to see, in a cognitive sense, where he's failed himself, but I have to be very careful not to explain too much to him, especially as he's a pretty intellectual fellow. What I do have to do is to appeal to his feelings and give him the feeling that he already is something, somebody. Now he happens to be a tall figure of a man with magnificent long flowing blonde hair. So we were talking loosely and casually about a number of things, and at one point I told him, which is true: "You remind me of one of those Wagnerian tenors I got to know and admire as a young man at the Vienna Opera." You see, this speaks to him and gives him the feeling that this is how he appears to people, that there is something attractive about him. So although the cognitive and the emotional are theoretically distinct, I try as it were to translate what I know into what he can feel, I try to reach out into the possibilities of the future at that level. There is, in practice, a constant intermingling of these aspects with a view to helping the client to *do* something with her life.

In this connection, you will remember that I've tended to speak of my approach in terms of a *Gesprächstherapie*, a dialogue therapy, whereas the dialogue is only half of the story and I ought more strictly to be speaking of *action*-therapy as well as action towards the future motivated by feeling. We need, at first, to be content with little things, not concerning ourselves straightway with long-term objectives. For instance, this young man mentioned that he would like to sing but felt very uncertain about his voice. So I said: "Look, I'm not a concert preformer, but I can sit down at the piano and tinkle away, so next time let's try out your voice." Something begins to move. Little by little we may be able to help self-confidence and a new feeling about the self to grow, always playing it by ear and finding the right tone. Does that answer your question, Marcus?'

'I certainly get the feel of what you're saying, Hans, and perhaps I ought to be content with that, but by now you'll know that I'm incorrigibly analytic and always want to make further "raid[s] on the inarticulate", as T.S. Eliot puts it – try to give more adequate and precise expression to the almost indefinable things of life.

While you were talking, another way of rendering what you call the intermingling of processes came to me. Your phrase "something begins to move" says the essential thing. For don't we need to push the analysis of what goes on within and between counsellor and client back to the mere fact of their being together at all in so far as this embodies their wanting to move? Doesn't the very coming together imply that they are already on the move? Their "working alliance", the fact that both desire something – although they may well not yet know what – is what enables even "mere" understanding to act at least as the removal of an obstacle to the impetus of the flow and therefore to have an emotional effect. To recur to your master-image, what is in question is not the flow but the blocking by the sluice-gate. What's in question is not, shall we say, libido in its etymological meaning of liking, loving, longing, being inclined, attracted, but what impedes it. So as soon as the blockage is removed, the potential flow is realised anew.

So perhaps we need to supplement the image of the water dammed up behind the sluice-gate with the image of two travellers, two mountaineers perhaps, negotiating obstacles in their paths, so that the question between them is not whether but, *presupposing the movement*, how the movement is to be effected. Or, to recur to the perhaps even more basic simile, the good parent's seeking to help the child help itself presupposes the child's own capacity and wish to get going again. Isn't it the pervasive presence of this endeavour or inclination that provides the "affective framework" which Sadler, Dare and Holder say needs to be provided in therapy and within which anything done by and between the counsellor and the client can be productive of movement and thereby change? Put more philosophically, where there is already movement, an "is" is in fact an "ought" – endeavour in the strict sense of en-devoir.'

'That way of seeing things certainly accords with my approach, Marcus, but, as so often, you have put it in a larger, almost a metaphysical way which, as you know very well, is just not my own thing.'

'Flattery will get you nowhere, Hans! More seriously, I'm encouraged by your ready acceptance of my difficulties to present yet another one! So far we've agreed that we must take account not only of the forward drive but of any drag of the past, and we've elucidated a little further the process of dealing with the "unlived life" so as to release the flow of life forward again. What I should now like to do is to essay a unified account which does justice to both these dimensions and in particular, to the way they interconnect and intermingle in the living, very variable process of therapy.'

'Well, Marcus, all I can do is to try to express how I handle things. For me there are definitely two elements: there is basically the forward drive, but there may also be various "Hemmungen", obstructions, and there may be what I call "unlived life". Now I bear both in mind, but I deal with the past, the obstruction or the unlived life, *in the light of the future*. To return to the woman of forty-two I was mentioning earlier, it was not just a matter of her doing what she might have done earlier; it was a matter of realising something unfulfilled which belonged to her nature but doing so in such a way that it led into the future. In another case it might have been a question of going back to have a love affair. That may well be necessary, but it can also be dangerous, even destructive. But if there is a forward drive already, the ego-forces will be in control to a greater or lesser extent. It all depends on whether people live through it in a positive and active way. To my mind, *any recapitulation – of education, culture, sex, whatever – which may be necessary needs to be done with mindfulness of the life as a whole, thoughtfully.*'

'Within a perspective of the future?'

'Yes, Marcus, within the perspective of the whole life.'

'So what you're saying, Hans, is, in my own words, that it may be useful and necessary to distinguish intellectually between successive phases in a single process of therapy, but that in concrete reality the potential for self-direction towards the future is present from the very beginning, even though it may for some time appear only fragmentarily and fitfully. The answer to my problem is therefore, that the two phases are phases of emergence or manifestation rather than of distinct and unrelated existence. The counsellor must therefore, be aware of this from the beginning, and to the extent that he is aware of this potential even when dealing with more immediate conflicts and inhibitions and pain, he will deal with them only as part of mobilising the future-oriented forces and so give assistance to every such movement into the future.'

'Yes, I can completely agree with this statement of what you call a unified view of the intermingling of the movements forwards and backwards. The point is that we cannot face the past and its pain without having something else to look forward to, and I in my turn should just like to sum this up in my own way with three more of my favourite quotations since they have, for a long time, sounded the depths of man's great

destiny and goal for me.

You may or may not have heard of Dr Friedrich Rittelmeier who was co-founder of the Christian community. Nevertheless, he had this to say in the last sermon he preached:

> An I is entrusted to us, a great and glorious good.[10]

A treasure is given into our care and keeping, something to guard, cherish, develop, a promise of a great future.

The second quotation is from the nineteenth century poet Christian Morgenstern, whom I have referred to before. He wrote:

> Man's true image must grow within him, and besides that nothing else matters for me.[11]

The last quotation will be familiar to you; it is from St Paul's letter to the Colossians:

> I became a minister according to the divine office which was given to me for you, to make the word of God fully known, the mystery from ages and generations but now made manifest to the saints. To them God chose to make known how great among the gentiles are the riches of this mystery, which is *Christ in you, the hope of glory.*[12]

For me, then, an evolutionary expectation, an instinct and a hope, a purposeful thrust, lives within every person, making for coherence amidst forces of disintegration. This is what makes human existence a being that is directed towards the realisation of her final end, her perfection. Goethe called it entelechy, from the Greek word *telos*, end: having an end within one. The crucial thing is that the inner direction of this dynamic is beyond his or her limited being. The essence of the forward drive is towards the person's higher self, the Christ in us.

It seems to me that the human being in his or her higher self subconsciously or superconsciously wants to be part of the whole forward movement of the cosmic process. So once the process of liberation from conflict, error, illusions is under way, a person becomes aware in his or her higher being that their personality partakes of the destiny of the whole earth. I believe too that this is not merely a speculative but a vitally practical matter in so far as these things have begun and will continue to break more and more into the lives of more and more people.

This, then, is the substance of the thing. But it has for me all sorts of expressions. May I indicate some of the ways in which I see this dynamic and expectation operating?'

'By all means, Hans. Now that I've got your main idea, I'd be very interested to learn how you see it manifested.'

'Well then Marcus, I'd like to begin the elaboration of this further aspect of my thinking in what at first sight may seem a rather far-fetched way, in the realm of more personal psychology again.

You know that I'm passionately interested in Arthur Schnitzler. Whenever I want "to go home", I read Schnitzler. This may surprise you since his general reputation, on the basis of his autobiography *Jugend in Wien*, Youth in Vienna, is of being "ein alter Erotiker" – in English one would no doubt say "a dirty old man"! Now he certainly had a weakness for the ladies – there always seemed to be a girl waiting for him in bed, like soup standing in the oven – but as a thinker and writer he went beyond this. The leading academic authority on Schnitzler, Martin Swailes, in his *Arthur Schnitzler*, maintains that he is above all a moralist. Interestingly enough he brings this out in his chapter on the relationship between Schnitzler and Freud. He begins by noting that Freud wrote to Schnitzler fairly late in his life to say that he had avoided meeting him out of a "Doppelgängerscheu", a timidity about meeting his double. Martin Swailes goes on to show very well that for Schnitzler it was, perhaps paradoxically, only fidelity in a relationship and the inevitable self-limitation involved that could bring man true self-fulfilment and this could be undermined and even destroyed by the exploration of those darker urges in man which seemed to be associated with Freud's enterprise. Thus the *Traumnovelle* evokes an absolute orgy of eroticism and yet it ends with the main actor finding his way home to his wife and to the purposeful, peaceful and meaningful life and structure of his family. It was thus for him only the freedom to overcome the tremendously powerful unconscious impulses to sexuality within him that gives meaning to man's life. This is how Martin Swailes puts it:

> There is one particular interesting moment in the Freud and Breuer *Studies*. In the case of Fraulein Elisabeth von R., Freud suggests to the patient that the cause of her pains and hysterical symptoms is her repressed love for her brother-in-law. She is outraged by this and Freud attempts to pacify her by using two arguments: "That we are not responsible for our feelings and that her behaviour, the fact that she had fallen ill in these circumstances, was sufficient evidence of her moral character." Freud here raises two issues – individual responsibilities, and morals – which are for Schnitzler an insistent dilemma, the cause for infinite reflection and questioning. From Freud's prespective they are in no sense problematical. *For Schnitzler, however, man must believe in his own free will and responsibility, in his existence as a moral agent, in order that the business of living should have meaning and value.*[13]

You see, here again, even in a man who had so fully experienced his impulse-ridden being, we see the affirmation of the possibility and the necessity of going beyond our impulses towards something higher by grasping the innermost core of our freedom.

Now it may be that it was Schnitzler's personal tragedy not to be able to live up to his insights as a dramatist and moralist, but we can see the process he intuited more positively attested by others. There is, for instance, what William James had noted about the utterances of St John of the Cross and St Theresa in his classic *Varieties of Religious Experience*:

> Saint John of the Cross, writing of the *intuitions and "touches"* by which God teaches the substance of the soul, tells us that – "They enrich it marvellously. A single one of them *may be sufficient to abolish at a stroke certain imperfections of which the soul during its whole life had vainly tried to rid itself*, and to leave it adorned with virtues and loaded with supernatural gifts ..."
>
> Saint Teresa is as emphatic, and much more detailed. You may remember a passage I quoted from her in my first lecture. There are many similar pages in her autobiography. Where in literature is a more evidently veracious account of the formation of a new centre of spiritual energy than is given in her description of the effects of certain ecstasies which in departing leave the soul upon a higher level of emotional excitment?
>
> "Often, infirm and wrought upon with dreadful pains before the ecstasy, the soul emerges from it full of health and admirably disposed for action ... as if God had willed that the body itself, already obedient to the soul's desires, should share in the soul's happiness ... For my own part, *I feel as if it would be a remedy for all our ill's*."[14]

This, to my mind, is all of a piece with *certain biographical fragments* which have much impressed me.

The case of Goethe is well-known. He worked on *Faust* for some sixty years in all, but his most creative period was at the end of his life when he worked on practically nothing else than what he called his *Hauptgeschäft*, the main business, of the second part of Faust, getting up at five o'clock in the morning. He completed the book, sealed the package of his manuscript and within a few months he was dead. It is therefore doubly interesting that Thomas Mann, in his turn, who also died in his eighties, in a Zürich hospital, said to his favourite daughter Erica, on a visit: "If I hadn't started to write *Dr Faustus* ten years ago, I should have died then." Then there's a number of incidents involving cancer. You probably know that Sir Laurence Olivier was told that he had cancer of the prostate gland and would not be able to act again. He was so fired with anger that he fought the illness, rallied and is still with us. Such was his tremendous will to live. Similarly Sir Francis Chichester was also told that he had lung cancer and was expected to die. The story goes that he literally crawled onto his boat. But the incredible happened. In coping with the adventure and in successfully circumnavigating the globe single handed in his boat, he came back after a few months more or less fit. In fact he made the journey a second time, though when he came back the second time he was dying and had to be picked up before quite completing his journey. Then, recently, a woman said on television that she had been told she was suffering from cancer, was given some six months to live, had set out collecting £2,000,000 for a scanner for the detection of early symptoms of cancer – and she recovered! She was asked how she had managed. Her reply was cautious: "Cancer isn't only a physical thing, it's also an emotional thing, above all it's a spiritual thing."

Do you see my point? In simple language, all that orientation towards the future, *being possessed of a sense of the future and so experiencing liberation of the energies of life and healing* – all that this means is having something to live for.'

'I must say that I find these "biographical fragments", as you call them, very striking too, Hans, and I'm particularly interested by the little stories about sufferers from cancer. The thing which most impressed me about the Bristol experience in dealing with cancer which was given wide publicity on television recently is that their little brochure is called "A School for *Living*": they have realised that coping with at least this disease, if not perhaps with all disease, is a matter of the revaluation of one's whole life. By the same token, I'm convinced that a medical friend of mine is on the right track in setting up a pilot research project in London involving three groups: those undergoing merely conventional therapy for cancer, those also having counselling, and those further having an opportunity for training in meditation and visualisation. For this experiment embodies the insight that we have not only a physical but an emotional and a spiritual dimension to our existence. This would again accord with your saying that the essence of the forward drive is the aspiration towards and intimation of a "higher self".'

'Exactly so, Marcus, but there's more to it than even this. The clue to what I want to go on to say is given in a little pamphlet by a certain Reverend Roy McVicar called *Healing through Meditation*. He says, on page 4:

> The need for purpose in living to enable one to find personal fulfilment is essential for health, for man is an integral part of the whole evolutionary process which through him is moving forward towards fulfilment. This means that the deep inner purpose of life is this forward movement.

You see, so far we have been talking as if the forward drive were only a matter of a process *within* the person, whereas McVicar is pointing out that this process within the person has to be seen to be part of the cosmic process. I think that this is what the so-called "spontaneous mystical experiences" and the "consciousness explosion" are really about. They are described, for example, in such books as *The Watcher on the Hill* and *Imprisoned Splendour* by Raynor C. Johnson. In the sort of "spontaneous mystical experiences" described by Raynor C. Johnson a man momentarily experiences the splendour of his higher being, released from the prison of his earth-bound body, and he suddenly becomes overwhelmingly aware of the glory of the cosmos. So what seems to be breaking out in more and more people is an awareness of responsibility for the whole earth. It's as if any profound interior transformation of their nature had to be transmitted mysteriously to the material life of the earth. Again I should like to quote you one particular expression of this new awareness from the pen of a certain Hans-Jürgen Baden in a little book called *Wissende, Verschwiegene, Eingeweihte*:

> The transformation of base matter into nobler stuff and above all into gold, now takes on a parabolic significance. Redemption too is a matter of man's renewal, of the new creature which bears the divine seal emerging out of the old. Is it therefore a big step for this transformation to be carried over to the very cosmos so that it now becomes alight and alive with the spirit? What else do the images of the new earth and the new heaven prophesied in the New Testament and glimpsed by believers mean than that the mystery of man spreads to the world and includes everything? Nor is the mystery of the depth of matter an obstacle to this process, for matter longs to cast off its heavy character as mere stuff and to change into a resplendent, ethereal medium. The alchemist with his experiments pursues the elevation of matter, so that it becomes transparent and lucid and as gold wins lasting worth. This redemption is not limited to the human realm. Matter is already meant to take a share in this lightness and spiritualisation to which it has a claim in the liberation of the alchemist. Matter presses beyond itself into the no-longer material, it takes on the radiance of the light, the weightlessness of the wind.
>
> It is from these golden, crystal, ethereal elements that the apocalyptic city glimpsed by visionaries is built. That dualism of spirit and matter which is built immoveably into so many theologico-philosophical systems is transcended. Spirit penetrates ever further into matter, into the sheer stuffness of things – and bascially waits to be overcome and illuminated by the former.'[15]

'If I might interrupt you again, Hans, I want to say that I find this way of looking at things very exciting too. For one thing, the bell which your remarks ring for me is the antique notion variously known as the Tao in Chinese culture, Rta in the

Hindu culture, natural law in the Western culture, and so evocatively caught in Wordworth's lines composed above Tintern Abbey:

> And I have felt
> A presence that disturbs me with the joy
> Of elevated thought; a sense sublime
> Of something far more deeply interfused,
> Whose dwelling is the light of the setting suns,
> And the round ocean and the living air,
> And the blue sky, and in the mind of man:
> A motion and a spirit, that impels
> All thinking things, all objects of all thought,
> And rolls through all things.

At the same time, what you say imparts to these primordial notions the contemporary feel for evolution, for ecology, for global inter-dependence and solidarity, and for the fulfilment of human destiny on earth.'

'Yes indeed, Marcus, and perhaps you'll see better how I've come to the notion of what I hope it's not too grandiloquent to call the eschatology of counselling – an awareness that people can and need to awaken into a responsibility for the "fate of the earth", to use the title of a recent best-seller by Jonathan Schell.'

'Could one then say that counselling nowadays can include as it were an initiation into the forward movement and destiny of planet earth itself, into the creative process of the cosmos – which we were really beginning to say last time, but are now saying in a fuller way?'

'That would be my meaning, yes, Marcus.'

'And if we're agreed on that, can we not add one more thing?

You've stressed, and rightly, that all this requires strenuous and unremitting effort, that even what you call the raising of the sluice-gate or the removal of obstacles requires such effort.

At the same time what results from this effort is an insertion or integration or subordination of the individual ego into something greater then the ego, a cause, what Esther Harding calls a "suprapersonal value", what people have traditionally called God. It's as if the innermost truth of human beings is that they open out into something beyond and greater than themselves and on which they depend, as if the real end of their self-actualisation is, as Victor Frankl has pointed out very incisively in an essay entitled "Beyond Self-actualisation and Self-expression",[16] their self-surmounting, self-transcendence. It's as if what you have called the "higher self" consists in being united to the Other. This is once again the truth at the bottom of the well, the individual wellspring's very reservoir. But this surely means that what has hitherto been experienced as effort, strenuous effort, *tapas*, energy, is felt more and more as a surender to this greater force or power or person – Life or Love or Truth itself. In that respect, therefore, one is passive. This is brought out in a very beautiful passage from Thomas Merton:

> At the centre of our being is a point of nothingness which is untouched by sin and by illusion, a point of pure truth, a point or spark which belongs entirely to God, which is never at our disposal, from which God disposes of our lives, which is inaccessible to the fantasies of our own mind or the brutalities of our own will. This little point of nothingness and of *absolute poverty* is the pure glory of God in us. It is so to speak his name written in us, as our poverty, as our indigence, as our dependence, as our sonship. It is like a pure diamond, blazing with the invisible light of heaven. It is in everybody ... The gate of heaven is everywhere.[17]'

'Yet this element of self-surrender – which would, I suppose, be called the receiving of grace? – presupposes a preliminary effort of strict discipline, the effort of making oneself a vessel which can receive grace, so that the effort of the self is a first stage. Don't you agree, Marcus?'

'I wouldn't put it quite like that. It's very difficult to talk about. I don't wish to say myself that at any stage there is unalloyed, unqualified self-effort to be then followed by grace. I believe that grace – God – is active all the time in the life of the individual and of the race, so that we have to find a way of talking about what goes on which does justice to both elements – the effort and the grace, the active and the passive – all the time. So I should prefer to talk in terms of the different phases of subjective experience. For me God is working in us and to that extent we are passive all the time, though in the initial phases we experience our active side of it, and it is only in subsequent phases that we have a more felt sense of the passivity which has nevertheless been present all the time. Any description in terms of effort and grace, activity and passivity, is a description of alternations of first one, then the other within us from our point of view. Something like that. Do you agree?'

'I do, Marcus, and yet we do also have to allow for the fact that we can, for example, get drunk or become involved in a passionate infatuation which damages and almost destroys us, so that God will have difficulty in working with us all the time. So in that sense this basic discipline, the rule of life, is applicable.'

'I must agree with that, Hans. I don't disagree with the facts, only with the description of the facts. I'm just trying to do justice to the presence of *both* God's working *and* our effort all the time and so hit off the relationship between them. I should still want to say that our working is in the last analysis our co-working with God, that any discipline we may develop is a discipline precisely of becoming more and more congruent with God, so that any activity of ours is passive in relation to his initiative, but I should also have to say that the degree of God's working in us is a matter of what we allow, so that, paradoxically, our effort is the measure of our becoming passive to God.'

'With that I can completely agree, Marcus.'

BACKWARDS AND FORWARDS

'Well, then, can we go one step further yet, Hans? Even if we can agree that the strenuous effort of moving into the future turns out of be a matter of the self-surrendering integration into the force of the future made present now, we have to acknowledge that it will always be only partial and liable to interruption, if only the interruption of personal death. But isn't this where the, say, Hindu notion of *jivan-mukti*, emancipation while still alive, as M. Hiriyanna puts it,[18] or the Christian notion of grace as the germ of glory, *semen gloriae*, finds its completion in the Judaeo-Christian intuition of the resurrection of the body: the new life of the future is inaugurated and anticipated now, but in such a way that it will be resumed and completed beyond any interruption?'

'I can again completely agree with that, Marcus. For me, since the Christ event there can be a "christing" of the personality which consists in the influx of supersensible life, light and love that gradually transforms the total personality in almost imperceptible stages, and such occasionally occurring phenomena as weightlessness, the odour of sanctity, the incorruptibility of the body are pointers to the final resurrection of the body. We have come back in our own way to St John's notion of "the new heaven and the new earth".

All this is, however, rather lofty. We may be over-reaching ourselves. I'd like to come back to earth. What sums up a good deal of what I've been saying today is something more homely, at least it is so for me since it is taken from the world of music which is so important for me. There's a little book about Mozart's "Die Zauberflöte" by Alfons Rosenberg and in it he first quotes Ludwig Börne's telling words about Mozart and then adds his own comment:

> "... Mozart's music reflects back everyone's own and present feelings like a mirror, but somewhat ennobled; we recognise in it the poetry of existence". In other words, ever since Mozart's time men have in his music recognised their true condition and state cleared of

everything that can tarnish it from without, the sensual man recognises himself as the godlike man he has been called to be by nature.[19]

That's the release of the drive towards the future in counselling in a nutshell.'

'I'm very content to end on this note today, Hans. Thank you.'

Notes

1. 25 September 1966, p.20. The italics are added.
2. p.204.
3. Quoted *Goethe, Wisdom and Experience* ed. N.J. Weigand, p.215.
4. pp.22 and 23.
5. *Our Adult World and its Roots in Infancy* (1960)
6. From *A Jung Anthology* ed. Jolande Jacobi, p.71.
7. (1979)
8. pp.115-120.
9. p.118.
10. *Die Christengemeinschaft* (1938), 'Letzte Predigt'
11. *Epigramme und Sprüche* (1922), p.113.
12. 1 : 25-27.
13. pp.125 and 126. The italics are added.
14. pp.413-415. The italics are added.
15. pp.100 and 101.
16. *Psychotherapy and Existentialism* (1973), pp.45 ff.
17. *Conjectures of a Guilty Bystander* (1968), p.158.
18. *Outlines of Indian Philosophy* (1932), p.19.
19. (1972), p.8.

Dialogue 8: Personality and Power

Go, release them, Ariel.
My charms I'll break, their senses I'll restore
And they shall be themselves ...

The charm dissolves apace;
And as the morning steals upon the night,
Melting the darkness, so their rising senses
Begin to chase the ignorant fumes that mantle
Their clearer reason ...
                    Shakespeare *The Tempest* Act V, Scene 1

'I'd like to take up a question today which is implicit in many of our previous discussions, Hans. You've often said or suggested that the counsellor's personality plays a very important part in the development of the client. It is a fact of therapy, as it is of life, that one person may indeed influence another enormously. But this immediately raises the question whether the counsellor does not, or may not, exercise undue influence on the client, more or less crudely impose himself, manipulate, violate the other, and this is really an ethical question. There are, therefore, two questions here: Does the counsellor exercise power? And, if so, how is he to exercise it in the client's interests rather than against them?

Now I'd like to take the first question first: Does the counsellor exercise power?'

'I think that he undoubtedly does, Marcus. This is implicit in my conviction, to which you've already referred, that the personality of the counsellor, what he is, quite apart from anything he does or says, can of itself be of decisive importance for the client. What we and other people discuss in terms of listening, exploring and guiding, enabling, encouraging and eliciting and so on, is the counsellor *in action*; but what I've come to realise more and more is that something can happen between people even before a gesture is made or a word is spoken. We've talked before about the mystery of the *Gespräch*, the dialogue; I now think we also need to take account of something we've not yet talked about, the mystery of the *Begegnung*, the encounter – the sheer meeting, the event of two entities, two entelechies coming into contact and communication. This is a mysterious happening in which the client takes in, certainly with a sensible but almost with a degree of supersensible perception, say, the very personality of the counsellor.

What is for me a wonderful and an almost archetypal illustration of this is given in *Twentieth Century Mystics and Sages* by Anne Bancroft, who had spent her childhood in the Quaker village of Jordans in Buckinghamshire before becoming a mother of four children and finally a lecturer and researcher in comparative religion. The saint or guru in question here is Ramani Maharshi who died in 1950. The book contains a photograph of him and it's important to see his face, it's important to see his eyes, because much of the mystery of the *Begegnung*, encounter, happens by virtue of seeing, gazing, rather than through talking. People came to him from all over the world, and he just sat there. Here is a description of the typical scene of the daily *darshan*, or audience, by a Buddhist monk who came to visit the ashram:

> By the time we arrived the Maharshi was generally established in his usual place on the couch at the far end of the hall, where he would either recline against a bolster or, though more rarely, sit up cross-legged. Sometimes we arrived early enough to hear the chanting of the Vedas by a group of Tamil brahmins, with which the morning

darshan began ... After the chanting was over, and the brahmins had filed out of the hall, not much seemed to happen. The Maharshi sat on his couch. From time to time someone would approach him with a question or a request, would receive a brief reply, sometimes no more than a look or a gesture, and would then return to his place. That was all. The rest of the time the sixty or seventy people sitting in the hall either simply looked at the Maharshi, which was what the word *darshan* literally meant, or else closed their eyes and meditated. Talking was by no means prohibited, and muted greetings would sometimes be exchanged between new arrivals and friends in the congregation, but for the most part the devotees sat quiet and motionless, hour after hour and a great silence reigned in the hall. One could not sit there for long without becoming aware that this silence was not mere absence of sound but a positive spiritual influence, even a spiritual force. It was as though a stream flowed through it, a stream of purity, and this breeze, this stream, seemed to emanate from the silent nodding figure on the couch, who did nothing in particular, only reading the letters that were brought to him or glancing, every now and then, at some member of the congregation with keen but kindly eyes. Sitting there in the hall ... I felt the stream flow over me, felt it flow over body and mind, over thoughts and emotions, until body, mind, thoughts and emotions had all been washed away, and there remained nothing but a great shining peace.[1]

Do you see: this is a heightened instance of what can go on between people even before and without words, it brings out the immense healing effects of coming into the mere presence of such a personality and any peace and spontaneity he may have attained. In this connection, I remember too how Steiner once visited a woman with a small handicapped child and said: "Es ist der Mensch der heilt" – "It's the human being who heals". So it's not only what the counsellor says or even knows which heals but above all what he *is*, the silent stream of his being and presence to the other. I firmly believe this, and of course, it emphasises for me the importance of preparation. Without it one is in danger of remaining one's ordinary self, and the time of preparation is at least an attempt to transcend this condition in the direction of being more open and peaceful.'

'I appreciate your distinction between the mystery of the *Gespräch*, the dialogue, and the mystery of the *Begegnung*, the meeting, Hans. I find your illustration enlightening. But in another sense what you say reinforces my difficulty. I'm as convinced as you are that what goes on between two people can be so subtle and full that it's ultimately ineffable, unanalysable, and can be referred to only by some such word as mystery or alchemy. At the same time, it's part of my bent – which will by now be familiar and perhaps even maddening to you! – to want nevertheless to try to make what is ineffable as articulate as possible, to reclaim for speech as much as possible of the mysterious. So while we have to recognise the limits of what can be said, we all have to try to push these limits back. We can and must talk about the mystery, and yet I persist in wanting to ask whether we can say anything more about it?'

'I think we can, Marcus, and I should like to mention a few facts which have struck me as particularly significant in regard to this mystery of *Begegnung*, meeting. Moreover these facts are factors of ordinary life since a meeting of the order of a *Begegnung* can, of course, take place there, so meeting in the context of counselling is once again only a heightened instance of essentially the same event. In life, then, people can gaze at each other and suddenly have the feeling – rightly or wrongly, but often enough rightly – that they have *found* each other. Meeting and gazing are also the mystery of finding. In this connection, I should like to mention a few examples.

You may well know that Sir William Walton, the composer, had many love affairs in his earlier life, then went to Ischia to deliver a lecture. The hall was full, and at the very edge of the crowded hall a girl was standing, an Argentinian girl. After the lecture Sir William Walton was asked how he liked their girls. He said: "You see that girl" – pointing to the Argentinian girl – "I'm going to marry her." She was overwhelmed, and thought he was mad. Within a few days he had convinced her that there was every reason to get married. They did, and they had a very happy marriage for thirty years. The mystery of gazing and finding. Similarly, Bruno Walter, the conductor, was on a ship, saw a girl, not particularly attractive, looked at her and said: "That's the girl I'm going to marry." Then old Hans Schauder himself, you know, when he was young, stood in a certain place, which he still remembers to this very day, and a girl who went to school with him spoke to him about another girl called Lisl Schwalb. He heard bells ringing and had the feeling that this was the girl he had been waiting for. It was.'

'You hadn't then even seen her?'

'No, I hadn't. I saw her later. Be that as it may, what is to me one of the most beautiful illustrations of the meeting which takes place in the depths of two people's being when they gaze at each other is taken from the life of Alban Berg – you know, Berg of the new Viennese school, the pupil of Schönberg, composer of *Wozzek* and modern atonal music. I'd like to show you two photos of Alban and Helene Berg, but before I do that I'll tell you the story attached to their meeting. Alban is an unusual name, even in German, but it so happened that Helene as a little girl loved fairy stories, as young children do, and her particular favourite was a story about a prince called Alban. Then, in later life, she met Alban Berg, they saw each other, gazed at each other and soon married. Here are two photographs of them looking at each other after their marriage. I think you'll agree that these pictures also bear out Hugo von Hofmannsthal's saying that the most intimate encounter is not the sexual one but the encounter of gazing into each other's eyes.

Now what I think takes place in such cases is not only gazing but an element of predestined finding, something in the nature of *karma*. In other words, there is, for some reason you can analyse as you wish, an expectation or foreknowledge of somebody one wants and hopes to find, it may be a spouse, or a lover, or a doctor. People do say to a doctor: "You're the person I've been looking for." They can even say: "I feel I've known you for a long time." As I say, you can explain this as you will, in terms of reincarnation or whatever. All I can say for myself is that when I had started to know Lisl I had one of the three big dreams of my life, in which I dreamed that I had waited five hundred and forty years to come to earth in order to meet her and to be there when she was here – and we were born and grew up within a mile of each other, across the little Danube canal. So for me part of the mystery of meeting and gazing is a deep undercurrent of personal destiny, a sense of finding or recognising somebody who belongs to you, who has been sent to you. When I look at a picture like that of Alban Berg I get the feeling that, unconsciously of course, they experience something that goes far beyond the ordinary perception of seeing each other, they recognise something which has been dormant or been buried in the abyss of time and which they discover – or recover.'

'These stories are truly remarkable, Hans. You have conveyed very clearly what you mean by the power and influence which can emanate silently from a person in what you call the mystery of the *Begegnung*, the encounter. I take it that for you this is the product not just of the immediate preparation for any particular meeting but of the preparation and discipline of a whole life. But this very fact brings us up against the second problem I indicated at the beginning, namely, how this power is to be exercised in the client's favour and not to her detriment. How is the power not to be manipulative but freeing? How is the client to avoid just joining the circle of the counsellor's admirers and followers – almost the charmed circle, because a person with a strong personality can keep another in thrall as if by a spell? Would you say that the way a counsellor can as it were return the client to herself is above all by dealing with, working through the "transference", to use a term taken from psychoanalytic practice and theory?'

'Yes and no, but perhaps you could first of all say a little more explicitly what you mean by "transference"?'

'Well, Hans, the topic is very well explained in the chapter of that title in the excellent summary of the Freudian tradition, *The Patient and the Analyst*, by J. Sandler, C. Dare and A. Holder. But I'll try to explain what I understand by this term in my own words. By tranference then, I understand the realisation of that tendency in us all to see and feel the new in the light of the old, the present in terms of the past, the tendency to assimilate what is offered us fresh now to what we have already experienced; therefore to see people in the present as if they were figures from the past, especially very significant figures, and so to relive the loves, hates, reactions and overreactions, dependencies etc. of the past here and now. Now this is a universal human tendency but it manifests itself more intensely and systematically in intimate relationships, and therefore in the therapeutic relationship. The intense form of this universal tendency in love and in therapy is well brought out by Monica Furlong in a book which is full of insights, *Travelling In*:

> "Into a transference a person will bring all his relationships". This was written by an analyst about the analytical situation, but it is equally true of the transference of the person in love ... The years which the locust hath eaten are restored. The pain of the old relationship with father and mother is relived, and we are born again, by the charity and the wisdom of the lover. A dual task is forced upon the lover, and acted out, sometimes in disguise, sometimes consciously; the infant returns again to the womb, to his mother's arms, to the breast, and is healed. To set off once again upon the journey.[2]

I hope that this is a clear enough indication of what I understand by transference. If so, I wonder whether you believe in transference and whether you deal with it?'

'Your indication, as you call it, is indeed very clear, and I recognise fully that what you have referred to in this way occurs in life and in therapy. Even if you are not an analyst, a patient will tend to *adopt* you in a certain role. Now my experience is that by and large a client has a need to do this. She doesn't do this because she's nasty or possessive – that she may be too – but because she has, for example, been deprived of a father or because, in the case of a woman, she has a very ineffectual husband or has no lover and has no one to turn to for guidance and care. So, speaking for myself, I long accepted it as inevitable that, to begin with, a client claims me in a certain role. The question is, what to do about it. This is a very subtle matter, and can be very delicate where, for example, it's as a lover that a woman wants to claim you. There's a little story which contains my response in a nutshell. I don't know whether you ever saw the film *Funny Face*, with Audrey Hepburn?'

'No I didn't.'

'Well, in it Audrey Hepburn played the part of a woman to whom a philosopher makes amorous advances and she said: "I thought you were a philosopher, you're just a man." In other words, the moment the therapist yields to the temptation of letting himself act in the role which the client wants, whether as father or as lover ...'

'By way of "counter-transference"?'

'Yes, this is counter-transference – then he's lost. But my point is that if I first accept the client's doing this as the expression of a need, then my reaction is to sit it out. I wait. I let the onslaught, as it were, go over me, if need be for a considerable time. I try not to reject the client's need and the fact of what he or she is doing. I think that this would be a mistake. I try to accept it within myself but I transform, transfigure it. So if I'm being asked to be, for instance, a father, then I begin, not by allowing myself to be cast in this role, but by accepting this potentiality of fatherhood in me out of my total humanity, *als Mensch*, as human being.

This, however, is only a beginning, and what needs in

principle to follow is again summed up for me in an experience of the whole process which I had when I still didn't understand it. I was seeing a woman, still a friend of the family, who had been deprived of good parents, had a completely unfulfilled marriage, and had no friend. She adopted me as a father figure and was desperate to adopt me as a lover. She was sometimes so disturbed that she couldn't open her month – because she is a very passionate woman. She wrote the most extravagant erotic poetry. But because I sat it out, she began to respect me as a human being who cared for her and could guide her. The point is that the energies released through the transference – and where loving and being loved are concerned, these are enormous – became transformed, redirected, rechannelled, in this case into studying, going to a teachers' training college, making an excellent career of teaching, in other words building her life. If she hadn't released her energies through the very emotional storm, and if I had tried to stifle this, which I didn't, she wouldn't have got on. So the transference, as you call it, is something which has to be welcomed and then rechannelled and transformed.'

'That makes very good sense, Hans. What you're saying is that, at least now, you recognise the phenomenon of transference.'

'Yes.'

'And the possibility of counter-transference as a trap?'

'Absolutely as a trap.'

'But the way you deal with it is subtly different from the psychoanalytic way of dealing with it. For whereas in the latter tradition the analyst deals with the transference by "interpreting" it (albeit "on the basis" of his "refusal to act in the role in which he is cast", as Sadler, Dare and Holder put it in a footnote[3]), you take the transference very seriously and sympathetically but in order to let it be transformed from within, and on the basis of an active awareness of the client's general human qualities and strengths. You note the transference, but go along with it rather than work with it?'

'That's right, I don't comment on the way the client acts towards me in one role or another. For instance, if I'd made a comment on the case of the woman I referred to, an explosion would have taken place. But I recognise the need and the character of what's going on and try to integrate and humanise it.'

'In this respect I think you're nearer to Jung. For although the Freudians have begun to take more explicit theoretical or official notice of the "human dimension in psychoanalytical practice", to quote the title of a recent book, Jung never, I think, attached so much importance to the transference, preferring to encourage the client's native and generally human resources, rather as you seem to do in your own way.'

'Yes, Marcus, for me the whole exchange is and must remain a profoundly human experience. I must live through it and work through the relationship and the trust. This is not something which happens automatically. I often say that, when a client comes in, I can so to speak smell whether he or she will relate to me. But if you for your part try to meet the other in a friendly way as a human being, without preconceived ideas, inhibitions or aversions – which takes a great deal of work – then the transference and the rechannelling of energies has a chance to take place.'

'I think you've given me a very complete account of how you deal with the reality behind the term transference. For you, then, transference is an opportunity to enable the client to release and realise her own innate energies, and since the basic problem we're dealing with is how the undoubted power of the therapist is to be made to serve the client rather than himself, this is a valuable contribution to seeing how this actually works.

Characteristically, however, I still feel that we haven't pushed the investigation of how the therapist's power communicates and deposits itself in the client as hers, the client's, power, quite far enough. You've spoken about the coming to a head and the redirecting of energies as if the process were a sort of discharge outwards and then a reflux back to the client, so that they are now available to his own purposes. But what are these purposes? And has the intervention of the counsellor and his personality and power anything to do with this further process? Put another way, your approach seems to consist in accepting the other's need for a father figure, or lover, whatever, into yourself, allowing it to resonate there with the corresponding possibilities within yourself, but, by retaining your own identity and purpose and so gently pushing the energy back to the client, encouraging it to move beyond where it was, according to its own dynamic. So, my question is: Do you think that the energies experienced in the transference do have an inner dynamic, and if so, what? You seem to believe in something very much like what Winnicott in *Playing and Reality* called "the natural evolution of the transference"[4], and so my question is also: Do you think that there is some inner direction to such a "natural evolution", and if so, what is it? Does anything more go on between counsellor and client than we have already seen?'

'I do indeed think that there is a dynamic, as you put it Marcus, and that it does have an inner direction, just as I also think that a lot more goes on between counsellor and client to help this forward, and here I must first repeat that putting another in the position of father, lover, whatever, is something which happens in ordinary life too, so that it's the expression of a human need deeply implanted in human nature and carried into the therapeutic situation. But there is more to it than such a human need to find a father, lover etc. What *is* more, to put it in an extreme form, is the need, conscious or half-conscious, to search for the *true image of the human*, something which transcends the ordinary frailties of human nature, something which has about it a sense of permanence, immortality. And in this connection, I should like to quote two wonderful lines from one of the less well known poems of Rilke, *Winterliche Stanzen*:

Fate like no other: dying yet to be, to be poised in a world of dwindling places.

You see, for Rilke, the destiny and fate of the human being is like that of no other – to overcome, transcend ageing, mortality; dying, yet to be, to lift himself up to and remain soaring or poised in a sphere which is durable. This is what the philosopher, the sage, the priest, the saint, represent. People feel that here is a being who has not been tarnished, corrupted by the inevitable ravages of mortality; although sick, ageing, frail, he or she still shares a destiny like no other. So when we do go on to ask what it is more precisely that people want their energies for, I suggest that they are looking for the true image of the human. This is surely to say in effect that they're searching for the essence of the religious.'

'Because the true image of the human being is then seen to include the fact that he or she somehow derive their being from God? Because the depths or heights of men and women are in the last analysis seen to consist in their dependence on God?'

'Precisely, Marcus, and in this connection I'm also convinced that Prabhavananda and Isherwood are right when they say in their commentary on the Gītā: "True religion is not taught but transmitted like light."[5] So people are looking for this light, and once they see it they feel that they've found what they'd been looking for.'

'I see what you're getting at, Hans. But isn't there an ambiguity in the way you're putting your point which needs clearing up? You say that what people are secretly looking for, beyond the figures of people they've missed, like a father or a lover, is the true image of the human being, which when met, is like a light from a transcendent source and is therefore something religious in character, in so far as it seems to be a participation in the divine. You say further that the counsellor can convey this true image of the human as made in the likeness of God in so far as he shares in something of the religious quality of the philosopher, sage, priest or saint. But are you saying that clients are searching for the true image of God as located in another human being, including the counsellor, or are they searching for it as something for and in themselves? In other words, is the other, including the counsellor, the object of the search for the imagehood of God or only the occasion? Must the other, including the counsellor, actually bear the image of God or can he somehow suggest and evoke it even despite any relative personal inadequacy, being perhaps an only too earthen vessel who nevertheless bears treasure which is not his own?'

'That's a very important distinction, Marcus, and it bears directly on the office of the counsellor and the raison d'etre of the relationship with the client. For it is precisely to the extent that a client's need becomes manifest as a need to find the true image of the human that she's in danger of locating this in the counsellor and *not* making it her own, and the counsellor is correspondingly exposed to one of the most insidious traps. For the more spiritualised a person becomes, the more attractive but thereby also the more powerful he becomes in relation to his client. Once again Prabhavananda and Isherwood put this very clearly in their commentary on the Gītā *How to Know God*:

> Up to a certain point, temptation increases with spiritual growth. As the spiritual aspirant ceases to be a mere beginner and gains some mystical experience, his personality becomes magnetic. He finds that he can exert psychological power over others, and also sexual attraction. At the same time, his senses grow keener and more capable of enjoyment. It is therefore easy for him to become involved in power- and sex-relationships which will make him forget his original purpose. The very people who are drawn to him because of the god-like quality they see in his nature may be the ones who are most responsible for his gradual alienation from God.[6]'

'So you seem to be saying in effect that the counsellor can indeed have great power, in fact that he gains in power in proportion to his spiritualisation, and that he has to make a conscious effort and choice as it were to return that power back to the client rather than to take it to himself?'

'Yes, that's what I'm implying.'

'Well, Hans, if that's so, then I think that I begin to see the solution to the problem I put at the beginning, namely, how the undoubted power of the therapist is not to be abused. The answer, it now seems to me, is, to put it briefly, that power needs to become more and more *shared*.

It's simple enough to state this conclusion, Hans. It's not so easy to convey how I've come to it. I ask you to bear with me as I try to explain my view.

The germ of the idea as to how power comes to be shared in the *Gespräch*, the dialogue, between counsellor and client had been sown in me, as I now realise, in a reading of *Introduction to Psychotherpay* by D. Brown and J. Pedder. For I had been struck by the way in which, at various points in this book, they referred to the gathering process of exchange between therapist and client in terms of a "culture" or language. In this they seemed to have been influenced by the conception of what goes on between the ordinary medical doctor and the patient developed by Balint. By "culture" they thus mean a way of talking, a way of looking at and dealing with things, a language and a "form of life" gradually developed and built up between therapist and client, at first largely under the leadership of the doctor or therapist but then gradually on a more equal basis.

Now this idea of what goes on between therapist and client is interesting enough in its own right. It becomes more inward when we follow the reference at least implicitly made here in the use of this term "culture" and trace it back to the work of the later Donald Winnicott and in particular to the way in which he uncovered the inner essence of the actual process of the making of a culture. For not the least of the discoveries which the later Winnicott made was that the making of a culture even in the larger social sense of the word and therefore also in a narrower bi-personal sense originates and is foreshadowed in the first exchanges between mother and child.

As I understand the inner force of Winnicott's thinking, as deposited in his last book so evocatively called *Playing and Reality*, he was gradually led by his persistent attention to the facts presented by his patients to break through his previous notions and so to become aware of a decisive change in the character of the relationship of a mother and her infant in the normal process of the growth of that relationship. He couched his successive discoveries in terms that have become almost technical: "transitional objects", and "intermediate area" between mother and child and between "subjectivity and objective observation", the "overlap" of personal space between the two, and the development of the capacity for ever more mutual play. But the essential realisation, it seems to me, was about the change from *mere gratification* on the infant's part to the first possibilities of the sort of cooperation he called *play* – and well called play, I think, because exclusive concern with gratification is a form of compulsion, so that moving beyond this creates a freedom in which the infant can begin to be concerned ever more disinterestedly in the other as other, and it is just such freedom that is associated with the term "play". So it was in this form of cooperation that he began to see the genesis and precursor of the making of culture in the larger social sense of that word.

The relevance of all this for us, it seems to me, is this: The developing relationship between the therapist and the client can be seen as an adult recapitulation of the process between mother and child. As Brown and Pedder put it very succinctly: "The transitional object is a joint action of infant and mother; successful therapy is a joint creation of patient and therapist."[7] But the making of culture is this sense is *also* a process of *the gradual relinquishing and divesting of power by the powerful figure* – the mother in the one case, the therapist in the other – and a process of divesting in the direction of an ever greater sharing, until the client is freed of compulsive ties, childish dependencies and such like spells, and so is in a position to form genuinely equal and reciprocal relationships with other adults.

My essential point therefore, is that the later work of Winnicott is a way of enabling us to see how the initial inequality of power tends to develop towards mutual freedom and therefore towards equalisation of power. The fact that Winnicott thought of himself as explaining the origin not so much of the process that goes on between therapist and client as of culture in its ordinary, and therefore more largely social sense, is not immediately relevant to our larger theme. For if culture, in its larger sense, can now be seen as the macro-social working out of what Winnicott had come to see unfolding at the micro-social level in the relationship of mother and child, then the *Gespräch*, in the sense of a dialogue between two adults, can be seen to stand half-way between the genetic form of the cooperative making of a common language and culture first established between mother and child and the greater social form of the making of culture, such as is described and analysed by, for example, Raymond Williams in his *Culture and Society, 1780-1950*. But this means that we're back to one of your master-insights, namely, that the relationship of therapist and client is only the crystallisation or paradigm of a more general process – in this case the process of conversing and arguing, of pitting and redistributing power which we call culture.'

'Once again Marcus, you've rather left me behind in your elaboration of my more homely meaning, but I do understand and respond with enthusiasm to your return to my intuition – my "master-insight", as you are pleased to put it – that the *Gespräch* expresses an archetype and that this is why it is what you call a "paradigm".'

'Yes, Hans, I admit that I tend to be drawn into these analyses. I should however, like to bring them at least a little nearer to more common ways of seeing things by suggesting finally that what I have been trying to analyse in terms of the process of making a culture is the inner explanation of a series of phrases which occur in ordinary speech. I refer to the term "world", in the way in which we say, for example, that we have a "world-view", a *Weltanschauung*, that so-and-so lives in a "world of his own", or that two people don't live in the "same world". Could we not say that the process of counselling, like the process of any true human conversation, of which, as you say, it is the crystallisation, consists in the counsellor learning to live in the world of the client – entering wholly into it, with his feelings as well as with his thought: this would then be the famous "seeing with the other's eyes", getting into her skin – and yet *not relinquishing his own world*, in such a way that the client can in her turn also come to share in the counsellor's world and they can thus progressively come to have at least an over-lapping and inter-mingling, if not an entirely shared world? Isn't this one of the ways of unpacking and understanding those haunting words of Herakleitos which T.S. Eliot placed as the motto of *Four Quartets*:

τοῦ λόγου δ'ἐόντος ξυνοῦ ζώουσιν οἱ πολλοί
ὡς ἰδίαν ἔχοντες φρόνησιν.

which I translate as follows: "There is a shared world and it makes sense as such, but most people live as though they had only a private understanding".

To put it in yet another and, because more poetically, in a simpler and more universal way, isn't it a matter of what Antoine de St Exupéry said to the effect that love is not so much looking at each other as looking together in the same direction?'

'With that, Marcus, I can whole-heartedly agree. I'm very happy to let you finish our exploration of the theme of the therapist's power with a quotation from a writer in the way you let me finish last time with the evocation of a musician!'

'Thank you very much, Hans.'

Notes

1. p.157.

2. p.32.
3. p.42.
4. p.101.
5. *How to Know God*, p.150.
6. p.198.
7. p.112.

Dialogue 9:
Growth and Morality

Even when in the grip of some dark force, a good man remains aware of the right way.

Goethe *Faust*

There is some soul of goodness in things evil
Would men observingly distil it out.

Shakespeare *Henry V* Act IV, Scene 1

'The subject I'd like to discuss with you today, Hans, is again one we have touched on before, that of growth and morality. By this I mean the conflict there can be between the demands of personal growth and the demands of a social code. The issue can be summed up very simply by an anecdote I seem to remember you telling me. It concerned a man who had always had a most unsatisfactory relationship with his wife but who decided to stay with her and could do so only because once a year he renewed acquaintance with a woman with whom he had a very deep rapport at every level, including the sexual one. Here, then was a man who could survive and keep his vitality and even, in a sense, a basic fidelity to his wife only through infringing common social morality.

Put in a more general way, I again see the problem in terms of a tension.

On the one hand, it must surely be a critical principle of counselling that we start with people from where they are and as they are, and thus as variously flawed and wounded, suffering from unlived life, unfinished business. We aim to help them move forward but from where they can really move, to facilitate their growth but from what their real growth-points are. But it may be a violation of this need to grow from where they are to expect immediate and complete compliance with a code of morality which is beyond at least their present strength. And this way of understanding the function of counselling is reinforced if we take the developmental view of human beings, the view that we come to our full stature and self-realisation through a *series of stages*, the skipping or only partial working through of which leaves tasks that have to be attended to at some time if the whole process of growth is not to be jeopardised. From this point of view conforming with a code of morality can seem to be an imposition from without, an inhibition of true growth from within. It is as if codes of morality were for mature adults whereas the client is, in some respects, deep down a child or even an infant.

On the other hand, the essence of any code of law and morality, and certainly in the Judaeo-Christian view as reformulated by, for instance, St Thomas Aquinas, is that it is ideally, in principle, educative, that it constitutes a schooling precisely to educe growth, the formed out of the unformed, and what is more, that it is the eliciting from without of what is within, according to the true dynamism and nature of the individual. Law in principle fits the individual as a glove fits the hand. This is why in the Judaeo-Christian tradition, as I understand it, the law can be made the object of praise and celebration, as in Psalm 119; it is *cantabile*, something to sing about. It is also the reason why for St Thomas Aquinas one of the master images of growing in faith is learning from a wise and kindly "doctor", teacher, who seems to know us better than we know ourselves. In this connection there is a recurrence of the essential idea involved in a most unexpected place. R.D. Laing, in his earlier work, *The Divided Self*, is talking about a schizophrenic girl who "was unable to sustain real autonomy because all she could be vis-a-vis her parents was a compliant thing". He then goes on as follows:

> Even when she began to "be herself", she could at first only dare to do so by completely mirroring the doctor's

reality. She could do this, however, since although his reality (his wishes for her) were still another's they were not alien to her. They were congruent with her own authentic desire to be herself.[1]

Do you see: this beautiful phrase, "congruent with her own authentic desire to be herself", exactly hits off the function of any code of morality in relation to the individual dynamic to growth. A system of law is thought of as a complement to, a drawing out of and a stimulus to growth, *not* its contradiction and thwarting.

Here, then, is the tension or dilemma. It is interestingly reinforced by the fact that you are a counsellor and I am a priest in so far as the counsellor in general estimation, I suppose, stands for the concept of growth, subjective need, whereas the priest stands more for the concept of law and morality, objective demand. The tension I have described is, therefore, embodied and even polarised between us two. I should, however, add that I do feel this tension within myself, even when wearing my priest's hat, in that I am somehow caught between encouraging growth even in the face of a code of morality and commending a code of morality as a challenge to growth. This however, is a refinement of the essential tension I want to indicate. I hope you follow.'

'I follow very well indeed, Marcus, and once again you have indicated very clearly the quick of a very real problem of life and counselling. I also completely understand your exposition of the problem in both its anecdotal and its more generalised form. You will however, not be surprised if I say that I prefer the anecdotal form, since all my thinking, as you know very well by now, has always started from concrete instances and cases and always tends to go back to them – it is case-based. At the same time, I don't as a matter of fact remember the particular story you attribute to me, and for that reason alone I'd like to start with another story, a true story, which illustrates more aspects of the problem. It highlights the hazzards of the dilemma facing anybody alive in our present age in which the individual has to free him or herself from the ties to collective society in order to find their own path.

As you may remember, I know a man who is now a prominent businessman. He was a very clever boy at school, but most unattractive – no girl ever looked at him. He was in his youth completely deprived of appreciation by girls, so that he was unfulfilled in this respect. It was therefore almost predictable that with his tempestuous disposition he would reach out, storm towards some solution sooner or later. Well, he became a tycoon and married a woman older than himself. The marriage was never very exciting, but he had many sexual relationships with women on his staff. His sexual relationships were thus for the most part episodic but he also had long-standing relationships outside business. Nevertheless he remained unfulfilled. I didn't hear from him for a long time, then had a letter which revealed a personal situation which to me was quite astonishing. He had met a woman who was twenty years younger than himself – a woman of fifty can still be very fresh! He had settled down to living with her in the city from Monday to Friday, as it were his working week, and returning at weekends to live with his wife in their country house. She had been loyal to him, supported him and had given him four or five children. So he had two women.'

'A wife at home and a mistress in the city. A classic case. Did his wife know about his other life?'

'He was very careful not to reveal too many details but it was clear that she knew his situation in general and I've no doubt that she had accepted it. Now the interesting thing is that he not only lives with his mistress in the city but every year takes her on world tours, leaving his wife at home. He said that, even before establishing this relationship, he had fairly strong feelings of guilt and there's no doubt that his wife suffers, to put it mildly. So, here is a man who has followed his own law and realised his unfulfilled eros and his own inner growth but he did so by breaking with a morality which was not here imposed from without since nobody bothered with his private life but which was a matter of ordinary human consideration.'

'Yes, Hans, this story does illustrate the conflict and all the more so because you state that this man felt guilty and that his wife suffered. I suspect that the fact of guilt in even so apparently a liberated man tells us something important. But I'm certainly concerned about the hurt and grief on the part of the wife. What is the validity of a so-called law of inner growth which inevitably results in one or more others being so hurt?'

'Of course, that concerns me too, Marcus. I'm saying, however, in the first place that one has duties to others but also duties to oneself, to life itself and that one therefore has to take on the responsibility of being a lawgiver to oneself, even though harm to others is inevitable. Take the case of Gauguin. He was a conventional Parisian banker and one day he packed it in and went to live in the South Sea islands, leaving his wife behind. Now who could say that a man who had such a tremendous artistic task to fulfil didn't act morally even though he undoubtedly hurt others in the process? I'm not, however, saying that one can do anything – that's the permissive society which I abhor. No, the question becomes whether one does only what is essential to one's own inner growth in a thoughtful and restrained manner to secure what one needs, or runs riot. My tycoon, for example, could have given up going on world tours with his mistress every year, out of consideration for his wife. There are cases where such behaviour can, at least if it is conducted thoughtfully, in fact encourage the wife's independence and growth. But the real point is that every such situation is very precarious and individual and that it requires a creative decision, something which cannot be prescribed beforehand; it requires a tact and a wisdom of an intuitive order.'

'I must agree that the matter is delicate, otherwise I shouldn't have posed the problem. While I feel the rightness of what you are saying about the veritable law of inner growth with all the fibres of my personal being, I still question the imperiousness of this law. Here I should like to return to the matter of this man's *guilt* since I believe that something more than personal and socially-induced guilt-feelings are involved. Let me put it in the form of what will no doubt at first sight seem to be a very abstract question: Granted the law of personal fulfilment, can one find one's fulfilment alone, without involving others? Isn't there a certain individualism built into your formulation? Put the other way round, doesn't happiness inevitably include others and if it does, then can there be fulfilment without regarding others?

I've formulated the problem in its most general form, because I want to go to the root of your friend's guilt. So I'd like, if I may, to pursue it a little at the same level. We can begin in a relatively simple way by turning to an article I came across in my capacity as English-language editor of an international theological journal. The article I have in mind was about Chinese ethics compared with Christian ethics. The author, Julia Ching, was talking about the central importance of the doctrine of *ren* (Jen), "human-heartedness", the moral virtue that makes a person truly human. She then went on:

> This word *ren*, itself a homophone of the word "human", is written with the radical "human" and another word signifying the number "two". It points to man's social nature, his relatedness to other men.[2]

These brief indications of Chinese thinking lit up for me what it is to be a human being: *being human intrinsically involves a reference to a second. Human-heartedness is an awareness of being half of two.* Couched in terms of the Chinese tradition, these two sentences nevertheless expressed an insight into human nature as such, universal human nature. We should therefore almost expect to find this perception recurring time and again in divers settings. I personally think immediately of two such expressions. The first is from the pen of the nineteenth-century English idealist philosopher T.H. Green. He wrote as follows:

> The idea of the end or unconditioned good is that of the self as realised. And this self is *social*; the good includes that of others, who are also conceived as ends in

themselves ... It [this social interest] implies the consciousness of a permanent well-being in which the permanent well-being of others is included.[3]

Essentially the same idea is developed in a peculiarly suggestive as well as personal way by the contemporary English legal philosopher John Finnis, who has done so much to recover and re-express the insight into natural law of Aristotle and Thomas Aquinas and who has, in the course of doing this, found a central place for the notion of *friendship*. He thinks of friendship as the working towards the maintenance of a new vantage point between the two friends:

> In friendship one is not thinking and choosing "from one's own point of view", nor from one's friend's point of view. Rather one is acting from a third point of view, the unique perspective from which one's own good and one's friend's good are equally "in view" and "in play".[4]

Do you see how all this helps us to understand your friend's guilt? These apparently high-flown abstractions allow us to see that what he was going against was not merely his socially-induced feelings, but, in so far as he was not valuing his wife equally with himself, not appraising things from the third point of view between them, he was going against his very nature. There is what might be called an ontology of guilt. In this connection, I should like to return to Schnitzler. For was it not his achievement as an artist to have been able to convey in convincing dramatic form the need of men and woman to be faithful for their very fulfilment, in the face of the urge to explore the darker side of their nature – even though it was also his tragedy as a human being that he was not able to live up to his insight but dissipated himself self-destructively in a multiplicity of relationships?'

'I absolutely agree with you when you talk about an ontology of guilt, Marcus, a going against the very order and structure of nature itself. At the same time I do want to insist that we have to go beyond text-books of moral theology and philosophy if we are to deal with the infinite complexity of real life, which is what makes an act of creative discernment imperative, an act which simply cannot be programmed in advance. Let me cite another sort of case. And since the cases I want to mention concern mature women, I should perhaps add that one of the complicating factors is that the creative decision I speak of is different at different ages while still being unpredictable. The problem of growth and morality is not the same in old age as it is in middle life or in youth. For in old age we need to retract our physical activities and go inwards, and the moral problem is what we owe our inner life and life itself. At the same time age does not dictate answers. Thus I have in my practice in the course of years met quite a number of women who, at a comparatively advanced age, were still virgins. Many of them I had reason to admire for the great moral courage they showed in determining, often after a long agonising struggle, that it would be right to enter into a relationship with a man. The risk of an upheaval in the woman's personal life and subsequent unhappiness is always great. But the most trying decisions had to be made in cases where a deep and sincere love existed between the woman and a married man. I remember with particular admiration several women who, disregarding convention, ultimately entered into such relationships which I for my own part felt to be based on a truly moral decision.

What I'm saying, then, is that there are cases in which individuals have to go against the traditional morality in the interests of their own growth, and in which at best they live with the conflict until they have a sense of moral intuition from deep within, from the wisdom of the higher self. There the task of the counsellor is to help people to that maturing of the inner life from which the creative moral judgement can proceed.

My main point here, therefore, is that there are no ready-made answers, that such an act is creative and intuitive, a work of the subtlest moral tact and wisdom, countering anything that is merely subjective, self-seeking, tempestuous, and as such it is open to all human beings. It is a human answer to a human problem. I have, however, long thought that *this general human phenomenon is highlighted by the case of so many artists* – and here I'm talking about great artists. The essential moral conflict may be the same but it occurs in an intense form in them. Let me give you a few examples.

Wagner is widely acknowledged to be a composer of genius. Yet in his private life he was a liar, a cheat, an egomaniac and an adulterer. He lied to King Ludwig and he stole Cosima Bülow from his best friend. He was utterly dependent on this woman in his life, confessing himself unable to work when she was away. Thus as a human being he was pathetic, even repulsive, and yet he did all these despicable things for the sake of achieving his works of art, which must surely be accounted masterpieces.

The case of Toscanini is perhaps even more interesting. He was a very intense and emotional man, a veritable force of nature, a conductor of radiant energy and genius. His performances were so demanding and high-powered that he had to have release. It is a fact that he had numerous and often tempestuous love-affairs, some casual, some not so casual. In his case he could not fail to be aware that he was transgressing traditional morality. There was one famous occasion when the leading soprano, an Italian woman, who was pregnant by him, was howled at on the stage. Another of his mistresses asked him to leave his wife, he flatly refused and the affair broke up. He allowed himself this freedom. With all this power and intensity he could not have remained a faithful husband in a conventional sense, he was an artist. Yet he remained utterly committed to the idea of the indissolubility of marriage. So he remained with his wife Carla, to the end. Not only that, it is one of the most intriguing features of his character that he rejected divorce so much that, if any of his friends did divorce, he never spoke to them again!'

'What did his wife feel about all this, Hans?'

'I think that basically she accepted the situation. She was a very calm, loyal, motherly woman, certainly not an exciting woman. Many women in such circumstances either are relieved because as a result the demands on them are less or else they just accept things. At the same time, I must admit that there always will be tension, there will always be pain on both sides, and guilt on at least one, not least some guilt on the wife's part for not being adequate. On the other hand, what would have been the alternative in, say, Toscanini's case? Suppression of his needs would have been disastrous to his artistic activities, let alone to him as a human being. Who is the better for it? A wife or a husband in such cases also has to be realistic and has to accept the best possible compromise in all the circumstances. They must seek a compromise which is least hurtful to both.

But let me go back to my next case, Marcus, that of Georges Simenon. I must admit that I'm a addict, and I hope it isn't only for that reason that I regard him as a great writer. He is of course, famous for his invention of the character of Maigret but he has written numerous other novels, touched into convincing life not only by his native penetration but by that voracious reading of books of psychology which is almost an obsession with him. They have a spontaneity and an inevitability which few other writers achieve. Do you know how he works? He is an extremely sensual man and cannot begin until he has been stimulated by some immediate sensation: a sound, a smell, a touch, an impression of light. This need, this artistic need amounting almost to an obsession with sensuality, has conditioned his whole way of life and his creative process. It is said about him that when a novel starts to stir in him, he seems to fall ill, and to become feverish, as with 'flu. The doctor may be called in and he says: "It's not 'flu, its a novel." Simenon then withdraws and writes for, say, eight to ten days and nights, almost non-stop. But once he has finished, then, in order to relieve the tension but also in order to reconnect with the lower, the crudely sensual element which he had taken up into the creative process, in the words of a fellow artist he just rushes to the brothel. He is said to have had thousands of women, as well as having gone through three wives. It could of course be said that he overdid it, for as somebody else said, he has the sexual habits of a commercial traveller. But the point is that sensual stimulation, even at the expense of conventional morality, was indispensable for his artistic being. In this respect, then, he was like Mozart, for he is the very by-word for the sublime and yet he could be very crude, even obscene in his behaviour and language because he needed to keep in touch with life even in its grossest form in order to remain creative. So again you see the predicament in moral terms, since he surely had an obligation to his art, and the problem of growth here is that of a person's growth as an artist.'

'I do take your point, Hans, that the case of the artist is a more vivid version of the conflict which many people experience between demands from within and demands from without, and I do agree that it is perhaps even more of a genuinely moral conflict than the case of other people in so far as a great work of art as an enhancement of life has a moral value in itself. I must admit that I do also have certain reservations. There is first of all the fact that your way of thinking and presentation are somewhat Romantic. But wasn't it your beloved Goethe himself who wrote these critical lines out of his reaction against the essentially Romantic *Sturm und Drang* and his refinding of the classical mood: They are rendered by Michael Hamburger as follows:

> Who seeks great gain leaves easy gain behind.
> None proves a master but by limitation,
> And only law can give us liberty.[5]

While he himself may not have been able to live up to the ideal glimpsed here, are there not more Classical artists who were, such as Milton, Bach, Jane Austen, Gerard Manly Hopkins?

There is something deeper which lies behind this reservation on my part. It's simply that I wonder whether you do not allow a place for an ideal of complete fidelity to commitments, whatever the cost? Isn't living for an ideal also a basic need?'

'I not only allow for such a need, Marcus, I give it *a quite central place*. Striving for the ideal is the supreme need, and for me anything else is only an approach to it. The supreme need of man is to be faithful to his higher self, which inevitably demands restraint and sacrifice. Even Schnitzler was able to practice these virtues in his artistic life, though not in his personal life. But even this conflict points to the fact that what we're talking about is a *process* – of *slow redemption*. People may have to live through the darkness and terror of some more or less orgiastic outburst before they can be liberated. So for me what I've previously called "schöpferischer Verzicht", creative renunciation, is the proto-phenomenon of human experience – that a man can be confronted with temptation but reject it. A simple example is the case of Galsworthy. As you may well know, he fell in love with a woman of eighteen when he was at the dangerous age of forty, but he said "No" because he wanted to remain faithful to his wife. What one has to do as a counsellor in any such situation is to assess whether there is any possibility of such a renunciation, any substance of strength to attempt this, and if there is the slightest chance of mobilising it, to challenge the person and to make the approach to the higher self. But in many cases this strength is not there, while the unlived life is very much there to torment a man or woman. In this case one just has to make the best possible, the least hurtful, the least self-seeking, the least subjective compromise. But may I repeat: the central case of human experience is the pursuit of the ideal. Any deviation is only a stepping-stone to the ultimate ideal.'

'Well, Hans, if you say this, then you've completely answered my initial question in so far as I talked about a tension and you have now spoken, and so vitally, about both terms of this tension. You began by arguing the need to follow what you called the law of one's inner being, you then stressed the central importance of the pursuit of the ideal, and so you have stated a reconciliation of principle, albeit in terms of process, struggle and pain.'

'Yes, and in this connection, Marcus, there is a brief saying of Christian Morgenstern, that poetic philosopher or philosophical poet, which perfectly sums up for me what you have expressed in those last words: process, struggle and pain. He once wrote a poem to guilt and addressed it as "Schuld, du dunkle Huld", "guilt, thou dark blessing".[6] You see, what he saw was that even guilt – guilt in what you call the ontological sense of hurting one's deepest self and life itself – guilt as suffering from doing even what one has to do, can be a stepping-stone to redemption, to a greater freedom, to the attainment of the ideal.'

'You know, Hans, I find this statement of your position wholly acceptable, and you may be surprised to learn that it happens to be, to my mind, a spontaneous recovery and personalised restatement of the teaching of Thomas Aquinas. For he says, in two crucial successive articles of his *Summa Theologiae* on conscience, that while one is bound to follow one's conscience, even if it is mistaken, one is not thereby necessarily excused from fault[7]. You see, in his dry scholastic way he too holds a balance between inner conviction and what I call ontological reality, nature, the objective order of things, what you tend to call certain basic, unalterable laws.'

'I didn't of course know that, Marcus, but naturally I'm delighted to be on the side of the angelic doctor!'

'Not only this time, Hans. May I take this further, and again, I'm sorry to say, in a more philosophic direction.

You know only too well that there is a great deal of talk nowadays about a new morality. It is couched at a more popular level in terms of the permissive society, at a more esoteric level in terms of the Aquarian age. I take it, however, from what you say that you, like me, are in favour of a new morality in the sense of investing the traditional codes with a deeper and a more personal meaning, regarding them as expressions of what you have here referred to as the law of inner growth, but that you are not in favour of it in the sense of sanctioning the pursuit of more or less untutored intuitions and wishes. I ask you for your opinion on this topic because I think that this division represents one of the great conflicts of value-judgement in our time.

As I see it, one value system believes centrally in *experience*. More and more widely people, and especially young people, are saying that they rely on experience to guide them through life rather than any code or tradition or the advice of others. This expresses at once a disillusionment with received systems and some sort of faith in their own creativity. "Experience" is thus one of the great words of our time, almost a rallying cry, a shibboleth of modernity. I recently had two pungent experiences of this – if I may use the word! Somebody was saying to me just the other day that she liked our previous book because it was based on experience, and two days later I happened to be distributing communion to a student when I noticed that the word machine-stitched above the pocket of her denim jacket was : "Experience" ... But I think of two more generalised expressions of this trend of thinking and feeling. One of the clearest I know of is Erich Fromm's in his justly acclaimed little book *The Art of Loving*, first published in Great Britain in 1957 but reprinted many times since:

> While irrational faith is rooted in submission to a power which is felt to be overwhelmingly strong, omniscient and omnipotent, and in the abdication of one's own power and strength, rational faith is based upon the opposite experience. We have this faith in a thought because it is the result of our own observation and thinking. We have faith in the potentialities of others, of ourselves, and of mankind because, and only to the degree to which, we have experienced the growth of our own potentialities, the reality of growth in ourselves, the strength of our own power of reason and of love.[8]

Carl Rogers speaks in a very similar vein in his *On Becoming a Person*:

> *Experience is, for me, the highest authority.* The touchstone of validity is my own experience. No other person's idea,

and none of my own ideas, are as authoritative as my experience. It is to experience that I must return again and again, to discover a closer approximation to truth as it is in the process of becoming in me.

Neither the Bible nor the prophets – neither Freud nor research – neither the revelations of God nor man – can take precedence over my own inner experience.[9]

Now experience is a notion that is not only very familiar but one that is very rich and intricate. It's only in our time that people are beginning to analyse the notion more systematically and they're finding it very complex. It's like what St Augustine said about time: We know what it is until someone asks us to define it ... I cannot therefore hope to do justice to it. There do, however appear to be at least two essential elements in the ordinary notion of experience: it somehow means both what one has learned *already*, some deposit from the past ("in my experience") and also something new that one encounters, something one has *yet* to learn ("its all experience"). There is a phrase in one of the leading studies of this and associated notions that hits off the presence of these two elements and the mysterious tension between them: "that strange fusion of memory and expectation into a whole that we name experience and that we acquire from experience"[10].

Thus when we appeal to experience we may have in mind something we have indeed experienced and so we do so with the thought of the element of the remembered past, or we may have in mind something yet to be encountered, and so we do so with the thought of the other element in the notion of experience, that of the new, or else we may have in mind something new to complement the past and so we do so with the thought of the new somehow of a piece with the past. It is precisely the apparent permission in the notion of experience to slip imperceptibly from one element to the other that constitutes a great deal of its plausibility. But reliance on the past imprisons one in that past and so is a limited guide, reliance on what is new is by definition reliance on something unknown and so cannot count as a guide, *at least in the same sense*, while reliance on what is new on the basis of what has gone before begs the question of how the new relates to the past. The very amalgam of past and new, memory and expectation thus hides the fact that the two main elements are disparate so that slipping from one element to the other to escape from the limitations of either is a logically illegitimate jump and the plausibility is spurious. This is why for me reliance on experience above all, in the spirit of Erich Fromm and Carl Rogers, is at the very least logically incoherent.

It is no doubt because of even the logical inadequacy of the notion of experience to take the full weight of being a guide and "authority" and "touchstone" of life that Cardinal Newman made an apologia for accepting the inevitability and the desirability of relying on guidance from the past, therefore from some tradition and some inherited code of belief and behaviour, though without thereby disallowing a place for experience. In, for instance, *An Essay on the Development of Christian Doctrine* and the *University Sermons* he referred to the "presumptive" character of so much of our actual life – the fact that we live out of the past, some pre-shaping of the new, out of anticipations, acceptance – in a word, presumptions – and hence out of *trust*: "we must begin by believing and … conviction will follow".[11] The essence of the alternative value system, therefore, is the frank and willing acceptance of some pre-guidance, some tutoring and directing of our projects, prejudice in the etymological sense of pre-judice, pre-judgement, *Vorverständnis* or pre-understanding. On this view we acknowledge the complex of received and learned attitudes and information with which we inevitably come to anything fresh, albeit only as an initiation which then *does* need to be tested in experience and so personally appropriated into conviction. Since such living initially out of trust is not irrational, then neither is the supreme case of such trust, namely, trust in what we take to be revelation by God himself. We then believe in order to understand, trust in order to become convinced, presume in order to experience.

So far I have tried to state the conflict of value systems in my own words and in terms of spokespersons of the Anglo-American tradition. In fact the conflict is a very profound one, as has been shown massively by the man whom I quoted a few minutes ago, the disciple of Heidegger, the German philosopher Hans-Georg Gadamer. In *Truth and Method* he describes the conflict I am indicating in terms of the running and continuing battle between the values of, on the one hand, reason, experience and individualism, and on the other, tradition, pre-understanding, pre-judice, faith in revelation that set in for us with the Enlightenment of the eighteenth century.

Not that this is an exclusively modern or even a Western problem. I was fascinated to discover recently that no less a person that Mahatma Ghandi experienced the conflict between faith and conscience, what we are here calling social morality and inner growth, acutely in his own life and person, though he experienced it against the background of the antique acceptance of a traditional code, in his case the eternal law expressed in the Vedas of India. This is how R.C. Zaehner puts it in his book *Hinduism*:

> In his frail person the ancient ideal of renunciation, "harmlessness" (*ahimsa*, translated by him as "non-violence") and truth met. He described himself as a *sanatani* Hindu, one who follows the *sanatana dharma*, the "eternal law" once embodied in the *dharma-raja*, Yudishthira. Ghandi's dilemma was the same as Yudishthira's: what and where *was* the *sanatana dharma* he claimed to follow? Was it in the heart or was it in what the Brahmans proclaimed? ...
>
> So it seemed only natural that he could say of the scriptures, "My belief in the Hindu Scriptures does not require me to accept every word and every verse as divinely inspired. Nor do I claim to have any first-hand knowledge of these wonderful books. But I do claim to know and feel the truths of the essential teaching of the

Scriptures. I decline to be bound by any interpretation, however learned it may be, if it is repugnant to reason and moral sense." The outraged conscience of Yudhishthira speaks through the lips of Mahatma Ghandi.[12]

This way of putting it reminds us in the Judaeo-Christian tradition of those extraordinarily revolutionary but yet traditional words of Jesus: "You leave the commandment of God, and hold fast the tradition of men."[13] It is as if he were saying that God's own teaching can come to us only through the vehicle of man's teaching and yet this very mediation can distort and betray it. The archetypal teaching therefore needs to be disengaged and rediscovered time and time again, in a searching interplay between trust and experience, code and conscience – but, I should say, and I think that here you agree with me, on the basis of an *initial* and initiating acceptance of the tradition and the moral code.'

'Yes, Marcus, I do indeed agree with you. For me there *are* certain basic and unalterable laws. These belong to the perfected moral nature of man, his higher self. For instance, adultery remains adultery and the higher self does not commit adultery. I do not want to sanctify and make permanent any deviation from these basic laws. What a counsellor does is to help a client to move, by slow stages, towards this ideal, and he has to accept compromise solutions, tentative answers which have to do with the lower self, developmental obstacles, and so on, but which can stimulate and promote growth. But these are only stepping-stones towards the ideal.'

'So you give a very interesting twist to the notion of movement towards an ideal in so far as you say that a counsellor has not merely to tolerate but in some sense to encourage what you call compromise solutions which fall short of the ideal, *provided* that they can be seen to stimulate efforts to grow beyond them ...'

'And ultimately leave them behind. Then the tension is ultimately resolved.'

'I see, Hans. You know that what you now say reminds me

of a distinction which has long been made in the Roman Catholic tradition and which was one of the first things which Cardinal Hume recalled after becoming archbishop of Westminster. This is the distinction between principle and pastoral application. He said that we have to be uncompromising on principle and infinitely flexible on application. This is the real pastoral skill, so that what you are talking about is as it were the secular equivalent of this pastoral skill.'

'What you say is most interesting, Marcus, and not only for its immediate content. For in comparing the counsellor to the priest you remind me of the contrast between their two roles which you drew at the beginning of this morning's discussion and so also of something I've thought for a long time. You see, for me the counsellor and the priest have different tasks and different resources. The priest has the possibility of addressing and challenging this higher self which is inactive or only partially awake and of doing so directly, and he has the resources of the sacred text, the sacraments, prayers, his whole presence, even his appearance and dress as a pointer to something beyond his individual and limited self. The counsellor, on the other hand, starts from the other end; his business is to help sort out the problems of the lower self in the way we've seen this morning, and he doesn't have the office or role – or the image – of challenging the higher self directly which the priest has; he can only open the way to the other becoming more receptive to the presence and influence of the higher self. Priest and counsellor, therefore, work together, but from different directions – and of course, the priest-counsellor has in principle both resources, like yourself.'

'I appreciate your saying that, Hans, but I have in all conscience to say that in actual practice when I'm using counselling skills in the course of performing my priestly role, I find that discernment of what emphasis I am to give in any concrete case very delicate to make. I find it difficult to know from which end I'm to begin, at what time I'm to make the challenge of which you speak so justly. I must also say that in my experience one can make a mistake in either direction:

either confronting the other with the spiritual challenge too soon or allowing him or her to continue in his or her experiments too long. Here too one has to accept the possibility of making mistakes. Perhaps the essential thing is to allow any sense of the infinite complexity of human situations and of the human struggle to be charged with the spirit of that statement of St Paul which you have quoted to me before: "Not that I am already perfect: but I press on ... forgetting what lies behind and straining forward to what lies ahead."[14] The key-word here is "straining forward", and I find it most interesting that it is precisely this passage and *this word* in particular which St Gregory of Nyssa, in his *Life of Moses*, uses to develop his novel idea of perfection as a continual progress. If we wanted to invent a word, we could shape it from the Greek original of "straining forward", *epekteinomai*, and say that we have to retain a sense of the individual's life being "epekteinic", a matter of ceaselessly straining forward.'

'I quite agree, Marcus. In my own terms the conflicts, the crises, the moments of decision, the darkness and the terror, the very guilt cannot be what I've called stepping-stones towards the ideal of the higher self unless a person has been alerted to it, is future-oriented, otherwise they'll just settle down and feel comfortable. But for me the other side of this coin is that one can also overstrain oneself. I remember a woman of my aquaintance saying so often "Why can't I be perfect, why can't I be perfect?" For myself I accept what human nature is, I accept what I am. I just ask myself what the next step is, and I accept the struggle.'

'I'm reminded of a succinct statement of Carl Rogers, and since I quoted him before in order to disagree with him, I'd like to cite him now, since this time I endorse what he says:

> I believe that I have learned this from my clients as well as within my own experience – that we cannot change, we cannot move away from what we are, until we thoroughly *accept* what we are. Then change seems to come about

almost unnoticed.[15]

This in turn recalls another passage which is very similar in meaning but which is couched in more dramatic and more religious terms. It is from Harry Williams' fine little book *The True Wilderness*:

> Human life is very largely a wilderness, a dry land where no water is ... once we thus accept our wilderness and no longer try to hide it from ourselves, there follows the miracle of resurrection. The desert become verdant. The stony ground itself brings forth rich pastures. It is, for instance, the man who faces and accepts his inability to love who discovers within himself a power of loving which nothing external can destroy or diminish. This is life through death.'[16]

'I for my part, Marcus, can wholly accept both these statements. Thank you very much.'

Notes

1. p.173.
2. *Concilium* 150 (1981), p.32.
3. *Prologomenon to Ethics*, 4th ed. (1899), p.xxvi.
4. *Natural Law and Natural Rights* (1980), p.143.
5. from a poem beginning 'Natur und Kunst ...'
6. 'An die Schuld', in *Epigramme und Sprüche*.
7. la. q. 19, articles 5 and 6.
8. pp.103-104.
9. pp.23-24. The italics are the author's own.
10. *Truth and Method* (1975), p.195.
11. Pelican Classics, 1974, p.343.
12. pp.170-171.

13. Mark 7:8.
14. Philippians 3:12-13.
15. p.17. The italics are the author's own.
16. p.12.

Dialogue 10: Sex and Contemplation

Love is an elemental means of self-satisfaction and a physical avenue, apart from mystical immersion, to possible transcendence.
          Rainer Maria Rilke Siegfried Mandel[1]

As in the Śaiva Siddhānta so in the Gītā and Rāmānaja God imprisons souls in matter only to release them and unite them with himself. This constitutes his adorable 'game' (krīdā, līlā).
          Hinduism R.C.Zaehner[2]

'The subject I should like to discuss with you today, Hans, is one which we have touched upon from time to time explicitly, and this is no doubt because in its essence it pervades everything we talk about. For our underlying theme, just as human beings, even more than in the roles we play out to and for each other as counsellor and priest, is *relationship and spirituality* under different aspects, and sex and contemplation are the intensest forms of these two things. They also sum up the paradox of relationship and spirituality because while sex and contemplation seem to be at emnity with each other, there is a recurrent intuition throughout history that they are also very close to each other. What is the truth of the matter?

When I ask for the truth of the matter, I mean, of course, practical not speculative or academic truth, because nothing could be more personal to each of us than our sexuality and our possible openness to what St Augustine unforgettably called the God who is "more intimate to us than we are to ourselves". It is at this level that I should like to put the question to you this morning.

For the subject is in the first place quite obviously of personal interest not only to me as a man but because I am a celibate member of a contemplative Order and so experience the problem in terms of a struggle within my own body and person. Yet I continue to try to pray, and I feel the need to experience life contemplatively, to make sense of it, even of frustration, pain, tragedy and sin as a very important need too. I value the opportunity to talk the problem over with you, especially as I assume that you experience similar tensions within yourself but from the different point of view of a man who has a happily married life of almost fifty years behind him and yet is also passionately committed to meditation and contemplation.

Moving to a more general level, I again see the subject of sex and contemplation in terms of a series of dilemmas or tensions. Thus, in the first place, we need Freud only to remind us, not to tell us, what so much experience and so much of the world's art testifies, namely, that sexual attraction is one of the great forces which moves the world, and that we fail to acknowledge it at our peril. On the other hand, we also know intuitively – which was surely part of the message of Freud himself – that an unregulated pursuit of sex is incompatible with being human, let alone with gaining access to the contemplative possibilities of our nature. Then again, to take the question from another angle, we may acknowledge that people are capable of contemplation, in fact that they deeply need to contemplate in order to come to the unfailing source of their being and find the true love of their hearts, and yet the experience of both of us in dealing with people who aspire to spirituality is that one of the most insidious traps on their path is a denial of their sexuality and bodiliness and so a premature spirituality and a false sublimation. So where is discernment and sanity in this matter? But perhaps this is enough to introduce the topic I have in mind?'

'It certainly is, Marcus, and I'd better stop you here so that I can begin to respond. And since you began yourself in so personal a vein, I'd like to begin myself by acknowledging a comparable tension in my own life. Now you put your own position as a celibate priest in the foreground of your introductory remarks, and this is of course only one aspect of the whole subject you have raised this morning. But since you have mentioned it, you may be surprised to learn that my contemplative nature asserted itself early in my life in so far as I wished to be celibate from my very teens. You know, in my school days I used to get up several times in the night pretending to be a monk with my Bible! In retrospect I now think that this may, at least in part, have been a reaction to what I saw of sex in earliest childhood. Such an experience of sex as ugly and distasteful is, of course, far from unique. Many people have such shadows over their sexuality.

One case which occurs to me is that of Mahler. As a young man he was living as a lodger in poor digs in Vienna and one day he came upon a fellow lodger, Alfred Grünfeld, a pianist, later to become famous, in the act of intercourse with the serving girl. Mahler was so appalled by what he found repulsive and *tierisch*, bestial, that he tried to haul the fellow off from the girl. He got a very bad reception and was sent packing. Whether this was the only cause, or only a factor, he certainly had a block about sex which later made itself felt in his relationship with Alma, his wife, twenty years younger than himself and one of the greatest beauties in Vienna when he married her. It was a difficult marriage and it is interesting that Mahler consulted Freud. Now Freud, you know, was a man of very regular habits who also insisted on taking his holidays which he much enjoyed. So when Mahler got in touch, Freud agreed to see him only on condition that Mahler accompanied him on one of his holiday walks. Mahler agreed and went, they walked for four hours, and Mahler felt much better about his relationship to Alma – whether as a result of what Freud said, or of what he just was, no one will ever know.

Anyhow, the point is that many of us have such dark experiences of sexuality. I certainly did, but apart from possibly inducing in me this almost life-long desire to be celibate, my childhood experience also aroused my sexual awareness very early. I long hoped that I would "overcome" sex, but one of the lessons of my life is that few, if any, can; certainly that I could not, and I just had to accept this. Sex is, of course, complex, and is readily confused with desire, which can make us feel guilty, but sex is not the same as desire. It can manifest itself as desire, but it first manifests itself at the lowest level simply as hunger, a need as physiological as hunger in the ordinary sense, which is how the Buddha spoke of it.

My question, therefore, becomes that of knowing how to manage this dual need – to reconcile a life-long need for contemplation with the need for sexual release, and here my personal question becomes a typical one. How to do justice to human nature and not stifle it, in such a way as to keep it in balance with a socially ordered and moral life that hurts neither others nor oneself and so retain one's mental and spiritual integrity and independence. Above all, how is one to arrange one's life so as not to suffer intolerable intrusions into one's contemplative life?

I've thought a great deal about this and lived it through in my own life, compared my own experience with other's and I've come to certain conclusions. In the first place, I believe that in order to be fully human everybody must awaken to sexuality and go through a basic sexual experience in youth, in the way that, for instance, the Buddha and St Augustine did. This learning experience or basic experience by itself liberates human potential. So far as the next phase in life is concerned, in my opinion, as I've already indicated, one must have a sexual partner, but if one also seriously wants to lead a contemplative life one's choice of such a partner is crucial. In this regard I have in my professional life dealt with more marital problems than with any other sort of problem and so I've come across couples who have experienced all the famed delights and ecstasies of sex but who, to my complete astonishment, have in most cases experienced little or no human contact or communication in their love-making and even more, are usually not given to contemplation. It's as if we could not experience everything in human nature. Certainly, for me personally, frequent and passionate excitement and the experience of delirious ecstasy is incompatible with any serious and sustained contemplative life, whereas the relief of basic sexual need, human contact, mutual helpfulness, companionship and the sharing of interests is conducive to it.'

'So it's as if there were several possible combinations of sexual and contemplative activities which could be thought of as forming a continuum – sexual ecstasy, settled domesticity, marital contemplation, celibate contemplation, Hans?'

'Exactly, Marcus, we have to establish our priorities and if we want to lead a contemplative, as well as sexual life, we have to choose a partner accordingly.

That, however, in not all that is necessary. A sexual comradeship must also be lived in the context of what I've previously called a *serene way of life* generally – refraining from unnecessary talking and blethering; ensuring quiet spaces during the day, especially before seeing anyone professionally; taking a minimum of bodily exercise; chastening one's senses; as far as possible keeping free from the overstimulation and titillation of the media; a suitable diet. This amounts to an ascetic, but not, I think, an unnatural way of life. This is the sort of way in which I envisage the appeasement of the passions in the interests of a contemplative life – the modest equivalent of the way in which St Jerome was able to study in his cell because the lion of his feelings had settled down quietly at his feet, next to his dog, as depicted in the engraving by Albrecht Dürer which I keep just inside the door of the room we are in, as you may have noticed.'

'As a matter of fact, I've often observed your other pictures as well as all the books here but I've never noticed this engraving, Hans, so I shall have a look at it when I leave this morning. But your discreet reference to the classical precedent only increases the fascination I felt on hearing you describe what you call the serene way of life that, in your opinion, is a necessary foundation and setting for a contemplative life. For what was passing through my mind as you spoke was another classical reference – St Thomas Aquinas' analysis of the inter-relationship between the active and the contemplative life in general and between the act of contemplation strictly so called, *simplex intuitus veritatis*, the "simple intuition of the truth", and the manner of ordering one's emotions and way of life and the very life of the imagination which dispose a man to this contemplation in particular.[3] But all this teaching was put more accessibly and engagingly by Fr Victor White OP in the admirable little commentary which he composed on one quantitatively tiny but qualitatively rich work of St Thomas, namely, the letter of advice on how to study which he wrote to a young Dominican student, Brother John. This is how Fr Victor White rendered his master's teaching:

> The natural desire to know of Brother John's mind must not be weakened, still less deadened; it is this that will provide the needed motivation for all his studies. But moderated – not in our sense of diluted, but in St Thomas's sense of being given "modus", order, direction – it must be. If Brother John wants to attain wisdom, he must not be impatient, in a hurry. It is slow work, and it cannot be done by cramming or by any slick technique. This may be damping and disappointing; but if Brother John thinks so, then there is worse to follow.

For two thirds of the remainder of the letter seem to have nothing to do with intellectual, scientific method at all. Brother John had asked how to *study*; St Thomas replies by telling him how to *live*. He continues: "Haec est ergo monitio mea de *vita tua*" ["This, therefore, is my advice on how you are to live"]. That "ergo" therefore, must seem strangely inconsequential until we remember what St Thomas, developing some ideas in Aristotle's Ethics, has to say about the relation of the life of virtue to the life of contemplation. *Essentialiter* [essentially] moral virtue had nothing to so with science, with the search for truth; but *dispositive, removens prohibens* [dispositively, by way of the removal of obstacles] it is indispensable: "For the act of contemplation is impeded both by the vehemence of the emotions, by which the attention of the soul is drawn from the things of the mind to the things of sense, and also by external disturbances. But it is precisely the task of the moral virtues to prevent the immoderate vehemence of the emotions, and to quieten the disturbances arising from the external business."[4]

So instead of some elaborate methodologico-pedagogical technique, what Brother John gets first of all from the great Master Thomas is a list of matter-of-fact commonplaces which he might have got any day from his novice-master. He must be careful about keeping silence, he must be slow to speak; he must embrace purity of conscience; he must not cease to spend plenty of time in prayer. Also, he must keep to his cell, love his cell ... He must think twice before wandering off to the common room; he must be on amicable terms with his companions, neither aloof from any nor too familiar with any; and he must not get himself entangled in the affairs of outsiders. Above all he must avoid "discursus" – which perhaps we can best translate by "rushing about" in the colloquial sense – and imitate the examples of the saints and other sound men ...

I confess that when I first read this letter, I was surprised that St Thomas, in this context of study, laid such emphasis on *fraternal charity*, and Brother John's attitude to his companions. But one cannot have lived for twenty years in houses of study without realising to how great an extent study is helped by satisfactory or hindered by mismanaged personal relationships ... A vigorous sense-life is not merely, for the student, a condescending concession to his "lower nature", it is a necessity for his studies themselves ...[5]

You see, Hans? Leaving aside the question of celibacy, which is a special problem, as you've indicated already yourself, it's as if you had out of your own experience of yourself and others spontaneously formulated a secular version of a monastic way of life ... !

There is however, one problem about your account of the way of life that is the necessary setting for contemplative activities. As you spoke, I was thinking of various people I have come across who were so restless and active that they just could not tolerate the regime of life which you and St Thomas describe. Nor is this only my own personal question. I'm again encouraged in this thought by recalling the perception of one of the witnesses St Thomas Aquinas quoted in this same sequence of reflections on the contemplative life, Pope St Gregory called the Great:

> It often happens that those who have been quite decently occupied in leading an ordinary human life have been slain by the sword of quiet ... There are some people who are so restless that they begin to feel crushed when they stop working, because the more leisure they have the more exasperated they become by the tumult of their heart.

St Thomas accepts this and says that "those who are liable to feel things intensely because they are temperamentally active are sometimes better suited to the active than to the contemplative life", whereas those who "are constitutionally quiet and calm are better suited for contemplation", to the point that they deteriorate if they are required to do nothing but work.[6]

You see, I think that we need to have the discernment of a St Gregory and a St Thomas if we are not to run the risk of extending a way of life which happens to suit you and me to people whom it might not suit, in fact whom it would definitely drive crazy.'

'I quite agree with you there, Marcus. I've already said that every person is unique, and that different people need different solutions. People do need to identify their own disposition. I would however, in the first place like to say that everybody, even the most active person, has at least the potential for contemplation somewhere within him or herself and so needs, if not space for contemplation in any strict sense, then at least what I call some "quiet time". Lotz has the wonderful image of the wheel which turns at its periphery but the axle of which remains still at the centre. Unless we find the still centre we shall only turn at the periphery. I do think that some minimum of withdrawal, standing back from the press of activity, some stillness, recollection, is necessary for leading any life that can be called human.

Subject to this however, I accept what you – and your illustrious predecessors – say. In fact I'd take it further, because for me the fundamental reason why the balance of activity and quiet must be adjusted to each individual is that we are dealing not merely with sexual impulses but with *every sort of disordered impulse* – what the Buddhists call "cravings" and what St John of the Cross calls "appetites". There may be appetites for, most simply, food, for restless movement, for power, or even for intellectual gratification, as well as for sex. It is such appetites we need to subdue and silence, these are the beasts we need to tame. I remember two lines of Goethe:

> What perturbs your inner being, you should not suffer to happen.

– whatever it may be. It is, therefore, just because this is so that I agree that work can for many people, perhaps for most people, be a most important way of combating their cravings. For any intense work and certainly work with people, uses up two things: first, one's physical vitality – one simply gets tired, exhausted even; and secondly, in the case of caring work, one's energy and resources of loving and caring. I certainly find myself that I'm much less conditioned by sexual demands when I work as hard as possible. Further such a giving and receiving of love is itself a redemption of even the sexual impulse.'

'I'm glad you go below the surface of the subject, Hans, and that you now state that your "serene way of life" and work is in fact a matter of an implacable battle with the deepest and darkest desires and fears of man's nature. I'm also very glad that you make at least a sidelong reference to the tradition of the East by your use of the term "cravings". For it seems to me that we're now talking about something central to the spiritual traditions of both West and East.

At first sight it seems that the traditions of West and East are strikingly similar. Thus in the West a distinction is made between the active and the contemplative life and they are variously symbolised by the figures of Leah and Rachel, Martha and Mary, Peter and John. The Eastern tradition similarly distinguishes between the way of knowledge or wisdom (*jñāna*) and the way of action (*karma*). Thus, for example, the *Bhagavad Gītā* says:

> In this world there are two roads of perfection, as I told thee before, O prince without sin: Jñāna Yoga, the path of wisdom of the Sankhyas, and Karma Yoga, the path of action of the yogis.[7]

When we come to look at the matter more closely, however, and see how the masters of either tradition seek to state how these two ways relate to each other and work out in practice, we become aware of a subtle but very important difference, it seems to me.

For, on the one hand, two of the great masters of the West do not just state the distinction but do so in the context of ranking them in relation to each other. Thus St Augustine writes in *The City of God*:

> The love of truth seeks holy leisure (*otium sanctum*), but the compelling force of love accepts due busyness. If nobody imposes this latter burden on you, give yourself up to the pursuit and intuition of truth. If it is imposed, however, you should take it up out of the compulsion of

love. And yet you should not completely desert the delight of truth, lest you lose its sweetness and become crushed by activity.[8]

St Thomas sums up his teaching in the very article in which he quotes this passage:

> We have to say that, simply speaking, the contemplative life is better than the active.[9]

On the other hand, Eastern texts state the distinction but leave the relationship between the respective terms unstated. Thus the *Bhagavad Gītā* says, for instance, the following:

> Stand fast in Yoga, surrending attachment;
> In success and failure be the same,
> And then get busy with thy works.
> Yoga means "sameness" and "indifference" (*samatva*).[10]

> Better one's own duty (*dharma*) [to perform], though void of merit,
> Than to do another's well:
> Better to die within [the sphere of] one's own duty:
> Perilous is the duty of other men.[11]

The teaching here implied is well summed up by Zaehner in his *Hinduism*:

> In the Bhagavad Gītā three paths to the Absolute are offered to the man who seeks liberation – the path of "knowledge" (*jñāna*), the path of action (*karma*), and the path of *bhakti*. By "knowledge" is understood not simply book-learning, which according to the Upanishads leads you nowhere, but the intuitive apprehension of Brahman – a term which is variously interpreted by the philosophers but which in the Gītā means the direct apprehension of the timeless Reality and the inter-

connection of all things as cohering in the "great Self" and therefore also in the individual "self" once it is liberated from its mortal bonds. To speak of a "path of action" as far as the Gītā is concerned is misleading, for this does not mean that the active life, as against the contemplative, has value of its own but that it is possible and desirable to pursue the life of contemplation while still engaged in an active life, be it the sacred ministration of the Brahman, the warfare of the Kshatriya, the business activity of the Vaiśya, or the menial service of the Śūdra. All these activities are good and each of the four great classes should carry out the duties of their station, for this is the *dharma* perscribed by the law books and the will of God, but the zealous performance of caste can never lead to liberation, for action breeds its own reward or punishment, and the 'fruits' or *karma* bind whether they be good or bad; they 'attach' to good or evil and therefore militate against detachment which is the *sine qua non* of liberation ... [12]

Thus the West gives a priority to the contemplative life but does so in making it alternate with the active life in a way that the East does not, whereas the East at first seems to put the active and the contemplative life on a par only then to suggest that it is, in Zaehner's key words, possible and desirable to "pursue the life of contemplation while still engaged in an active life", which suggests an effective priority of the contemplative life over the active after all. The initial similarity seems on closer inspection to dissolve and this is all the more puzzling as a basic agreement seems nevertheless to lie hidden somehow in the very blurring.

The way to unravel this tangle would seem to consist in realising that the masters of the West couch their insight in terms of a way of spending time, a form of behaviour, whereas the Eastern texts speak directly about an inner attitude of mind. We therefore have to make a distinction between outward expression and the inner spirit informing any such expression. Then in the light of this distinction we can say that the East has seen more clearly what St Augustine and St Thomas have also seen but not stated so sharply, namely that the essential thing is a certain attitude of mind, but that St Augustine and St Thomas have stated correctly that this attitude of mind does have priority and should be the object of our striving.

We can go on to say what this attitude of mind consists of. We seem to be in a position to say that in both West and East the essential thing in life from moment to moment is *neither* contemplation *nor* any particular activity as such but what can variously be called being devoted, dedicated, selfless, acting without being attached to the fruits of one's action, loving, doing the will of God, being abandoned to God, sacrificing oneself, cleaving to God, being joined to Him and therefore practising yoga in the etymological sense of being yoked – to the Origin and End of all things. At the same time we have to win through to such as inner attitude of mind and this is what detachment is about – which is therefore ultimately detachment from one's narrow possessive ego. So, to return to what you were saying, what the gradual overcoming of "cravings" and appetites is about is the detachment that liberates the one thing necessary, the inner state of mind that has been called devotion in the traditions of both West and East.'

'You have deepened and broadened what I was saying, Marcus, and as a result I can understand a little more clearly another passage from the *Bhagavad Gītā* which I wanted to bring out next, although I can now also see better just how much struggle is in fact involved in what is stated so simply, almost blandly:

> But the soul that moves in the world of senses and yet keeps the senses in harmony, free from attraction and aversion, finds rest in quietness.[13]

You see, even this classical spiritual text is not suggesting total abstinence. No, it states that it is possible for an individual to reach a state of purification such as to be able to surrender to his or her sensuality without being humiliated and pulled down by it.'

'I had overlooked that particular text, Hans, and yet I have lived for some time now with the more ancient text which I think must lie behind this one. It is the opening words of the *Iśā Upanishad*:

> All this, whatever moves on earth, is pervaded by the Lord. Renounce it first, and then enjoy.

This is the way in which Zaehner himself translates it, in his *Hinduism* again, but the real excitement of the message comes out when we realise that a subtly different translation can be given. This emerges from the fact that Gandhi translated it differently. Here is what Zaehner says:

> In his later years Gandhi was asked what he considered to be the essence of Hinduism, and he replied that the whole of Hinduism was contained in the first verse of the *Iśā Upanishad* which he translated as follows:
> All this that we see in this great universe is permeated by God.
> Renounce it and enjoy it.
> Do not covet anybody's wealth or possession.[14]

You see, Hans, the essential thing for me is that in Gandhi's rendering there is no mention of a before and after: *first* renounce, *then* enjoy. It's therefore as if in the concrete complexity of life either could come before the other, or they could even alternate indefinitely or be mingled with each other, so that the attitude which is being set before us as the goal of our seeking and struggle is an enjoyment *in* renunciation or a renunciation *in* the very enjoyment, a commitment which is nevertheless detached, a detachment which is nevertheless shot through with delight and laughter, a whole-hearted involvement with the world which is nevertheless so free as to amount to play. Is this perhaps what the Divine Comedy and the Hindu līlā/game, *homo ludens*, man as playful and Śiva Nataraja, Lord of the Dance, are all about?'

'I think that you may have penetrated to the essence of what we're talking about, Marcus. I can here, add only two further attempted formulations of the attitude of mind which a "serene way of life" is meant to bring about. The first is again from Steiner, in a passage where he is talking about the development of the state of consciousness called the six-petal lotus flower:

> Still greater difficulty attends the development of the six-petalled lotus flower in the centre of the body, for it can be achieved only as the result of complete mastery of the whole man through consciousness of self, so that the body, soul and spirit are in perfect harmony. The functions of the body, the inclinations and passions of the soul, the thoughts and ideas of the spirit, must be turned to perfect unison. The body must be so ennobled and purified that its organs impel the individual to nothing that is not in the service of the soul and spirit. The soul must not be impelled, through the body, to desires and passions which conflict with pure and noble thinking. But the spirit must not dominate the soul with its laws and moral precepts like a slave-driver; the soul must follow these laws and duties out of its own free inclination. The pupil must not feel duty as a power hovering over him to which he unwillingly submits, but rather as something he does because he loves it. He must develop a free soul standing in equilibrium between sense-existence and spirituality. He must reach the stage where he may safely give himself over to his sense-nature, because this has been so purified that it has lost the power to drag him down to its level. It should no longer be necessary for him to curb his passions, because they will follow a right course of their own accord.[15]

The second passage contrasts strongly with it in tone, although not really in substance. Do you know Somerset Maugham's *The Razor's Edge*? It's about a young American, Larry, who is in search of illumination. He's an extremely entertaining character, liberated from the start and yet not a saint – an ascetic, if you like, but by nature and endowment and not by grace and struggle. He remains basically uninvolved although he is open, sociable, friendly. He is free even from sexual cravings, but because of his attractive temperament, he finds that women just crawl up to him, even into his bed, and he is kind enough to oblige. Here's the passage in which this state of mind is described by a woman who fell for him:

> "I went upstairs and undressed and then slipped along the passage to his room. He was lying in bed reading and smoking a pipe. He put down his pipe and his book and moved to make room for me."
>
> Suzanne was silent for a while and it went against my grain to ask her questions. But after a while she went on.
>
> "He was a strange lover. Very sweet, affectionate and even tender, virile without being passionate, if you understand what I mean, and absolutely without vice. He loved like a hot-blooded schoolboy. It was rather funny and rather touching. When I left him I had the feeling that I should be grateful to him rather than he to me. As I closed the door I saw him take up his book and go on reading where he had left off."[16]

So here's a personality who's open, kind, free and completely untainted by the dark side of life and who acts out of a natural response to life.'

'That brings us down nice and easily from the heights we had ascended, Hans!

More seriously, I'd like to ask you a question which arises from all this. What you're here saying in effect is that we can have both a sexual and a contemplative life provided we fully recognise and appease the reality and insistence of sex in the context of a supporting way of life. Would you, therefore, say that there is in principle no conflict between sex and contemplation?'

'No, Marcus, I would not go as far as that. What I should say in this connection is two things. First, I now recall how many of the people I've dealt with and habitually move among, do practise meditation as an important part of their lives but experience absolutely no conflict as a result. I was for a long time very puzzled by this, and I can only explain it by making a distinction between meditation and contemplation strictly so-called and saying that the meditation the people I have in mind practise, remains enclosed within the life they lead, whereas contemplation for me is a matter of gradually withdrawing from sensory and emotional stimuli, impressions and images and so disposing oneself to receive an influx of what St John of the Cross calls "the limpid light of God", being touched, in at least some measure, by pure spirit, and here one inevitably gets into conflict and struggle.'

'I see, Hans, so for you meditation as you now speak of it tends to be a confirmation of the rest of life, whereas contemplation is a challenge to it, one is a sealing of ordinary life, the other is a breaking out of it, and this essentially because contemplation is an opening up to, a surrender to another, the Other, whose ways are not our ways? In other words, you would then, I think, endorse the searing words of the nineteenth-century Russian master, Theophan the Recluse, recorded in that golden book about prayer, *The Art of Prayer*:

> God's grace, coming first at a man's initial awakening, and afterwards visiting him during the whole period of his conversion, cleaves him in two. It makes him aware of a duality within himself, and enables him to distinguish between what is unnatural and what should be natural; and thus it makes him resolve to sift or winnow all that is unnatural, so that his God-like nature should be brought

fully to light. But obviously such a decision is only the beginning of the undertaking. At this stage it is only with his will and intention that he has left the domain of alien unnaturalness, rejecting it, and aiming at the naturalness which he expects and desires. But in fact his whole structure remains as before – that is saturated with sin; and passions dominate his soul in all its faculties and his body in all its functions, just as they did before – with only this difference, that formerly he chose and embraced all this with desire and pleasure, but now, it is not desired or chosen, but is hated, trampled on, rejected ...[17]

'Yes, Marcus, I do strongly endorse this, and what you so aptly quote brings me to the second thing I wanted to say in response to your question about conflict between sex and contemplation. You see, the goal of the contemplative pursuit is indeed to be open to the influx of the "limpid light" but the very effort has to pass via the tumult of emotional impulses, facing the monsters of the deep, particularly but not exclusively sexuality, also anger, resentment and so on; in fact it seems to provoke them in a most daunting and terrifying way. St John of the Cross is very clear and blunt about this:

Such, as we have said, is the night and purgation of sense in the soul. In those who have afterwards to enter the other and more formidable night of the spirit, in order to pass to the Divine union of love of God (for not all pass habitually thereto, but only the smallest number), it [the way of illumination or infused contemplation] is wont to be accompanied by formidable trials and temptations of sense, which last for a long time, albeit longer in some than in others. For to some the angel of Satan presents himself – namely, the spirit of fornication – that he may buffet their senses with abominable and violent temptations, and trouble their spirits with vile considerations and representations which are most visible to the imagination, which things at times are a greater affliction to them than death.[18]

William Johnston is entirely within this same tradition when he writes as follows:

> When one begins to love profoundly at a new level of awareness (as often happens in deep intimacy between a man and woman) it may happen that latent or suppressed forces rise to the surface of the mind: hatred, jealousy, fear, insecurity, anger, suspicion, anxiety, unbridled eroticism and the rest surge up from the murky depths of the unconscious. And all this, it is well known, can coexist with true love. This violence, unleashed in human relations, can be unleashed also in the divine – the two are not so distinct, and divine love is incarnate. And one is liberated only by continuing to love. By fixing one's heart on the cloud of unknowing with deep peace, one becomes detached from these turbulent uprisings; and then they wither and die, leaving only love. It is by loving at the ultimate point, by going beyond all categories to the deepest centre, that one is liberated from jealousy and hatred and the rest. But this is an agonising purification.[19]

Just to indicate that once again we are dealing with something universally human, I'd like also to quote you another passage from Prabhavananda and Isherwood's commentary on Patanjali's *Yoga Sutras*:

> When a spiritual aspirant begins to practice concentration, he meets all sorts of distractions. You never realise how much junk you have in the house until you start to clear out the attic and the cellar. You never realise how much rubbish has accumulated until you make the attempt to concentrate. Many beginners therefore become discouraged. "Before I started to practice concen-

tration," they say, "my mind seemed fairly clean and calm. Now it's disturbed and full of dirty thoughts. It disgusts me. I'd no idea I was that bad! And surely I'm getting worse, not better?" They are wrong, of course. The very fact that they have undertaken a mental house-cleaning, and stirred up all this mess, means that they have taken a step in the right direction. As for the calmness which they imagine they have hitherto experienced, it was nothing but apathy – the stillness of a pool which is choked with mud. To the casual observer, sloth and serenity – tamas and sattwa – may sometimes look alike. But to pass from the one to the other, we have to go through the violent disturbance of active effort – the phase of rajas. The casual observer, watching our struggles and our distress, may say: "He used to be much easier to get along with. I liked him better the way he was. Religion doesn't seem to agree with him." We must not mind that. We must continue our struggle, with all its temporary humiliations, until we reach that self-mastery, that one-pointedness of concentration, of which Paranjali speaks.[20]

'I see, Hans. So for you there's a scale and gradation of interests and activities, a process of moving from one stage to another, each of which must be respected and worked through before passing on to the next: the emotions must be satisfied and put in order, the sexual appetites must be appeased and humanised, meditation must be practiced and only then can we hope to become open to the contemplative experience. In fact this progression is strikingly reminiscent of the *Stufenfolge*, as you call it, the stairway, of movement from character training, through meditation and knowledge into the final liberation of the spirit in union which you expounded in chapter 5. It is that same stairway or scale but now with the specific inclusion of the sexual domain.

In this respect however, I have a question. So far we have spoken about sex and contemplation as being in conflict and about sex reconciled with contemplation, but we have not spoken about whether sex can be said in some way, to be taken up into the very essence of contemplation – the vexed subject of sublimation. We have moved, if you like, from sex *versus* contemplation, to sex *plus* contemplation, but we've not reached sex *into* contemplation. I could put this in terms of the famous vision of St Theresa, recorded in her autobiography and made the subject of a sculpture by Bernini:

> Our Lord was pleased that I should sometimes see a vision of this kind. Beside me, on the left hand, appeared an angel in bodily form, such as I am not in the habit of seeing except very rarely ... He was not tall but short, and very beautiful; and his face was so aflame that he appeared to me to be one of the highest rank of angels, who seem to be all on fire. They must be of the kind called cherubim, but they do not tell me their names. I know very well that there is a great difference between some angels and others, and between these and others still, but I could not possibly explain it. In his hands I saw a great golden spear, and at the iron tip there appeared to be a point of fire. This he plunged into my heart several times so that it penetrated to my entrails. When he pulled it out, I felt he took them with it, and left me utterly consumed by the great love of God. The pain was so severe that it made me utter several moans. The sweetness caused by this intense pain is so extreme that one cannot possibly wish it to cease, nor is one's soul then content with anything but God. This is not a physical, but a spiritual pain, though the body has some share in it – even a considerable share. So gentle is this wooing which takes place between God and the soul that if anyone thinks I am lying, I pray God, in His goodness, to grant him some experience of it.[21]

The really significant thing to my mind, for our present purposes, is that the mystical experience is couched in explicitly sexual terms: the talk of wooing, the penetration of the phallic spear, the mixture of pain and delight, so that there is here an instinctive realisation on St Theresa's part of the truth that sexual powers are not pitted against contemplation but, on the contrary, are in their very essence taken up into the mystical experience. There is not conflict but transformation. Do you see?

'I do, Marcus, and the question is very interesting. To take up your first point first, I should not only say that the scale, the gradation, the stairway of progress through sexual life into contemplation that I have evoked is the same as the stairway or scale which I had expounded before on the basis of the saying of the Buddha; I should go further and say that there is a sense in which the very act of love over a lifetime is inscribed with the same law of progression and is a foreshadowing of the act of contemplation.

You may remember that we identified four stages on the spiritual path: moral discipline, meditation, contemplation and union when the spirit becomes free. Now in making love we first learn to treat the other with consideration, feeling, tact – it will not do for the man, for instance, to come at the woman like a steamroller, as one woman once complained to me about her husband. This corresponds to the Buddha's stage of "character training" in life as a whole. Again in love-making we must not rush at the desired and loved object but need to approach gently, gradually probing, finding and penetrating; this corresponds to the Buddha's second stage of meditation, since this is a matter of approaching gently, weighing things, exploring, getting to know. The third correspondence is quite obvious because the chief word the Bible uses for sexual intercourse is knowing: He went into her and knew her. So this phase of intercourse, when we are sufficiently practised to find that we get to know each other in making love, corresponds to the Buddha's third stage of knowledge. Finally, the climax of love-making, the ecstasy, at least when there is a mutually achieved orgasm, corresponds to the Buddha's fourth stage of union. At the same time, I have to say that while the contemplative experience is forward-moving, developing and transforming, the sexual act, in my view, can be enjoyable and, for some couples, ideal, but it remains essentially repetitive. It is not the mystical way, only a shadow of it, a premonition of the life of the spirit.

I realise that I am left with the puzzle that it seems to be precisely those who experience sexual ecstasy who are so often not spiritual and not open to the spirit. I can only explain this to myself by thinking that the germ of such openness to the spirit is in all of us but that its flowering into the realm of the spirit depends on so many factors and accidents. This brings me to the importance of the counsellor but also to his limitations. For he can, by his awareness or lack of the dimension of the spirit within himself, facilitate or stunt the possible germination. At the same time it is not strictly his office directly and explicitly to waken this possibility, whereas it is that of the priest, as we have said before. So we have to recognise that the therapist strictly as therapist, by virtue of his training and outlook, does not go beyond psychic equilibrium and natural wisdom. It is up to the individual to realise that there is something beyond – stimulated, perhaps, by the priest.

Staying, however, with the counsellor, I do want to insist that he should be aware of this potentiality for the spirit in us all, and even of the extraordinary reach of this potentiality. This brings me to the main part of my response to your question. You asked whether there is a sense in which sex can turn *into* contemplation, whether the very sexual impulses and forces can be transformed into spiritual energy.

I have already suggested that it is precisely when a person begins to enter into the contemplative and mystical realm that sexual forces gather. It is as if these forces were threatened, and so mustered to resist, *but by this very token* became available to the victor.

At the same time the very absorption of sexual energies seems to be itself a matter of degrees. In this connection I have been very much struck by the difference of tone and language between, say, St Augustine, on the one hand, and St John of the Cross and St Theresa on the other. Take, for instance, this passage from St Augustine's *Confessions*:

> But what do I love when I love my God? Not material beauty or beauty of a temporal order; not the brilliance of earthly light, so welcome to our eyes; not the sweet melody of harmony and song; not the fragrance of flowers, perfumes and spices; not manna or honey; not the limbs such as the body delights to embrace. It is not these that I love when I love my God. And yet, when I love Him, it is true that I love a light of a certain kind, a voice, a perfume, a food, an embrace; but they are of the kind that I love in my inner self, where my soul is bathed in light that is not bound by space; when it listens to sound that never dies away; when it breathes fragrance that is not borne away on the wind; when it tastes food that is never consumed by the eating; when it clings to an embrace from which it is not severed by fulfilment of desire. This is what I love when I love my God.[22]

It's very lovely, but it's still saturated with the memory of sensual experiences. Contrast this with St John of the Cross or St Theresa:

> Accordingly, a person should not mind if the operations of his faculties are being lost to him; he ought to desire rather that this be done quickly so that he may be no obstacle to the operation of the infused contemplation which God is bestowing, that he may receive it with more peaceful plenitude and make room in his spirit for the enkindling and burning of the love that this dark and secret contemplation bears and communicates to his soul. For contemplation is nothing else than a secret and peaceful and loving inflow of God, which, if not hampered, fires the soul in the spirit of love, as is brought out in the following verse:

SEX AND CONTEMPLATION

Fired with love's urgent longings.[23]

> So tranquilly and noiselessly does the Lord teach the soul in this state and do it good that I am reminded of the building of Solomon's temple, during which no noise could be heard; just so, in this temple of God, in this Mansion of His, He and the soul alone have fruition of each other in the deepest silence. There is no reason now for the understanding to stir, or to seek out anything, for the Lord who created the soul is now pleased to calm it and would have it look, as it were, through a little chink, at what is passing. Now and then it loses sight of it and is unable to see anything; but this is only for a brief time. The faculties, I think, are not lost here; it is merely that they do not work but seem to be dazed.[24]'

'So for you, Hans, the stairway or scale continues even in the contemplative realm itself? I find this very interesting. The essential idea however, is that of this stairway or scale, of a progression of stages. What occurs to me therefore, is that the way of life and human development which you envisage is strikingly like what has been incorporated into the very organisation of Hindu society. This is how K. M. Sen, a disciple of Rabindranath Tagore, puts it in his admirably simple account of Hinduism in the book of that name:

> According to Hindu doctrines, the ideal life consists of four stages (*āśramas*): *brahmacarya*, the period of discipline and education, *gārhasthya*, the life of the householder and active worker, *vānaprasthya*, retreat for the loosening of bonds, and finally, *sannyāsa*, the life of a hermit. *Brahmacarya* is an active period of education and hard work ... *Gārhasthya* is not looked upon as a less important period of life than the later ones, even though renunciation is such an important Hindu value. In a sense *gārhasthya* is considered to be the mainstay of the four *āśramas*, for it gives unity and cohesion to the entire

structure, and the other *āśramas* depend on it for their sustenance. The Hindu is supposed to lead an active, married life at this stage, when ideals of social living are held to apply with particular force. It is often said that the Hindu ideal is inactivity, but in fact a considerable part of the Hindu scriptures discusses the value of an active life ... However, success in the wordly second period of life is not considered sufficient ... The successes of the material world, great as they are, are not considered sufficient, and it is here that the ideal of *moksha* or *mukti* comes in. This ideal of liberation is not a negative state. It is a state of completeness, of fullness of being, free from the bondage of *karma* and, thus, from rebirth ... The Hindu is supposed to loosen his association with the social life at the third stage, *vānaprasthya*, and later to lead the life of a hermit, *sannyāsa* ... Renunciation thus becomes an important part of ideal human life ...[25]

Now for me as a Roman Catholic, this extension of your own insight to become the principle of structuring the social life of the whole community is particularly fascinating. For, by means of this principle, the value of sexual renunciation is built into the very fabric of society as is it into the Roman Catholic regime of life, and yet this value is built into Hindu society in an importantly different way from the way this same value is built into the Roman Catholic community. In the difference lies the rub. For in the Roman Catholic way of seeking to honour and combine both values, sexual renunciation is recommended as an alternative to a sexual life for at least a few, where in the Hindu way it is seen as the culmination of sexual life for all. Moreover, in the Roman Catholic system, sexual renunciation is imposed as a way of life on all those who wish to be priests or religious even before they can be considered to have reached sexual maturity: sexual renunciation is a way of maturing in the Roman Catholic system and not only the fruit of maturing. I take it, however,

SEX AND CONTEMPLATION

Hans, from everything you've said that you would be totally opposed to this as going against human nature and its slowly ripening and developmental character? To be honest, to go back to where I started this morning, this is where the question of sex and contemplation becomes a daily anguish. This is why I find so much of what you say painful personally.'

'I, in my turn, Marcus, found your opening, more personal remarks, almost too painful to bear myself. But, if you will allow me to say so, this really reinforces my point. I've already said that I value celibacy. I should go further and say that this truly noble ideal can be practised by a few. I think, for instance, again of my beloved St John of the Cross who certainly knew sexual temptations, as his very plain words show, but who had the gift of overcoming them and so manifesting to the rest of us a sublime ideal to which we need to strive in our own way. I think personally, that his very bodily constitution – and for me it is relevant that he was physically a very small, short man – must have been of a particularly fine and delicately balanced character, so that he was not bothered and burdened by his body. But then he was also very spiritually centred. Be that as it may, I still think that this is for the very few and that we have to adapt the ideal to the vast majority precisely in order to make it accessible to them. All I can say is that in professional experience of priests, monks and nuns and those aspiring to the celibate life, I have witnessed such human misery, such chaos of perversions and substitutions, such ruin of the personal and even the religious life that I cannot speak strongly enough of the wrongheadedness of the system as an imposed system, regardless of individual human needs, wounds and weaknesses.'

'I recognise what you mean from my own professional experience, Hans, and yet I'm still bothered or borne up – I don't know which – by the thought that the Church cannot have been completely wrong for at least a thousand years to impose celibacy on aspiring priests, monks and nuns.'

'I agree, Marcus, you may be surprised to learn. For I have an immense regard for the wisdom of the Church and the sublime teaching of its greatest saints. But I'm talking about the Church as an establishment, which, as an establishment, can perpetrate – and to my mind has perpetrated – untold and unnecessary unhappiness on so many people and in this area in particular.'

'Alright, Hans, limiting ourselves to the Church as an establishment, let me say that the nub of my difficulty about your statement when I'm squarely faced with it in terms of human development and happiness is that you talk as if a way of life – in our case a way of life which includes sexual renunciation – should be thought of only in terms of expressing something already possessed or gained, not a way of becoming what one can be, a form of practising what one wants to become. Yet surely there are certain important experiences in life which one can't prepare for adequately and which we therefore just have to embark on. We have to start doing them and learn in the doing. I mean, isn't, for example, marriage an experience in relationship which teaches one what one's capacity for reciprocal equality is about? In parenthood isn't it by being a parent that one practises what one is gradually able to become? As the French proverb well puts it, "C'est en forgeant qu'on devient forgeron", it's in doing the work of a smith that one becomes a smith. There are things in life, it seems to me, regimes, institutions, which are not realisations, expressions of what one already is but which are meant to be conducive to, bring out, what one can become. In the end they may become expressions of what one has become but they begin by being acts of trust and hope, means to becoming, ways of being initiated into what one wishes to be and can be. So, in a similar way, couldn't sexual renunciation be a way and a means towards, a practice of something one hopes to become and not just the expression of something already achieved? I find it interesting that some such view is to be found even within Hinduism. This is how M. Hiriyanna puts it in his excellent account of Hindu philosophy:

The hexterodox held that man should once for all turn

away from the world whatever his circumstances might be. But the orthodox regarded the ascetic ideal as only to be progressively realised ... The contrast between the two ideals is set forth in a striking manner in a chapter of the Mahābhārata known as the "Dialogue between Father and Son". Here the father, who represents the orthodox view, maintains that renunciation should come at the end of the āśrama discipline, but is won over to his side by the son, who holds the view that it is the height of unwisdom to follow amidst the many uncertainties of life such dilatory discipline and pleads for an immediate breaking away from all worldly ties.[26]

After all, you have yourself already stated that contemplation even within the context of a sexual life needs a "serene way of life" and that the purgative of work can include the spending of the vital and emotional energy of caring for and loving others. The practice of celibacy could therefore be seen as an extension of the "serene way of life" and as the cultivation of this work of caring.'

'I must say that I'm impressed by your counter-arguments, Marcus. At the very least they compel me to clarify certain things.

In the first place, I don't want to be taken to suggest that a sexual life – by which I mean a disciplined sexual life, above all in marriage – is a soft option. I can remember how shocked I was when I was having some analysis and the analyst said that marriage was the most difficult vocation. How green I must have been to be so surprised! Experience has taught me that sustained sexual life imposes its own requirements and that this is part of the necessary humanisation, let alone the spiritualisation of sex. It is indeed a training-ground for character and virtue in which inconsiderate habits gradually have to be weeded out and tolerance cultivated.

Secondly, I want to insist that when I say that everyone, in my opinion, has to pass through a sexual phase before aspiring to renounce sexual life, I don't necessarily mean a life-long sexual union. There are what I call *token* experiences. To take a fairly light-hearted example from my own experience, I can remember so vividly how, when I was fifteen year old, one of my uncles told me it was time to go with a prostitute and gave me the money – I can still see the very spot in the coffee house where he took me in hand. Well, I duly went to where the girls were parading and received their invitation, "Kommst du mit, Bubi?", "Are you coming, laddie?" but I found them so made up and odd, poor creatures, that I couldn't go further and that was my experience of prostitutes for life. More seriously, what I have in mind is again something Steiner wrote in response to Friedrich Eckstein. He, you may know, was a very remarkable man, full of ancient wisdom, and he was to be seen holding court in the Kaffee Heinrichshof, opposite the Opera House, for half a lifetime. Steiner was told that Eckstein had decided that in order to experience life as a whole he would give himself up to unrestricted enjoyment. Steiner was appalled but significantly, he waited to mature his response and then wrote as follows:

> The part of your letter which concerns Eckstein has shattered me. I have for a long time been aware that Friedrich Eckstein is in the grip of a fateful mistake. This consists of his understanding the sentence "A man must live his life through in all its fullness" in a wholly quantitative sense as if for him it were necessary to experience all the accidental and adventitious forms in which life's course manifests itself. This notion is mistaken in so far as it is tied to a misunderstanding about the quality of all being. For I too believe that the man of understanding must assume the substance of life and the world in all their forms into himself, but he must do this qualitatively, through deepening his experience more and more, and not through rushing around in all possible directions. This is not the way happiness lies since it leads to an infinite regress. The man of understanding must indeed live everything, but he must

get his experience in the right places, not just wherever he happens to be pushed.[27]

You see, he was talking about a qualitative and not a quantitative testing of life.

All this said, however, I still maintain that celibacy is just not possible, except for the very few, and then as something freely chosen and grown towards as part of an individual self-determination. Personally I think that whatever may have been the situation before, people are no longer physically constituted the way they used to be. At the physical level alone, there are just more demands on the nerve centres of the brain. Take children. I've worked with children all my adult life and I have to say that they are now capable of grasping things – cars, computers, the new maths, the new astronomy – which leaves me feeling like a village idiot. But it's an established fact that the greater the intellectual work, whether academic work or say, the work of a brain surgeon, the greater the nervous tension and also the sexual excitations, so that some relief is necessary. This is the sort of thing I have in mind when I talk of a change in people's constitution, the way they are incarnate and experience the balance of body and spirit.'

'Well, Hans, I must say that I still find myself torn between the evidence of so much human unhappiness caused by the attempt to impose celibacy on those unfitted for it and the intuition – instigated and reinforced by the Church – that celibacy can be a valid part of a whole way of life and training as well as the fruit thereof. I realise, of course, that there's more to sex than celibacy. Yet the issue of celibacy focusses the issue of sexuality, making us concentrate on what sex is really about. I therefore do not regret our having included this issue in our present discussion, even at some length.

On this topic you have, it seems to me, presented one side, on the basis of a coherent view of human development, while I have sought to present the other side, without anything like so convincingly an articulated a view to support that. Yet I feel that we have both shifted from our initial position and that we are groping towards some intermediate position which nevertheless still eludes us. I am tempted to say that this mediating position is to do with a view of human development and a regime of life which borrows something from, but lies beyond, the perceptions embodied in Hindu, the Roman Catholic and the Orthodox systems: the Hindu position that the sexual renunciation is the fruit of sexual life, the Roman Catholic position that sexual renunciation can be part of a whole way of maturing, and the Orthodox position that marriage is open even to priests but that celibacy is a condition for becoming a bishop.

At the same time I also feel that this would still be grappling with the problem in too external a way. What we seem to need is some deepening and interiorising of the already current distinction between genital and general sexuality, and the perception – first just attained in its essence, then gradually embodied in appropriate structures – that the real choice and alternative is not between sexual life and sexual renunciation, but between *two modes of accepting and living ones' sexuality*. It may be that those who will show us this middle way will be not those dedicated either to marriage or virginity but those who feel such a lively attraction towards both counter-sexual friendship and God simultaneously that they have chosen the single state as another way of living their sexuality. It's just because such people are undistracted by the merely external rules and demands of either of the other two states that they can concentrate on the only thing that can sustain their constantly renewed choice, the inner substance of *both* marriage *and* consecrated virginity: the need for another human being in one state, the need for the source of selfhood in the other state, and the freedom *within* sexuality of both. It's this latter that seems to be the essential thing: freedom from the compulsive power of sexuality and therefore freedom in its regard, and in so far as we're talking about the freedom of getting beyond mere self-gratification, we seem to have come back to the idea of commerce with people and the world as *play*.

Be that as it may, for myself I must continue to struggle for my personal answer, conscious as I am in it that the celibacy I try to live is a discipline which could be changed, so that my personal struggle may be part of a more general travail towards a different way of organising the balance between the two modes of living sexuality I've already indicated, and towards a more subtle and humane way of discerning those who are psychologically capable of either state and those who are not.'

'With those last words of yours, Marcus, and especially with their very personal tone we seem to have come full circle. So I think that this is a suitable place at which to stop this morning. I should myself just like to say two last things.

First, before you had begun your final remarks I had myself already been thinking that there is more middle ground between us that may sometimes have appeared. And I was thinking in particular that we seemed to be agreed on two important things: that contemplation in some form must be an essential part of any fully human life, and that the prerequisite of any such contemplative life was what you called, by reference to St Thomas Aquinas, the need to be "quiet and calm". Where we differed was on the question whether it was possible to be "quiet and calm" without appeasing the sexual urge and attraction.

This is what I was beginning to formulate within myself. But having now heard your final remarks, I realise that what I really want to say by way of conclusion is to agree that the essence of what we've been talking about does still escape us, as you've said. At the same time, I think that our approaching the question of sexuality from opposite ends, as you said at the beginning, plus the further fact that we have indeed modified our initial views, have brought us a little closer to the heart of the matter. Perhaps that's the most we can hope for from our conversations: to focus on the live issues with as much purity of feeling and clarity of thought as we're capable of and then leave the working through to further discussions – and, above all, to life itself!'

'I'm quite happy to conclude at this point, Hans, as it were with a series of dots into the unknown ...'

Notes

1. p.121.
2. p.99.
3. He does this in questions 180 and 183 of the 2a. 2ae. of his great *Summa Theologica*.
4. 2a. 2ae. question 180, article 2.
5. pp.18-19, 21, 23.
6. in question 183, article 4.
7. III, 3, in the translation of Juan Mascaró.
8. Book XIX, quoted in the *Summa*, in question 182, article 1, in the reply to the third question.
9. 2a. 2ae. question 182, article 1.
10. Book II, 48.
11. Book III, 35, both in the translation of R.C. Zaehner.
12. pp.125-126.
13. II, 64, in the translation of Juan Mascaró.
14. p.180.
15. *Knowledge of the Higher Worlds*, pp.137-138.
16. p.186.
17. p.140.
18. *The Dark Night of the Soul*, I, Chapter 14, p.82.
19. *Silent Music*, p.120.
20. *How to Know God*, pp.78-79.
21. *The Life of St Teresa*, translated by J.M. Cohen, p.210.
22. in the translation by R.S. Pine Coffin, Penguin Classics, 1968, pp.211-212.
23. *The Dark Night of the Soul*, I, Chapter 10, p.318.
24. *Interior Castle*, VII, iii, p.143.
25. pp.22-23.
26. pp.20-21.
27. *Zu Rudolf Steiner's Lebensgang*, I, (1971), p.136.

11: The Open End

The announcement of another chapter followed by a largely blank page is more than a trick; it is a symbol. The absence of a further dialogue is only apparent. The void is what the Japanese would call plenary. The white open space suggests the dialogues continued between Dr Hans Schauder and myself, or within ourselves, or with others. It is thus the expression in type of the Zen Buddhist notion of the return to the market place of ordinary life once the oxen have been herded and caught. It is only once you have something that you can give it. The blank is thus, variously, the symbol of continuation; of return to contact with others who are in turn in contact with yet others; of the recycling and circulation of ideas and life energy; of the progressive inwardness of all this; but therefore and through it all of that final liberation to which Dr Schauder alluded in Dialogue 5: The Spirit Becomes Free.

Concluding Personal Postscript on Counselling and Friendship

Readers who have persevered so far will want to tie things together each in his or her own way. Any such gathering together of meanings and associations will be highly personal and I hope it will not intrude if I offer my own thoughts on re-reading what precedes. I want to foster such a process of recollection rather than distract from it.

My first thoughts then, as I pondered the way our conversational explorations had gone, was to recur to one of the central themes of the book, namely, what it is to be human, and in particular to the fact that being human intrinsically involves a reference to a second, another. Being human is being one of at least two, becoming human requires the acknowledgement of another. I came back time and again to the late Professor John MacMurray's seminal intutition that 'the unit of the personal is not the "I" but the "you and I".'[1] Human-heartedness, as I found myself putting it, is an awareness of being half of two. We are insufficient to our sole selves. No man is an island, but a piece of the main. Anybody who has ever been in love implicitly knows this. One of the great poets of lyric love, E.E. Cummings has expressed his own variant of this discovery:

> One's not half two. It's two are halves of one:
> which halves reintegrating, shall occur
> no death and any quantity.

CONCLUDING PERSONAL POSTSCRIPT

Finding one's other half is the first fulfilment of the pursuit and desire of the whole.

It is for this reason that dialogue is an enactment of what it is to be human. We engage in dialogue because we have a dialogical nature. Talking with another, ultimately playing with another, is exercising our human nature. We converse because we are constitutively conversational creatures: imitating, questioning, challenging each other, agreeing and disagreeing with each other, discovering and constructing a world with each other because we are inherently connected with each other. Language is a form of life precisely as shared. Dialogue is the form of our human nature before it is a literary device, a more or less diverting if tricky option. Its appropriateness as a literary form derives from its ontological – my friend Dr Schauder would say its 'archetypal' – status.

In the light of this, however, the special characteristic and importance of counselling or psychotherapy shine out with renewed clarity. For it is a dialogue and is as such the exercise of our dialogical nature. At the same time it is not a simple unimpeded dialogue but one that includes the impediments to an easier flow in its rationale. It is a conversation like any other but one that gathers the very difficulties into its own progress. It is like practising for full dialogue. It is to the extent that it thus pauses to work at the knots in relationship that it has a purpose and an authority of its own. It is concentrated. It is in principle free of such distractions as aimless chatter, mere gossip, ego-trips, even ego-trips *à deux*. This is how it is circumscribed, has its own boundaries, as the jargon has it. It is thus a conversation that takes place initially on the basis of various inequalities but that progressively comes to be on a more equally shared basis. In this sense it can be seen to be in the nature of an initiation into what it is to be more authentically human. We see better why *Gesprächstherapie*, talking therapy – at least when it is part and parcel of action-therapy, therefore indeed a 'form of life' – has privileged status. It is like art and theatre in relation to life: a mirror of life's deeper structures and patterns held up so as to return it to itself, more aware, more freely functioning, more compassionate.

The concentrated form of life that is therapy is thus meant to return us to ordinary life much as art does. But a distinction therefore remains between life in its privileged, intensified form and its daily, more diffuse form. At the same time our need for dialogue continues, in fact it is reinforced. So here a more piercing consequence of our dialogical being appears. To the extent that therapy successfully elicits the dialogical potential of any human being, it works with the capacity for relationship in us all but then it has to let the other pursue its completeness elsewhere, for the counsellor cannot *as such* be a friend in the ordinary sense of the word too – though he can become one once the specific task of therapy is concluded. The very experience of counselling or therapy can bring out capacities and raise expectations which cannot then be further fulfilled *in the therapy*.

By one of those strange coincidences that is, no doubt, not a coincidence, I learned this for myself in an acute way the very week I began writing this postscript. For it was during this time that I happened to be ending my own analysis after six years. I had felt at last that I had to cast off and yet I found it painful to do so – presumably because I had in the very experience of the relationship of analysis learned more deeply what relationship is, only then to realise that my analyst could not *qua* analyst reciprocate as an equal friend. The poignancy – and the chance – was that, for this, I had to look elsewhere.

So it tends to be in all therapy: the very contract and concentration points us beyond – in this case to the fulfilment of relationship that is friendship in its ordinary, daily sense.

For such friendship *is* the fulfilment we most deeply desire, isn't it? This is the logic of our being dialogical by nature, even more importantly it is the logic of our hearts: human-heartedness is the awareness of being half of two, and its natural name is friendship. In the light of this conclusion of head and heart alike, therapy and counselling themselves take on a different look. There are different theories as to what

CONCLUDING PERSONAL POSTSCRIPT

therapy is about – listening, catalysing, holding, transference, companioning, and so on – but these theories rise and fall, mercifully so, since the reality of relationship is more complex and mysterious than is dreamt of in any philosophy. So can we not say, both more simply and more complexly, that therapy is not this element or that, but all of them? It is not, say, holding, but then neither is it, say, withholding, nor empathy, acceptance or congruence, exploring or waiting, confronting, befriending, accompanying, attending, enjoying. It is not any one of these alone, it is all of them. But we can now see that it is also all these as rehearsals and adumbrations of the flow of friendship in all *its* moments and positions. For in the growth and gradual deployment of human relationship there is feeding and playing, suckling and rearing, taking in and giving out, incorporation and evacuation, withholding and releasing, touching base and exploration, the rhythm of withdrawal and return, going in and coming out, in and out, coupling and uncoupling, the various making and loosing of affectional bonds, whatever, what have you. All these can be seen as so many trailers and variants of the central mystery of the self and other – the play and interplay of my mother, my self, me and you; the struggle between gratitude and envy, omnipotence and impotence, self-sufficiency and dependence, the sin of Lucifer and the merger of individuality; the aspiration to union without fusion, as all this receives its consummation in friendship – sexual friendship usually, and yet not only.

For there is a still further pointer beyond. This thought too emerged for me as I re-read our dialogues. In the eighth dialogue my friend Dr Schauder was talking most movingly about certain meetings which operate primarily through gazing and which have about them an air of being predestined. As I re-read this, I thought again of John Donne's poem 'The Good Morrow'. He began by asking, much as the lovers Dr Gregory mentioned might have done:

> I wonder by my troth, what thou, and I

Did, till we lov'd? Were we not wean'd till then?

Then at the end of the first stanza he answers:

If ever any beauty I did see,
Which I desir'd, and got, t'was but a dreame of thee.

This is a metaphysical enough sentiment as it is, but suppose we were to take the essential insight and transpose it onto an even higher metaphysical plane? The poet perceives that any previous loves are but an anticipation of the definitive love between two human beings. Can we not prolong this thought and say that the delicate, intimate and seemingly predestined sort of human meeting that sometimes occurs is itself only an anticipation and foreshadowing of the final face-to-face with God?

If this is so, then certain other things also fall into place. The reason of the heart even more than reason itself is to realise the need of a dialogical other, to find the peer and companion of one's heart, to be able to say with another contemporary poet, Elizabeth Jennings, 'I felt myself, acknowledged you', and yet to realise that even with such friendship the heart is restless until it rests in God.

Not that it is a matter of a friend *or* God. No, most vehemently no. Just as therapy can prepare for ordinary friendship and friendship in turn for God, so God's most urgent desire and work is to make us more and more fully human and therefore more and more capable of exercising human relationship in all its forms. It is a human being fully alive and truly human that is the glory of God; grace perfects nature, and grace, as St Thomas Aquinas saw, is a *law* which precisely as such integrates individuals into society, makes them social, associated, so that morality is being patient of progressively but creatively assuming the mores of one's tribe and people and, finally, the human race. In this light, the effect of therapy can, therefore, be so to promote growth into being human and therefore relating more and more generously that it culminates in our becoming, in R.S. Thomas' phrase, "as generous as bread", sharing in God's very being and self. Contrariwise, the effect of any spirituality we may be granted is in principle so to centre us in our most radical relating that we flower into human relationships. Under either aspect, there is in principle no more split than there is between inner and outer, centre and radii, root and flower, metaphysics and *physis*/nature.

Really? This *is* being very metaphysical, not to say solemn. Yet these remarks only represent gropings, attempts to catch in one particular idiom a sense of that something other and lighter that can arise from human dialogue of head and body and heart, dialogue, at its most concentrated and intimate. For *doesn't* this tend towards play? Isn't the end of reality playing? And because this play is ultimately cosmic play, the *krīdā*, *līlā* of ancient India, isn't it in the nature of a sharing in the song and dance of the universe, thus in one formulation, the play and inter-play of the two and the third between them?

We have been here before. I think we may well gravitate back here again sometime, when we meet again – in dialogue, in trinity.

Note

1. *Persons in Relation* p.61.

Index of Works Cited

Anselm of Canterbury (1033-1109) *Cur Deus Homo*
Aquinas, Thomas (1255-1274) *Summa Theologica* (Eyre & Spottiswode, London, 1976)
Augustine *Confessions*
Augustine *The City of God*

Baden, H.J. *Wissende, Verschwiegene, Eingeweihte* (Herder, Munich, 1981)
Bancroft, A. *Twentieth Century Mystics and Sages* (William Heinemann, London, 1976)
Beckh, H. *Buddha und seine Lehre* (Verlag Urachhaus, Stuttgart, 1958)
Beckh, H. *Der Hingang des Vollendeten* (Verlag Urachhaus, Stuttgart, 1960)
Bhagavad Gītā
Brown, D. & Pedder, J. *Introduction to Psychotherapy* (Tavistock Publications, London, 1979)

Cox, M. *Coding the Therapeutic Process: Emblems of Encounter* (Pergamon Press, Oxford, 1978)
Cummings, E.E. *Selected Poems 1923-1958* (The Penguin Poets, Harmondsworth, Middx, 1963)

Dante (1265-1321) *La Divina Commedia* (Oxford University Press, London, 1971)
Donne, J. *The Extasie*

Fiedler, L. *Max Reinhardt* (Rowohlt Taschenbuch Verlag, Reinbek bei Hamburg, 1975)
Finnis, J. *Natural Law and Natural Rights* (Oxford University Press, Oxford, 1980)

Fromm, E. *The Art of Loving* (George Allen & Unwin, London, 1975)
Furlong, M. *Travelling In* (Hodder & Stoughton, London, 1971)

Gadamer, H.G. *Truth and Method* (Sheed & Ward, London, 1975)
Goethe *Faust*
Goethe *Iphigenie auf Tauris*
Goethe, J.W. von (1749-1832) *Das Märchen* (Deutscher Taschenbuch Verlag, Munich, 1968)
Goethe, J.W. von *Wilhelm Meister's Lehrjahre* (Deutscher Taschenbuch Verlag, Munich, 1968)
Goethe, J.W. von *Faust* (Deutscher Taschenbuch Verlag, Munich, 1968)
Goleman, D. *Varieties of Meditative Experience* (London, 1978)
Green, T.H. *Prolegomena to Ethics* (Oxford University Press, Oxford, 4th edition, 1899)
Gregory, Pope *Moralia in Job*

Harding, E. *The Way of All Women* (Rider & Co., London, 1971)
Heyer, C.G. *Der Organismus der Seele* (Ernst Reinhardt Verlag, Munich, 1951)
Hiriyanna, M. *Outlines of Indian Philosophy* (George Allen & Unwin, London, 1932)

Igumen Chariton of Valamo *The Art of Prayer* (Faber & Faber, London, 1966)

Jacobi, J. *Jung, Psychological Reflections* (Pantheon Books, New York, 1953)
Jacobi, J. *A Jung Anthology* (Pantheon Books, New York, 1953)
James, W. *Varieties of Religious Experience* (Longman, Green & Co., London, 1910)
John of the Cross, *The Dark Night of the Soul* (Burns & Oates, London, 1953)

Johnston, W. *Silent Music* (William Collins Sons & Co., Glasgow, 1974)

Klein, M. *Our Adult World and its Roots in Infancy* (Tavistock Publications, London, 1960)

Laing, R.D. *The Divided Self* (Penguin Books, Harmondsworth, Middx, 1965)

Lewis, C.S. *The Four Loves* (Fontana, London, 1963)

Lotz, J.B. *Erfahrungen mit der Einsamkeit* (Herder, Freiburg-im-Breisgau, 1972)

MacMurray, J. *Persons in Relation* (Faber & Faber, London, 1961)

MacVicar, R. *Healing Through Meditation* (Scottish Centre of Christian Healing, Boness, n.d.)

Mandel, S. *Rainer Maria Rilke* (Southern Illinois University Press, 1965)

Maugham, S. *The Razor's Edge* (Penguin Books, Harmondsworth, Middx, 1963)

Merton, T. *Conjectures of a Guilty Bystander* (Doubleday Books, New York, 1968)

Morgenstern, C. *Epigramme und Sprüche* (Piper Verlag, Munich, 1922)

Newman, J.H. *An Essay of the Development of Christian Doctrine* (Penguin Books, Harmondsworth, Middx, 1974)

Paul, *Epistle to the Colossians*

Plato (427-347 BC) *The Symposium*

Prabhavananda & Isherwood, C. *How to Know God – The Yoga Aphorisms of Patanjali* (Vedanta Press, Hollywood, 1966)

Rayner, E. *Human Development* (Unwin Hyman, London, 3rd edition, 1986)

Radhakrishnan *Indian Philosophy* (Vols. I and II, Allen and Unwin, London, 1923-27

Reiter, U. *Meditation: Wege zum Selbst* (Mosaik Verlag, Munich, 1976)

INDEX

Rilke, R.M. (1872-1928) *Briefe an einen jungen Dichter* (Insel Verlag, Frankfurt-am-Main, 1955)
Rilke, R.M. *Winterliche Stanzen* (Insel Verlag, Leipzig, 1957)
Rittelmeier, F. *Die Christengemeinschaft* (Letzte Predigt, 1938)
Rogers, C. *On Becoming a Person* (Constable & Co, London, 1967)
Rosenberg, A. *Die Zauberflöte* (Prestel Verlag, Munich, 1972)

Salzberger-Wittenberg, I. *Phycho-analytic Insight and Relationships* (Routledge & Kegan Paul, London, 1970)
Sandler, J., Dare, C. & Holder, A. *The Patient and the Analyst* (Maresfield Reprints, London, 1982)
Sen, K.M. *Hinduism* (Penguin Books, Harmondsworth, Middx, 1981)
Shakespeare, W. *Henry V*
Shakespeare, W. *Macbeth*
Shakespeare, W. *The Tempest*
Silva, J. & Miele, P. *The Silva Method of Mind Control* (Grenada Publishing, Herts, 1980)
Stafford-Clark, D. *Psychiatry for Students* (Allen & Unwin, London, 1979)
Steiner, R. *Knowledge of the Higher Worlds and its Attainment* (Anthroposophic Press, New York, 1947)
Steiner, R. *Practical Training in Thought* (Anthroposophic Press, New York, 1947)
Steiner, R. *Die Welt der Sinne und die Welt des Geistes* Rudolf Steiner Verlag, Dornoch bei Basel, Switzerland, 1959)
Steiner, R. *Knowledge of the Higher Worlds* (Rudolf Steiner Press, London, 1969)
Steiner, R. *Zu Rudolf Steiners Lebensgang*, Bildband I (Verlag Die Kommenden, Freiburg im Breisgau, 1971)
Storr, A. *The Art of Psychotherapy* (Secker & Warburg/Heinemann, London, 1979)
Swailes, M. *Arthur Schnitzler* (Oxford University Press, London, 1971)

Theresa of Avila *The Life of Saint Teresa* (Penguin Books, Harmondsworth, Middx, 1958)

Theresa of Avila *Interior Castle* (Sheed & Ward, London, 1974)

Thomas à Kempis (c.1380-1471) *De Imitatione Christi*

Underhill, E. *Mysticism* (Methuen, London, 1904)

Vatican II *Lumen Gentium* (The Documents of Vatican II, edited by Walter Abbott S.J., Geoffrey Chapman, London-Dublin, 1966)

Weigand, H.J. ed. *Goethe, Wisdom and Experience* (Routledge & Kegan Paul, London, 1949)

Whistler, L. *The Initials in the Heart* (Rupert Hart-Davis, London, 1966)

White, V. *How to Study* (Aquin Press, London, 1966)

Williams, H. *The True Wilderness* (Fontana & Collins, Glasgow, 1965)

Wilson, C. *New Pathways in Psychology: Maslow and the Post-Freudians* (Victor Gollancz, London, 1973)

Winnicott, D. *Playing and Reality* (Penguin Books, Harmondsworth, Middx, 1982)

Wordsworth, W. *Lines Composed a Few Miles above Tintern Abbey*

Zaehner, R.C. *Hinduism* (Oxford University Press, Oxford, 1980)

Zaehner, R.C. *Hindu Scriptures* (J.M. Dent & Sons, London, 1972)

Zweig, S. *Die Welt von Gestern* (Fischer Teschenbuch, Berlin & Frankfurt-am-Main, 1965)